LOCKE AND FRENCH MATERIALISM

Locke and French Materialism

John W. Yolton

CLARENDON PRESS · OXFORD
1991

Oxford University Press, Walton Street, Oxford OX2 6DP
Oxford New York Toronto
Delhi Bombay Calcutta Madras Karachi
Petaling Jaya Singapore Hong Kong Tokyo
Nairobi Dar es Salaam Cape Town
Melbourne Auckland
and associated companies in
Berlin Ibadan

Oxford is a trade mark of Oxford University Press

Published in the United States
by Oxford University Press, New York

British Library Cataloguing in Publication Data
Yolton, John W. (John William) 1921–
Locke and French materialism.
1. English philosophy. Locke, John, 1632–1704
I. Title
192
ISBN 0–19–824274–3

Library of Congress Cataloging-in-Publication Data
Yolton, John W.
Locke and French materialism / John W. Yolton.
p. cm.
Includes bibliographical references and index.
1. Locke, John, 1632–1704—Influence. 2. Materialism—France—
History. 3. Philosophy, French—17th century. 4. Philosophy,
French—18th century. I. Title.
B1925.M25Y64 1991 146′.3′094109032—dc20 90–39833
ISBN 0–19–824274–3

Typeset by Joshua Associates Ltd., Oxford
Printed and bound in
Great Britain by Biddles Ltd.,
Guildford and King's Lynn

Robert Shackleton
1919–1986

Preface

T H E research which has resulted in this study was conducted over a number of years. While working on my 1984 *Thinking Matter: Materialism in Eighteenth-Century Britain*, I became aware of some of the appearances of the British debate across the Channel. As soon as that book was completed, I made plans to continue the exploration of Locke's suggestion about thinking matter in France. Yearly short visits to the Bodleian Library at Oxford and the British Library in London kept the research moving, but many of the titles and references I was uncovering were unavailable at those two libraries. A visit in 1984 enabled me to spend time in the Bibliothèque nationale in Paris where some but not all of the books I needed to consult were found. A leave from Rutgers in 1986 led to a visit to the Bavarian State Library in Munich and the library at the University of Amsterdam where still other titles were found. In the United States, the eighteenth-century collection in the Yale University libraries, especially the Beinecke Library, provided me with additional titles. The collection at the University of Pennsylvania also proved useful. The last two chapters and many additions to earlier chapters were written while holding a Fellowship from the National Endowment for the Humanities during the academic year 1988–9.

Portions of Chapters 2 and 3 have been presented at various institutions: the University of Amsterdam and Tilburg University in the Netherlands, the universities of Windsor and Calgary in Canada. Two presentations at meetings of the Northeast Society for Eighteenth-Century Studies gave me other audiences to react to my material. Earlier versions of the same two chapters have appeared in the *Journal of the History of Philosophy*, 25 (1987), and the *Revue internationale de philosophie*, 42 (1988).

I have benefited from advice and reactions to various parts of this study from James G. Buickerood, Carol Blum, and Ann Thomson. My wife's bibliographic skills and her keen eye for readable prose have played a major role in bringing this study to completion. Our friendship with the late Robert Shackleton, and frequent conversations the three of us have had, usually over a fine meal, have provided me with information and inspiration.

Contents

Introduction

L o c k e 's suggestion that there is nothing inconsistent in the notion that God could superadd to matter the power of thought gave rise to a running debate in eighteenth-century Britain. There were a number of features in Locke's writing which led many of his readers to charge him with favouring materialism, the view that there is only one substance which has the dual attributes of thought and extension. Bishop Stillingfleet forced Locke to respond in some detail to his charge on this point. The exchange between Locke and Stillingfleet helped spread the interpretation of Locke as a brilliant but dangerous writer. The debate in Britain was watched and chronicled by a number of French-language journals. In my recent *Thinking Matter*,[1] I tried to survey and analyse the extensive literature in eighteenth-century Britain on this controversy, with a few glances at some of the French writings on the topic, 'can matter think?' In that work, I also gave some indication of the coverage of that debate by some English- and French-language journals. Locke's books had, of course, been quickly translated into French, and a few appeared in Latin. German translations appeared later. Locke was a well-known author, both in England and on the Continent.

For French readers, the long abridgement of Locke's *Essay concerning Human Understanding* in Le Clerc's *Bibliothèque universelle et historique* in 1688, which appeared before the publication of the full work itself in 1690, may have alerted some French readers to that work, but it was Pierre Coste's translation in 1700 of the

---

[1] *Thinking Matter: Materialism in Eighteenth-Century Britain* (Minneapolis, Minn.: University of Minnesota Press; Oxford: Basil Blackwell, 1984). This controversy was much broader than Locke's suggestion of thought being added to some kinds of matter. It was a debate that ranged over physics (the nature of matter, passive or active), religion (God's causal role and his omnipresence), and physiology (the causal role of mind or thought in action). Questions about the nature of space and its extension, with the possible extension of the soul, were also debated. Fears about man's becoming viewed as a mechanism, as an automaton, issued from traditional defenders of the immateriality of the soul.

2   *Introduction*

complete *Essay*, following the changes made by Locke through the fourth edition, that brought this work within easy access of the French reading public. That translation was reprinted a number of times in the eighteenth century; there were even several pirated editions. Coste in his second edition of 1729 (based on the fifth English edn. of 1706) made available in a note the relevant passage between Locke and Stillingfleet over the thinking-matter suggestion.[2] Besides this major source for French readers of Locke's ideas and doctrines, there were a number of biographical sketches in French, most of which contained brief summaries of some of his doctrines in the *Essay* and other writings. Jean Le Clerc's 'Eloge du feu M. Locke' in his *Bibliothèque choisie* in 1705 was the first such sketch; the entry, 'Locke, Philosophie de' in the Diderot–d'Alembert *Encyclopédie* (vol. ix, 1765) was not the last. In between, there are several more biographical accounts with varying attention to his doctrines.[3]

The transmission of Locke's doctrines on to the Continent in these ways (translations, reviews, and debates in journals) is fairly well

[2] One other handy source available to French readers was J. P. Bosset's *Abrégé de l'Essay de Monsieur Locke, sur l'entendement humain* (1720). The English abridgement by Wynne (1696) omitted the 4. 3. 6 passage on thinking matter, but Bosset's abridgement included a brief reference to that suggestion. Wynne does give an extended account of 4. 10, where Locke argues against the materialists who held that matter was eternal and might think. Many of the contentions about thinking matter are discussed by Locke in that chapter, but Wynne omits the earlier suggestion about the limitation of our knowledge not enabling us to rule out the possibility that God could add thought to matter. The Italian abridgement by Francesco Soave (3 vols., 1775), which states it is a trans. of Wynne, follows Bosset on the 4. 3. 6 passage. Another significant difference in the French and Italian edns. is the inclusion of Le Clerc's summary of bk. 1 of the *Essay*. The 1688 abridgement which appeared in the *Bibliothèque universelle et historique* did not include that book, the rejection of innate ideas and principles. When Le Clerc reviewed the 1st edn. of the *Essay*, he turned that review into an abridgement of bk. 1 (*Bibliothèque universelle et historique*, 17 (1690), 399–427). Both Bosset and Soave refer to that bk. 1 summary as 'Le Clerc's abridgement'. It would be easy to confuse that reference to an abridgement with the 1688 abridgement of the *Essay* itself. Soave also adds in a note a long quotation from Condillac on this topic. (See *Essai sur l'origine des connoissances humaines* (1746), I. i. i. 6–7.) In that passage, Condillac expresses amazement that Locke could have entertained that possibility.

[3] See e.g. Jean-Pierre Nicéron, 'John Locke', in *Mémoires pour servir à l'histoire des hommes illustres dans la république des lettres*, i (1729); Pierre Bayle, 'An Account of the Life of John Locke, Esq: Extracted from Mr. Bayle's Historical and Critical Dictionary', *American Magazine*, 2 (1744), 540–4; Jacques G. Chaufepié, 'Locke, Jean', in *Nouveau Dictionnaire historique et critique, pour servir de supplément . . . au Dictionnaire historique et critique de Mr. Pierre Bayle* (1753), iii. 100–6.

known, but there is a side to this transmission which has not been given much detailed attention, the thinking-matter issue. In his important study *Diderot and Descartes: A Study of Scientific Naturalism in the Enlightenment* (Princeton, NJ: Princeton University Press, 1953), Aram Vartanian remarked, about Locke's suggestion, that 'A monograph on its picaresque fortunes across the Channel would make both entertaining and instructive reading' (p. 300). To my knowledge, no one has undertaken to write that story. This study is an attempt to trace the transmission to France of that suggestion, with the reactions to it. As well, the story will include the attention given in French-language journals to the British debate around that suggestion. I suspect that there are other facets to this story than I have uncovered. There is room for others to follow different aspects of this intriguing tale elsewhere in France, and also in Portugal.[4]

The story of the adventures of Locke's suggestion across the Channel is interwoven with the accounts in French-language journals of the British debate aroused by Locke. I have indicated briefly in my *Thinking Matter* the coverage of that body of writings by Jean Le Clerc's *Bibliothèque choisie*. Three other journals are of equal importance in putting before their readers many of the books and tracts in that long debate, together with Locke's suggestion: the *Bibliothèque raisonnée*, the *Bibliothèque britannique*, and the *Journal helvétique*. It was not just Locke's suggestion which travelled to the Continent, it was the extensive literature surrounding it as well. Locke's suggestion was not an isolated notion; it was embedded in controversy *pro* and *contra* which was still expanding in Britain as the French-language journals recorded it.

Locke's suggestion was also linked with other doctrines, prime among these being different accounts of the relation between mind and body. The French-language journals carried many articles devoted to this topic. Of the three different accounts—occasionalism,

---

[4] For a useful discussion of 18th-century Portuguese reactions to Locke's 'materialism', and the adoption of some of Locke's doctrines, see Joaquim de Carvalho's introduction to the 1st Portuguese edn. of Locke's *Essay* in *Boletim da Biblioteca da Universidade de Coimbra*, 20 (1951), 1–212. This edn. was a trans. of Wynne's abridgement of bk. 2 preceded by an adaptation of Le Clerc's abridgement of bk. 1 (see n. 2 above), and was made in the 18th century but not allowed to be printed because of the materialism associated with Locke. José Mayne's *Dissertação sobre a alma racional* (1778) contains extensive discussions of and attacks on Locke's suggestion, with many references in British writers such as Henry Dodwell, William Coward, Hobbes, Toland.

pre-established harmony, and what was referred to as the 'system of physical influence'—Locke was linked with the last. The role of the physiology of the body in perception and action was another ingredient in the French discussion of Locke's suggestion, especially among his critics. While the nature of matter plays a key role in the materialism associated with Diderot, as it did in the British debate, it seems to be much less apparent in the writings of Locke's French critics and 'disciples'.

The one doctrine of Locke's thought most often cited when discussing eighteenth-century French philosophy is the stress on sensation as the origin of ideas. The so-called 'sensualism' or 'sensationalism' of Locke's doctrine has been taken as characteristic of 'empiricism'. This one-sided reading of Locke, overlooking as it does his equal stress on reflection and mental activity as a source for ideas, *is* cited by his French critics, but it is often the causal aspects of that doctrine that they reject: the causal theory of perception and action which says objects cause ideas, and that mind or soul can cause the body to move. The worries about the causal theory were that, if true, it would detract from the mental features of the perceiver and actor. Physiological causation within the body and physical causation from objects to mind were equally seen as threatening and as leading to materialism. Locke's philosophy was seen as accepting both types of causal connections between mind and body.

Condillac gave some prominence to the sensory aspects of Locke's account of the origins of human knowledge in his *Essai sur l'origine des connoissances humaines* (1746) and in his more detailed *Traité des sensations* (1754). These two works are filled with references to and discussions of various Locke doctrines. There are also some references to Locke in Condillac's attack on abstract systems of philosophy, *Traité des systêmes* (1749), an attack which reminds us of some of Locke's rejections of traditional metaphysical terms and concepts. Condillac was more concerned than was Locke with specific explanations of phenomena, but the stress on experience-based accounts is similar in both writers.

Earlier, Claude Buffier had included in his various books discussions of Locke; for example, discussions of probability, of clear and distinct ideas, of the origin of ideas (*Principes du raisonnement* (1714), pt. 2, art. xxiv). At the end of his *Traité des premieres véritez* (1724), Buffier added a series of 'Remarques' on the metaphysics of Descartes, Locke, Malebranche, and Le Clerc. In those remarks on Locke, he praises what he calls the 'metaphysic of Locke' as history, in contrast to the 'fictions' of Descartes and Malebranche. The doctrines Buffier singles out for brief description include the ideas of space, judgement, simple ideas. His comments are made on certain aspects of Locke's argument against innate principles, on reflection, on the soul not always thinking, on liberty, on language, and on the concept of person (which Buffier misunderstands). Buffier's works themselves are rather traditional in subject-matter but modern in the attention paid to the sensory basis of some of the materials of knowledge. That Locke takes his place in Buffier's writings alongside Descartes and Malebranche, that Locke's doctrines are often praised over those of the two French writers, is some indication that by the 1720s, Locke's reputation in France was well established; he was considered to be an important author.[5]

Before mid-century, it is difficult to find French authors attacking Locke, although some of his doctrines here and there received critical examination. When the attacks did come, starting in 1735 and growing after 1750, they came from those who were sympathetic to Malebranche. There seems to have been, as Jørn Schøsler has recently suggested,[6] a revival in France of interest in and respect for Malebranche around 1750. Between 1720 and 1750, French-language journals were covering the British writings which attacked Locke's suggestion about thinking matter. It is probable that the circulation of that British debate in these journals contributed to the attacks against Locke mounted in France after the rehabilitation of Malebranche. We can witness this change in Locke's reputation in France in a succinct way by examining one of the more important journals, the *Bibliothèque raisonnée*. Schøsler's excellent monograph on this journal illustrates the importance it had in the dissemination of Locke's doctrines and in reflecting the changes in attitudes towards them, especially those views which were seen as tending towards materialism.

Locke was often in the centre of the attention given by those

---

[5] Writing against the use of general principles as a source of knowledge, Condillac makes a reference to Locke's attack on maxims in *Essay*, 4. 7. 9–10. He reminds the reader that Locke has given reasons for saying maxims are not useful for acquiring or enlarging our knowledge. Condillac then says that he does not need to repeat Locke's arguments against maxims, 'parceque son ouvrage est entre les mains de tout le monde' (*Traité des systêmes*, p. 13 n.).

[6] *La Bibliothèque raisonnée (1728–1753): Les Réactions d'un périodique français à la philosophie de Locke au XVIIIe siècle* (Odense: Odense University Press, 1985).

journals (mainly the *Bibliothèque raisonnée* and the *Bibliothèque britannique*) dedicated to announcing and reviewing British books. When not at the centre, his views are frequently in the background and may have, as Jørn Schøsler suggests, determined which books were to be reviewed. Whether it is his rejection of innate ideas, his minimalist religious views, or the more disturbing denial that immateriality is not necessary for the immortality of the soul, 'le publique cultivé français' was given detailed accounts, analyses, and occasionally criticisms. Schøsler's useful pamphlet traces the coverage of and reactions to Locke's doctrines in the *Bibliothèque raisonnée* during its run from 1728 to 1753. In almost every volume, there are several articles on Locke or on books dealing with doctrines of Locke. In some cases, a book reviewed bears directly on one of the controversial issues in which Locke was entangled, even though Locke may not be mentioned. Schøsler cites the review of Humphrey Ditton's *A Discourse concerning the Resurrection of Jesus Christ* (1712), with its important Appendix attacking thinking matter, as an example. Schøsler is undoubtedly right in saying that, while Locke's name is not cited in this view, 'les lecteurs de la B.R. n'ont aucun mal à reconnaître les arguments de Locke dans l'exposé que donne le journaliste de la critique de Ditton' (*La Bibliothèque raisonnée*, p. 8).

This particular controversy had already been well covered by the *Nouvelles de la république des lettres* (the Locke–Stillingfleet exchange on that topic) and Bayle's *Dictionnaire historique et critique* (1697). As Schøsler points out, Voltaire's Letter XIII in his *Letters concerning the English Nation* (1733; French edn, 1734) gave prominence to Locke's thinking-matter suggestion. Locke's name and suggestion are cited and used in other French materialist works, even in some of the clandestine tracts. In the 1741 volume of the *Bibliothèque raisonnée*, one of the strongest critics of Voltaire's Letter XIII, David R. Boullier, is discussed: his *Trois lettres relatives à la philosophie de ce poète*, which was appended to Boullier's *Lettres sur les vrais principes de la religion* (1741). The first of Boullier's 'Trois lettres' had appeared in 1735 in another journal, the *Bibliothèque françoise*. The reviewer in the *Bibliothèque raisonnée* defends Locke against Boullier, but only after a careful presentation of Boullier's arguments. That article is followed by one on Formey's *La Belle Wolfienne* (1741), which also discussed the nature of the soul, pre-established harmony, and the general question of mind–

body relation. Again the reviewer supports Locke's scepticism about not knowing enough about the soul to deny that thought might be a property of the brain. A related doctrine, Locke's version of the sensory basis for knowledge, which was often seen in France as aiding materialism, became embroiled in a notorious incident in the Paris Faculty of Theology when the Abbé de Prades's thesis was condemned.

Another work which was directed at Locke, *Two Dissertations concerning Sense and the Imagination* (1728), (the *Bibliothèque raisonnée* carried one of the few reviews of this important anonymous work attributed to Zachary Mayne), is presented in another article. That discussion is sympathetic to the author and reveals, Schøsler says, 'une méfiance apologétique à l'égard de la métaphysique de Locke' (*La Bibliothèque raisonnée*, p. 11). Similarly, the review of a dialogue between the Swiss theologian Turrettini and Bionens in the second volume is critical of Locke's *Reasonableness of Christianity* (1695).[7] That review is so structured as to show clearly, Schøsler thinks, 'que le livre de Locke est dangereux parce qu'il prête à des interprétations dangereuses' (p. 12).

Schøsler takes us through issue after issue of this journal revealing reviews that either support or attack Locke. He divides the coverage of Locke into three phases: a period from 1728 to 1740, where some criticisms of Locke are tentatively made; a second period, 1741–9, where Locke is defended; and a third period from 1750 to 1753 where Locke is criticized and replaced in praise by Malebranche. Schøsler calls attention to a long review in 1750 of Condillac's *Traité des systêmes*, which provides the reviewer with an opportunity to take issue with some of Condillac's comparisons of Locke and Malebranche. One unusual feature of this review is a long footnote (40 (1750), 136–9) in which the reviewer inserts comments on specific points made by Condillac. Malebranche is favoured in each case over Locke. Schøsler sees this review as leading the rehabilitation of Malebranche. He mentions Antoine-Martin Roche, whose two-volume *Traité de la nature de l'âme* (1759) launched an extended attack on almost every doctrine in Locke's *Essay*. Schøsler might

---

[7] Turrettini was Professor of Theology and Ecclesiastical History at Geneva. The identity of Bionens is not known. In the review of the exchange between Turrettini and Bionens in the *Bibliothèque raisonnée*, he is said to be Theodore Crinsoz (he used the initials T.C.), 'qu'on appelle ordinairement Monsr. De Bionens' (2 (1729), 312). The editors add in a footnote that in another work Bionens describes himself as '*destitué de tout Emploi*' (p. 313 n. *b*).

have mentioned Gerdil's earlier *L'Immatérialité de l'âme démontrée contre M. Locke* (1747), or Jean Astruc's *Dissertation sur l'immatérialité et l'immortalité de l'âme* (1755), both of which were criticisms of Locke from a Malebranchian point of view. A number of so-called French materialist disciples of Locke are discussed in these books. Thus, a Malebranchian revival which figured in the French criticisms of Locke influenced the attitudes of the reviewers in the *Bibliothèque raisonnée*.

In each of the chapters on these three periods, Schøsler gives us a detailed and judicious account of the attitudes embedded in the articles of this journal. He believes that the *Bibliothèque raisonnée* contributed 'dans une large mesure, à répandre le lockisme jusqu'au plein épanouissement du matérialisme lockien dans l'*Encyclopédie*' (p. 68). Whether it is Lockian materialism that surfaces there, or whether the Lockian version (and its extended analyses in the British debate) joined an already indigenous French materialism, is a question I shall address in this study.

I shall begin the reconstruction of the cross-Channel voyage of the British debate over Locke's suggestion, and of those doctrines of Locke's that were seized upon in France as materialist-inclined, by tracing an extended exchange of articles in another journal, the Swiss *Journal helvétique*, over the relation between mind and body. Locke as a proponent of the system of physical influence appears in many issues of that journal. I shall then explore Voltaire's role, in his private correspondence as well as in Letter XIII, in the dissemination in France of Locke's suggestion. Chapter 3 is a presentation of three occasionalist critics of Locke who identified what they took to be a number of Locke's French 'disciples' or 'partisans', writers who were for the most part labelled as 'materialist' and 'radical'. Chapter 4 examines 'l'affaire de Prades' and the association of Locke's stress on sensation with the de Prades thesis; an important digression on sensation by David R. Boullier; and some medical men whose research on specific physiological processes in nerves and brain were considered as supporting the system of physical influence. Chapter 5 takes a rather comprehensive look at the work of Boullier, an overlooked and undervalued writer, especially on the mind–body relation. Chapter 6 examines a number of lesser-known writers, both traditional and radical, whose works will help to give us a larger sense of the context in which Locke's doctrines were placed in France. Chapter 7 surveys the discussion of British books, especially those that played a role in the British debate over materialism and immaterialism in the *Bibliothèque raisonnée* and the *Bibliothèque britannique*. Chapter 8 then addresses the question: 'how does the British debate relate to the more widely known materialism of the French *philosophes*?'

1
The Three Hypotheses

ONE of the articles in the running debate carried by the *Journal helvétique* over the question of the relation between mind and body indicates that all accounts of this relation agree on several features: perceptions of the mind correspond to changes in sense organs of the body, all ideas depend on these sense perceptions, and ideas form the basis for reasoning and thinking.[1] These points of agreement apply whether we say that 'perceptions are carried to the mind by a physical influence on sense organs; or that God excites them in the soul each moment, on the occasion of changes made in sense organs; or that the soul is equipped from its creation with faculties for representing the universe'.[2] These three alternative accounts were often cited as 'les trois Hypothèses', namely the systems of physical influence, of occasional causes, and of pre-established harmony.[3]

Jean-Henri Samuel Formey in 1741 gave a brief history of the three systems:[4] the first was in vogue up to Descartes, Descartes introduced the second, and Leibniz added the third (*La Belle*

---

[1] N. Beguelin, 'Aux journalistes: A l'occasion de la philosophie de Mrs. Leibnitz & Wolff', *Journal helvétique* (Jan. 1738), 36–7. This journal was part of the *Mercure suisse*, edited by L. Bourget. The *Mercure* ran from 1732 to 1782. From 1738 to 1769, it included the *Journal helvétique*. Between 1737 and 1745, there were over a dozen articles, varying in length, on the topic of the relation between mind and body. The articles were usually in the form of 'Letters'.

[2] Beguelin, 'Aux journalistes', p. 37.

[3] See e.g. in *Journal helvétique* (July 1738), 36: 'Seconde lettre à Mr. Meuron, Conseiller d'Etat & Commissaire général de S.M. le Roi de Prusse sur la philosophie de Mr. le Baron de Leibnitz', by Bourget.

[4] Jean-Henri Samuel Formey, *La Belle Wolfienne, avec deux lettres philosophiques, l'une sur l'immortalité de l'ame, & l'autre sur l'harmonie préétablie* (1741–53). This ambitious work went to 6 vols. The first 2 parts, together with 2 philosophical letters, form vol. i. I have used the text of the facsimile repr. in Wolff's *Gesammelte Werke* (Hildesheim: G. Olms, 1983), xvi and xvii. Formey was a prolific writer and translator. Among his works relevant to this study are his trans. of Reinbeck's *Réflexions philosophiques* (1744), discussed in ch. 2, and his preface and notes to J. B. Mérian's trans. of Hume's *Philosophical Essays concerning Human Understanding* (1748; translated as *Essais philosophiques sur l'entendement humain* (2 vols., 1758)).

Wolfienne, i. 165). Formey goes on to point out that Leibniz proposed his system for the first time in the pages of the *Journal des sçavans* in 1695. Various writers then discussed and criticized Leibniz's system in other journals, with replies to some of them from Leibniz. Bayle's article 'Rorarius' in his *Dictionnaire historique et critique* (1697), attacking pre-established harmony, attracted much attention. Formey writes to explicate this system, as it was formulated by Christian Wolff. The first supposition of this system, Formey points out, is that 'the soul, by a force which is proper to it, produces the series of continual perceptions and desires' (i. 167). This force is natural and essential to the soul, not the effect of some external principle such as is required by physical influence or occasional causes. It follows from this supposition that 'it is not necessary for material ideas to be presented to the brain in order to excite ideas and perceptions'. Even were there to be no body, the soul could represent to itself a world which does not exist. It was, Formey observes, this feature of the pre-established system that led idealists to a false conclusion, that there is nothing material existing.

Formey also remarks that the main reason given by Leibniz for rejecting occasionalism was that it supposes a continual miracle (i. 176). A miracle 'suspends the course and laws of nature. God acts immediately and all the time.' For Leibniz and Wolff, bodies are a result of natural laws and a mechanism which may not be entirely intelligible but which is still not miraculous. The only miracle occurred at creation when God associated the soul and body, establishing laws for their respective actions. Formey identifies one of the false notions about this system, that all is mechanical, 'that the motions of our body, even those we call voluntary, are the result of a pure mechanism' (i. 179). Other objections are mentioned: that it is atheistical, that it denies freedom. Formey uses a nice phrase for characterizing the relation between soul and body on this hypothesis: the soul is, 'as it were, the interpreter of the body, its modifications explicate the modes of body' (i. 163).

Formey's comments were contained in the second letter (at the end of vol. i) on the pre-established harmony system. The first letter, on the immortality of the soul, reveals one of the prevalent worries about the nature of the soul: is it an *accident* of a living, organized body, or is it a *substance* (i. 137). If the former, it will then perish with the body, since accidents of bodies are only the results of the dispositions and workings of the machine of the body (i. 138). This notion of the soul is the one held by libertines. It was also the charge associated with Locke's suggestion of thinking matter, although Formey does not mention this fact. To draw the conclusion that the soul is an accident is similar to concluding that the organ music that I hear is made by the organ itself. All I am entitled to conclude is that when the organist touches the keys of the organ, the tune occurs. An example given against Leibniz was that pre-established harmony would be like a ship that navigates without a pilot. Formey says that to call attention to machines which can be made to operate by themselves (e.g. Vaucanson's flute-player) is beside the point, for no one can or has been able to show, by examining the mechanism of the human body, that it can think, reason, or reflect solely by means of that mechanism (i. 139). The conclusion is that the soul must be a substance: body and soul are two different substances which compose 'a single being called "man"' (i. 140).

A reviewer of this volume of *La Belle Wolfienne*, writing in the *Bibliothèque raisonnée*, agrees that no one *has* been able to show any such connection, but he rejects the conclusion about the soul being a substance. We do not know enough about the soul or body to enable us to prove the impossibility of thought resulting from the organization of the body. Nor can we say body and soul are two substances. The wise course to take is to withhold judgement.[5]

THE DEBATE IN THE *JOURNAL HELVÉTIQUE*

These three systems were the subject of extensive debates in the *Journal helvétique* in the years 1738 to 1745, and a few years earlier in the *Mercure suisse*. The focus of a number of these articles was the pre-established harmony system of Leibniz and Wolff. This system was, as Bourget said, well received by a great many 'Savans en *Allemagne*; mais la plûpart des *Anglois* & des *François* la rejettent entiérement'.[6] He points out that this system had generated much controversy in the Republic of Letters. The ridicule of Leibniz's

---

[5] *Bibliothèque raisonnée*, 27 (Oct.–Dec. 1741), 267–74. Another review appeared in the *Journal littéraire d'Allemagne, de Suisse et du nord*, 2/2 (1743), 402–26. This journal was the successor to the *Bibliothèque germanique*. See also *Bibliothèque françoise, ou Histoire littéraire de la France*, 32 (1739), 136–61.

[6] See his remarks at the end of an article in the Dec. 1737 issue of *Mercure suisse*, pp. 97–8. These remarks introduced a short letter from a partisan of Leibniz, signed 'Neûchâtel le 31 Decembre 1737 B . . .' (i.e. Beguelin).

system by J. P. de Crousaz, in his critique of Alexander Pope's *Essay on Man*, also stimulated many reactions, some in the pages of the *Journal helvétique*.[7] Crousaz found in Pope's *Essay* some Leibnizian themes: that this is the best of all possible worlds, that everything in the universe is related, and that all events unfold according to a prearranged plan formed by God. Pope scholars have noted that Crousaz worked from poor and distorting translations of Pope's *Essay* (there were two, the second apparently better than the first[8]) and thus have raised questions about the soundness of Crousaz's charges. The main charge was fatalism. Of greater importance for the debate over the relation between mind and body are the vivid rhetorical examples of spiritual automata developed by Crousaz in his *Examen*. These examples were supposed to reduce pre-established harmony to absurdity.

Pope's *Essay on Man* and Crousaz's *Examen de l'Essai de M. Pope sur l'homme* were the subject of a short article in the *Journal helvétique* for March 1738. The author of that article (it is signed E.M., probably Meuron) attempts to show that there is some truth in each of the three systems.[9] He tried to play the role of peacemaker by smoothing over the differences. In that effort he was unsuccessful; the controversy in this journal alone ran into the year

---

[7] See his *Examen de l'Essay de M. Pope sur l'homme* (1737). Elizabeth Carter made one of several English translations of this work in 1739. Crousaz was also the author of an important logic, which shows the influence of the Port Royal logic and Locke's *Essay: Système de réflexions qui peuvent contribuer à la netteté et à l'étendue de nos connoissances* (2 vols., 1712). This logic was translated into English in 1724. Crousaz also wrote a work on the soul, *De mente humana: Substantia a corpore distincta et immortali* (1726), which was translated into French in 1741. Of especial relevance is his *Réflexions sur l'ouvrage intitulé La Belle Wolfienne* (1743).

[8] The *Bibliothèque raisonnée*, 21 (July–Sept. 1738) reviewed Pope's *Essay* and Crousaz's *Examen* (pp. 215–27). The reviewer points out that the translation used by Crousaz was by de Silhouette (it was a prose translation), but that the Abbé Resnel had made a better (verse) translation. Crousaz then wrote a commentary on that translation as well. For more information on these translations, and on the damage done to Pope by Crousaz, see Maynard Mack's intro. to his edn. of *An Essay on Man* (1950; repr. in Mack's *Collected in Himself: Essays Critical, Biographical and Bibliographical on Pope and Some of His Contemporaries* (Newark: University of Delaware Press, 1982), 197–246. See also Richard G. Knapp, *The Fortunes of Pope's Essay on Man in 18th-Century France*, ch. II (Studies on Voltaire and the Eighteenth Century, vol. 82 (Oxford: Voltaire Foundation, 1971)).

[9] 'Lettre à Monsieur B. A. de B. & de C. Sur les variations de la Philosophie, & sur l'assoupissement des Philosophes, à l'occasion du début de la Lettre de Mr. Pope au Lord Bolingbrock, en ces termes: Réveillons-nous, Milord, laissons les petits objets à la basse Ambition, & à l'Orgueil des Rois', pp. 245–60. For a good statement of the three systems, see pp. 252–3.

1745. An earlier unsigned article is a response to an article in the *Bibliothèque germanique*, as well as a corrective to some misunderstandings of Leibniz in an article by a Professor B. (perhaps Beguelin) in the *Mercure suisse* for September 1737.[10] The anonymous author explains that, for Leibniz, there are no connections between the two substances, only an 'accord' arranged by God at the creation (p. 68). Nevertheless, this author finds one difficulty in Leibniz's account which he wishes could be explained, a difficulty which appears in later articles as well.

autant que j'ai compris l'*Harmonie pré-établie*, les impressions du Corps, suivant ce Sistème, n'ont aucune influence sur l'Ame. Cela étant, je demande comment nous pouvons nous communiquer nos pensées les uns aux autres, faire connoitre nôtre Volonté à nos semblables, & entendre leur réponse? Ce n'est point par la voie de nos Organes, puis qu'ils ne peuvent agir sur l'Ame. Il semble que ce ne peut être par aucune autre voie; l'Ame se serviroit-elle d'un moien qu'elle ne connoit pas? Tout cela ne seroit-il qu'illusion? (p. 78)

A somewhat similar difficulty is raised in January 1738 by N. Beguelin. In that article, wherein he attempts to defend pre-established harmony despite this difficulty, Beguelin points out that this system is offered by Wolff only as a hypothesis, not as a demonstrated truth (p. 34). Beguelin summarizes Wolff's account of the actions of the soul in terms of the correspondence of perceptions with changes in the body, the connection of ideas in the imagination, and the workings of syllogistic reasoning (p. 36). Wolff is able, Beguelin claims, to explain 'why the soul, at this particular moment has precisely this thought rather than another'. Using 'ame' and 'esprit' often interchangeably, Beguelin explains that Wolff defined the soul as 'a substance which represents the universe' (p. 38). He argues later in this letter that the hypothesis of pre-established harmony is the best explanation of the relation between mind and body, but an objection had been raised about the representative function of the soul. The objection was that while the soul could represent the characters of a book, the *ideas* signified by those

[10] *Mercure suisse* (Sept. 1737), 64–79: 'Reponse aux remarques critiques de Monsieur J. B. P. & Pr. en Th. à Genève, sur le 1er. article de la *Bibliothèque germanique*, T. XXXVI'. The *Bibliothèque germanique* article is a long defence of Wolff against a number of charges, among those that Wolff made the soul a machine. See 33 (1736), 1–34.

shapes have no relation to the organized body; thus, the parallelism between mind and body breaks down (pp. 43–5).

Beguelin's reply to this objection contributes some interesting notions about sign and signification. He agrees that, in reading a book, 'the soul is only able to represent the paper and characters'. It is the faculty of imagination that, when I see these characters, recalls to my mind 'the terms or sounds of which these characters are the arbitrary and artificial signs'. How does the soul get to the signification of those sounds? Beguelin appeals to *natural signs* (e.g. gestures) used by persons of different languages when they want to communicate some request but are unable to use each other's language. He also appeals to what he takes to be the method we use to help children learn the names of objects.

On montre l'Objet, on en exprime en meme-tems le nom; l'Enfant retient l'un & l'autre. Montrez-lui ensuite l'Objet, il en prononcera le nom; dites lui le nom sans lui montrer l'Objet, l'Imagination, par une loi constante, lui représentera l'objet qu'il a vu autre-fois, dans le tems qu'il entendoit ce son. (p. 45)

So much for learning the names of physical objects. How to account for learning and understanding phrases and sentences? Is this method of associating objects with the sounds of their names adequate to 'make known to the soul the meaning of each word' or phrase? Perhaps the context will help, once the sense of some words has been acquired. Beguelin thinks this topic of language-learning is well worth investigation. He suggests that we may need to start with writing, especially with hieroglyphics.

The relevance to the pre-established harmony hypothesis of these brief suggestions on how we move from the sounds or shapes of words to their meaning lies in the question of what ideas (the sense or meaning of words) express about the body, what the events are in the body that correlate with understanding the meanings of words. There were a few writers in the eighteenth century (medical men) who constructed theories of specific brain events for every thought or feeling. The question raised is one relating to the mind or soul and its body. Another objection brought against pre-established harmony was that it leads to idealism. Beguelin agrees that that theory does not establish the existence of an external world, but neither does it rule out its possibility (p. 47). Moreover, Beguelin believes that Wolff adopts definitions which leave open the question of idealism or realism. For example, Wolff talks of 'the order of successives', leaving it open for the idealist to substitute 'the order of successive perceptions', or for the materialist to talk of 'the order of successive changes in the universe' (p. 48). Truth for Wolff is defined as 'the order of phenomena', leaving open the question of whether the phenomena are real or not. All Wolff needs, Beguelin assures us, is to treat the body as a phenomenon, a fact which sceptics and idealists do not deny. The anticipations of Kant here are intriguing.

In a long article of February 1738, P. Roques argues that Leibniz's principle, which says, in the version given in his *Theodicy* (1710), that 'the body acts when the mind wills', means in effect that the body is, for example, like an architect watching masons construct a building, a building which the soul plans, which plans the masons never consult: the two work independently of each other.[11] The same conclusion applies to books: they are written by hands reflecting the soul's plot and narrative but without any contact or knowledge of the soul's conception. Even Leibniz's books and articles have been produced by laws of mechanism. Orators speak without the direction of the soul, managing without any direction to produce the sounds which express the ideas that the soul has (p. 108).

In his *Examen de l'Essay de M. Pope*, Crousaz constructed a number of similar scenarios entailed, he thought, by Leibniz's system. One of these examples involves a session with his secretary.

I believe that I am now thinking and dictating Expressions to my Amanuensis, proper to excite Ideas conformable to my own in the mind of my Readers. I imagine, too, that my Expressions raise Ideas in the Soul of my Amanuensis, and that it is from hence that the Regularity of his Strokes proceeds, which are exactly such as I would have them. No, say they, there is nothing in all this. Our two corporeal Machines have no need of the Influence of our Souls, in order to give one of them the Motion of dictating, and the other that of writing, as we do. All the parts of the Universe are so well connected, and so inevitably subjected to Motions following one another in a Series, that my dictating Machine was, by the Concatenation of certain Successions, found

---

[11] 'Lettre à Mr. Ruchat, ministre du St. Evangile & célèbre professeur dans l'Académie de Lausanne, sur le sistème de Mr. Leibnitz', 104–45. Roques may have in mind the *Theodicy* passages in 'Essays', pt. I, §§ 60–5, where Leibniz outlines his system. In an earlier letter to the same M. Ruchat, the author seems to think that all the thoughts, feelings, and sensations of the soul are *caused by* the soul intentionally and consciously. This is a misreading of Leibniz's notion of the unfolding of the various properties of a soul. See 'Lettre à Mr. Ruchat, ministre du St. Evangile & célèbre Professeur en Théologie dans l'Académie de Lausanne', *Journal helvétique* (Dec. 1737), 63–97.

near a Machine which should write conformably to what I pronounce, though it heard nothing of it. (pp. 20–1)[12]

The example used by Roques of Leibniz's books is also found in Crousaz.

It would have signified nothing for human Bodies to have cast their Eyes on the Books that bear his Name: These Books were incapable of causing any Idea in the Souls of those who read them; it was necessary that at a season-able Time a great Number of Souls should perceive these Ideas to arise in themselves, and should imagine that they were furnish'd with these Ideas by reading certain Books. Neither Mr. *Leibnitz*'s Soul, nor the Soul of his most zealous and indefatigable Adherents, could ever have had a Power of instructing the Souls of those who reckon themselves his Disciples; neither immediately, for a Soul does not act in this manner upon another Soul; nor yet mediately, for one Soul has no Action upon another by the Interposition of Bodies incapable of acting upon Thinking Substances. (pp. 62–3)

Crousaz and Roques are reflecting a similar criticism made against Leibniz by Pierre Bayle: Caesar goes to the Senate on a particular day and gives a specific speech without the soul making any impression on the relevant parts of the body (hands and voice), a body which does not have any awareness of the specific soul associated with it. Roques draws a sharp distinction between a body moved by the impressions of objects acting according to the laws of mechanism, and most of the actions of men (*Journal helvétique* (Feb. 1738), 110). He goes on to offer a number of useful examples of human actions, contrasting the uniform, predictive nature of bodies moved by mechanism with the unpredictable, free actions of men. It is only the soul which makes the difference. Choice, reasons, even caprice operate to move the body in action (pp. 111–13). Leibniz's system makes freedom impossible; it also results in scepticism about other minds (pp. 117–18) and renders uncertain the existence of our body and an external world. It even eventuates in 'égoisme' (p. 122). Roques ends his detailed critique by saying the

---

[12] I am using the 18th-century English translation of Crousaz by Elizabeth Carter, *An Examination of Mr. Pope's Essay on Man, Translated from the French of Mr. Crousaz* (1739). There are other intriguing and complex examples of this sort on pp. 55–60, 126, 158. Leibniz uses an example in his *Theodicy* (which he credits to Jacquelot) similar to Crousaz's amanuensis: 'And Mr. Jacquelot has demonstrated well in his book on the *Conformity of Faith with Reason*, that it is just as if he who knows all that I shall order a servant to do the whole day long on the morrow made an automaton entirely resembling this servant, to carry out to-morrow at the right moment all that I should order . . .' ('Essays', pt. I, § 63).

so-called 'union' of soul and body on this hypothesis is not a *real* union; it is only a 'metaphysical' or 'ideal' union. A real union requires some dependence of both parts on each other.

In May and July 1738, the editor of the *Journal helvétique*, Bourget, gave a careful explication of Leibniz's system, with an eye on some of the objections that had been raised in this and other journals.[13] The July article in particular takes up the criticisms of Crousaz in his 1737 critique of Pope and in his *Examen du pyrrhonisme* (1733). The article by Roques is also discussed and answered. Bourget, an admirer of Leibniz, writes to defend pre-established harmony against the other two hypotheses, believing it to be the best explication of phenomena. Roques contributed a brief response to Bourget in November 1738.[14] He remarked that great minds are not above making mistakes. He recognized that Leibniz *says* his system allows freedom, but the question is, is freedom possible within the principles of that system? He reiterated his earlier claim that Leibniz's doctrine makes the motion of bodies necessary, as necessary as the hands of a clock (p. 418). A free action has a certain contingency about it, the power of an intelligent agent to do or not to do the action (p. 419). In Leibniz's system, all bodies, including the human body, are moved of necessity in accordance with the original plan of God. Correspondence does not make for freedom.

Bourget then replies in December with a long and detailed article, perhaps the most important in this series.[15] He names some of the critics of pre-established harmony: the Abbé Foucher, Monsieur Bayle, the Fathers Lami (François Lamy) and Tournemine, Messieurs Newton and Clarke, and Doctor Stahl, a list of some of the most outstanding theologians and scientists of the day. Other critics fail to pay sufficient attention to Leibniz's replies, content merely to repeat what those writers have said. Moreover, each of them writes from a particular bias. Foucher writes from a very traditional point

[13] 'Lettre à M. Meuron, Conseiller d'Etat & Commissaire général de S.M. le Roi de Prusse à Neûchâtel, sur la philosophie de Mr. le Baron de Leibnitz', *Journal helvétique* (May 1738), 393–419; continued as 'Seconde Lettre' in July, pp. 15–36.

[14] 'Lettre à Monsieur Bourget, savant & célèbre Professeur en Philosophie à Neûchâtel, membre de l'Académie roïale de Berlin &c., pour servir de réponse aux deux lettres qu'il a publiées dans le Mercure suisse, au sujet de la philosophie de Mr. de Leibnitz', pp. 413–43.

[15] 'Lettre à Monsieur Meuron, Conseiller d'Etat, & Commissaire général de S.M. le Roi de Prusse, sur les hipothèses, concernant l'union de l'ame avec le corps', pp. 521–56.

of view. Bayle is subtle in argument but tends to sophistry. Father Lamy favours the system of occasional causes, Father Tournemine supports a modified version of physical influence. Newton and Clarke were too caught up in their antipathy towards Leibniz's general metaphysics to give him a fair reading. G.-E. Stall has his own view of the living body, with the soul as its unique agent, and is thus not disposed to understand or accept Leibniz's account. Bourget only asks for a fair hearing.

Je suis néanmoins persuadé, que tous ceux qui se donneront la peine de lire avec un Esprit libre & atentif le *Traité de l'Harmonie pré-établie de Mr. Bülf-finger*, qui renferme les Réponses aux Objections des Savans, dont on vient de parler, & ce que Mr. *Wolff* dit sur la même Matiére dans sa *Psichologie Rationelle*; je suis, dis-je, persuadé, que s'ils n'adoptent pas l'Hipothèse de Mr. *de Leibnitz*, ils la laisseront au moins aller de pair avec l'*Influence Phisique* & les *Causes ocasionelles*. (p. 523)

In this article, Bourget addresses a series of topics, the first being the operations of the soul. He reaffirms the Cartesian point that we cannot conceive of that which thinks in us being different from our-selves. Being aware of one's self is a unique act, but we cannot form any 'image' or 'representation' of that which thinks. Bourget is close to saying we cannot have an idea of the soul-substance, only of its acts and operations. What we find in our understanding when we pay attention and reflect are representations of objects which are intimately present to the understanding. The term 'idea' is used as a synonym of 'representation'. These ideas are formed in the under-standing without any distinct act of representation. The ideas of objects differ entirely from the perceptions we have of ourselves (p. 525). The soul attributes these ideas to the object as properties of the object but, Bourget reminds us, Descartes has shown that sensible qualities really belong to the soul. Hearing, seeing, tasting are operations of the soul; sounds, sights, and flavours are ideas (p. 526). The operations of the soul are three: (1) the natural representation of physical objects, (2) comparing and combining the ideas that represent objects, and (3) selecting some of these ideas for particular attention.

The second topic of Bourget's article is the operations of the human body. That body is a mass of organized matter, both as a whole and in its various parts (p. 528). All its operations are mechanical, 'that is, they consist of different motions' (p. 529). There

are three kinds of bodily motion: those internal motions that we have
in common with plants and animals; those the body has in common
with animals, of moving and changing place; and voluntary movements. The partisans of all three systems agree on the first two.
Bourget also believes that no one could be so unreasonable as to
deny that the third sort of motions are also mechanical, that is, that
they are 'the effects of the admirable structure of nerves, tendons,
muscles, fluids, etc.'. The question for the three systems (and
Bourget's third topic) is, whether the soul when it wills is 'the efficient
and physical cause of voluntary motion' (p. 530). Similarly, we need
to ask, 'are the organs of the body the efficient cause of the representations or ideas in the understanding?' The system of physical
influence gives an affirmative answer: there is causal influence from
body to mind and vice versa (p. 530). How are we to understand
such reciprocal interaction?

We can get some understanding of the claimed nature of physical
influence by examining the effects of external objects on the human
body and the effects of the human body on external objects. Science
agrees that all bodies act only by impulse and motion. When some
observed effect cannot be traced to the motion of gross bodies,
science has recourse to insensible particles. Vibrating strings on a
violin, the bells in clock towers, act physically on auditory nerves.
The understanding *responds* to these physical disturbances of
nerves with the *perception* of sound (p. 531). How is this perceptual,
cognitive response related to the physical motions in the environment and to motions inside the human body? How is it possible for
the ideas and volitions of the soul to activate the body? Is it not
evident that there is a physical influence of external objects on the
understanding, as well as on the body (p. 532)? Bourget agrees with
Leibniz that such claimed influence is only apparent, since it is
impossible for physical motion to be transformed into ideas, or for
ideas to produce bodily motion. Since the defenders of physical
influence agree that the soul is immaterial, they should agree that
there can be no influence of material bodies on the immaterial
understanding (p. 533). All that this claim of physical influence
amounts to is that there is some 'accord' or 'agreement' between
mind and body and between external bodies and the mind. Physical
influence does not explicate this accord, this relation between
motion in nerves and awareness of ideas.

Physical influence attributes to the soul and to bodies powers they do not have. It was because they worried about such attribution of powers incompatible with bodies and souls that some ancients and some recent defenders of physical influence have said we cannot prove that the soul is immaterial. Most striking among recent defenders of the system of physical influence is Locke, who said the nature of substances is unknown, even suggesting that certain sorts of organized matter could be made to think by God (p. 534). Bourget reads Locke's suggestion as saying either that the soul can think if God wishes without ceasing to be material, or that it is the organized body which thinks. Bourget, like so many who opposed Locke's suggestion in Britain, insists that representations or ideas which are clearly not material cannot be caused by matter in motion. Hearing and seeing are not material acts. In every instance of seeing or hearing, there are two actions: the motion of molecules of air or light which are represented by colour or sound and the action of perception, of being aware of the colour or sound. To confuse these two acts, to confuse physical with cognitive processes, is to say that particles of air or light would understand and think. No materialist has so far made such a bold claim.

Malebranche and his followers avoid the absurdity of thinking matter by going to occasional causes, with a firm denial of any interaction. Leibniz deals with the problem by defining the human mind as 'a representative being, representing the universe as well as God' (p. 543). Bourget might have said that representation is a cognitive act which does have some relation with the physical processes of the body and with external objects. Unlike occasionalism, which cuts the mind off entirely from any interaction with bodies, limiting the cognitive interactions to God, pre-established harmony stresses the double existence of ideas and objects. The suggestion made by Descartes and Arnauld of two kinds of interaction, causal and cognitive, is not developed by Leibniz explicitly, but it seems to be in the background. Bourget does link the duality of physical and cognitive to Leibniz's talk of two worlds. Man as mind, as free agent, as cognitive representation of the world, follows final causes and is a citizen of the intelligible realm or the 'Monde des Esprits', and a member of the City of God (p. 546). Man as biological body is a mechanism, composed of many smaller organic machines, and follows efficient causes, causes founded on and correlated with the law of agreement imposed at the Creation by God.

LOCKE'S DOCTRINES IN THESE DEBATES

As the exchange of articles continued in the *Journal helvétique*, many of the same points were made by defenders and attackers of Leibniz. Locke's name gets drawn in more frequently, not always over his suggestion of matter thinking. Roques briefly discusses his notion of reflection in February 1739 in a reply to Bourget's November 1738 article. In May 1739, a M. Guisi enters the debate, remarking that since we do not know the nature of mind (*esprit*), it may be composed of a kind of matter that we have not experienced.[16] He states that he does not want to say, or to give occasion for anyone believing, that the soul is material, as some accuse Locke, that 'ingenious English metaphysician', of doing (p. 416). Nevertheless, he claims that no one has shown that there is not a different sort of matter which is the substance of mind. Thus, how can we say that a substance about which we have no clear, precise, or complete knowledge is or is not material (p. 417)? Before we can decide if two beings are incompatible, we need to have an exact and perfect idea of both. He goes on to suggest that our body is more than matter. We *can*, he says, conceive that God has given to the understanding the power of acting on bodies.

In March 1740, Bourget replies to an earlier letter of Roques where Leibniz's notion of innate ideas was discussed. Bourget remarks that Locke's argument against innate ideas holds only against those who accept the system of physical influence (p. 206). The whole of Locke's *Essay* is based on this system of physical influence, to which Locke was attached. Bourget links this attachment to the opinion of the materiality of the soul. Locke's attack against innate ideas assumes also that ideas must be actually conscious to the mind. All ideas for Locke come from the senses, caused by external action. Leibniz's innate ideas are dispositions. An idea for Leibniz, he repeats, is a representation of sensible objects. In October 1740, Locke's name appears again, this time in connection with the discussion Locke had with Limborch over the liberty of indifference.

Locke's role in these discussions comes to a head with the

---

[16] In the remarks by the editor of *Journal helvétique* (referred to above, see n. 6) Guisi is identified as the author of *Démonstration de la réligion chrétienne contre les athées & déïstes*, and also of *Pensées, ou Conjectures sur l'union de l'âme avec le corps*. The editor explains that Guisi, who is from the town of Aarau, accepts the system of physical influence (p. 98). I have been unable to find these works or to identify M. Guisi.

announcement in October 1741, and the subsequent publication, of a four-volume work by Caspar Cuenz (or Cuentz). Much of that work was a defence of Locke against the charge of materialism. This work was announced in the *Journal helvétique* as 'Essai d'un Système nouveau en Metaphysique, ou pour mieux dire le Système de l'*Influence Phisique* réhabilété et rectifié'. In February 1742, this journal published a 'Projet de Souscription, pour un Ouvrage intitulé, Essai d'un Sistème nouveau, concernant la Nature des Etres spirituels, fondé en partie sur les Principes de Mr. Locke, célébre Philosophe Anglois, dont l'Auteur fait l'Apologie'. This 'projet' was given some fanfare since the *Journal helvétique* was sponsoring the four-volume study. Further attention was given to Cuenz's work, and to his discussion of Locke's doctrines (including thinking matter), by Cuenz himself in detailed outlines of all four volumes in another journal, *Bibliothèque françoise*, for 1743–4.[17] Subsequent issues of the *Journal helvétique* carried summaries and references to Cuenz's study. Then, in November 1742, Cuenz contributed a long article defending himself against an attack by M. Sandoz, Commissaire général at Neuchâtel. The immediate cause of this article was Sandoz's questions about the newly discovered polyp, questions about how to account for life in the divided material parts. If the principle of life is said to be in the parts, as he thought Cuenz's general position would say, Sandoz saw Spinozism in that answer. Cuenz writes against another critic, this time said to be a theologian from a nearby village. Locke's talk of intuitive and sensitive knowledge is cited and discussed (pp. 343–51), the question being whether intuition reveals an agreement or compatibility between the idea of a soul and the idea of that soul being non-extended. Cuenz finds the notion of a non-extended soul odd, since he follows a rather common tradition in believing that all beings (including space, some writers said) must be extended in some way. How does the critic know, Cuenz asks, that the nature of a soul is incompatible with some form of extension? Apparently, Cuenz's critic had suggested that Cuenz did not really agree with Locke, despite his apology for him. Cuenz admits that he does go farther than Locke. He admits that Locke never says the eternal thinking being (God) is material, nor does Cuenz believe this is true, so long as 'material' means the matter we are familiar with in ordinary experience (p. 438). Nor does Locke think that if matter were spiritualized as much as we

---

[17] See vol. 38 (1744), 82–106, 106–30, 262–86, 287–309.

wish, it would then have thought as a property. Cuenz assures his critic that he also does not attribute thought to ordinary matter, only to matter in a modified form.[18]

Cuenz received some help from an anonymous writer in May 1745. This writer praises Cuenz as well as Locke. He says that he studied medicine under Boerhaave, and that he read Locke, Spinoza, and other similar writers without falling into materialism. Materialism was, he says, the vogue among young students (p. 413). He gives a sort of intellectual biography of himself, explaining that he first entertained the notion that God gave thought to matter, but then swung the other way and favoured spiritualism. He finally reached a view of his own which conceives of the soul as a very subtle substance parallel to the body, having parts and even nerve fibres. He even seems to have flirted with the notion of a universal soul. He ends his article by using one of the analogies often employed, comparing the soul to a stringed instrument (p. 429).

The extended exchange of articles on the three systems even entered the realm of poetry. In June 1739, J. B. Tollot published a poem dedicated to Roques's daughter: 'Epitre à Madelle. Sophie Renée Roques, sur les trois hipothèses de l'union de l'ame & du corps' (pp. 517–23).[19] Tollot, who favours occasionalism, prefaced the poem with a defence of using poetry for such abstract topics. He also discussed the various writers on this topic, both those who have published in the *Journal helvétique*, and the main figures of Leibniz, Malebranche, Clarke, and Locke. Of Locke, he says: 'Mr. *Loke*, dont l'Esprit étoit si juste & si pénétrant, croit que nous ne connoissons pas encore toutes les proprietés de la Matière, & que peut être n'est-elle pas incapable de penser' (p. 512). The charge against Leibniz is repeated, that he makes the soul an immaterial automaton. The poem itself attempts to speak of the three systems, posing problems for each and ending by glorifying the soul. On physical influence, which was usually seen as leading to materialism, Tollot writes:

> Je cherche a démêler, par quels secrets ressorts,
> Mon Ame est unie à mon Corps;

---

[18] There is a very similar letter, presumably written by Cuenz, replying to the same critic, in an issue of the *Bibliothèque françoise*, 37 (1743), 229–347. There, he locates the attack in the *Nouvelle Bibliothèque, ou Histoire littéraire des principaux écrits* (Nov. 1742), a review of Cuenz's 4 vols. See below, ch. 3, pp. 76–84.

[19] The introductory letter covers pp. 501–16. It is addressed to the editors of the journal, 'sur l'Epître à Madelle. Sophie Renée Roques'.

Une mutüelle influence
En produit-elle les acords?
Mais comment concevoir qu'une brute Matière,
Pesante, insensible, grossière,
Puisse agir sur l'Entendement?
Je ne connois le Corps que par son mouvement,
Par son repos, sa couleur, sa figure;
C'est un Etre étendu qu'on divise aisément.
Tout autre qualité fausse, incertaine, obscure,
S'ofre à mes yeux, moins clairement;
Mais nôtre Ame aperçoit, forme un raisonnement,
Compare des Objets la grandeur, la Structure,
Et porrant ses regards sur toute la Nature,
En observe le cours, l'ordre & l'arrangement.
Comment des Corps sans sentiment
Feroient-ils naître nos Pensées?
Comment produiroient-ils ces diverses Idées
Sur lesquelles l'Esprit porte son jugement?

This poem also appears, along with the introductory letter, in the *Bibliothèque raisonnée* in the July–September 1748 issue.[20] This article is unsigned but it is clearly a revised version of the remarks found in the *Journal helvétique*. The revisions take the form of more detail about the disputes in the *Journal helvétique* (it serves as a useful summary of those articles, thus giving them a wider visibility to the reading public) and some attention to other critics of Leibniz. More detail is also given to the account of Leibniz's system. The writer compares pre-established harmony to a universe of marionettes run by a master 'machiniste' (pp. 84–5). The poem is reprinted virtually unchanged except for some alterations in spelling and capitalization and some slight variation in the placement of lines on the page.

TOURNEMINE AND THE *JOURNAL DE TRÉVOUX*

The Jesuit *Journal de Trévoux* is a source for traditional, orthodox views on most topics that touch on religion and theology.[21] Father

---

[20] Art. IV, 'Epître sur les trois principales hypothèses de l'union de l'ame & du corps à 'Madlle. Sophie Roques, fille de Mr. Roques, très célébre pasteur de l'eglise françoise à Basle: précedée d'une lettre au pere au sujet de cette Pièce adressée à Madlle. sa fille', pp. 72–97.

[*See p. 26 for n. 21*]

Tournemine was a frequent contributor, writing on a variety of topics but specifically concerned with the relations between mind and body. In the 1730s, he published a very strong attack against the materialism of Locke's suggestion and against Voltaire's praise of Locke. In volume 7 for May 1703, Tournemine rejects satirically the scholastic treatment of mind and body (at least, that doctrine as taught in the Schools), advancing a rather novel view of his own. He tells us that in the Schools, what is said to unite the two substances is an entity which is part corporeal and part spiritual, an intermediary between mind and body. Cuenz's notion of an extended soul may reflect this earlier view. The animal spirits of seventeenth- and eighteenth-century physiology may also reflect this notion, since the animal spirits were corporeal but very refined, rarified bodies. Tournemine charges that the appeal to a third entity, an inter-mediary, does not *explain* union. Nor is he happy with what he characterizes as the Cartesian talk of mutual correspondence, since he believes such correspondence or parallelism is the result, not the cause, of the union of soul and body (p. 866). The response which some Cartesians make, that the soul and body are united because God wills this union and established laws for their correspondence, is, he says, devout but insufficient philosophically. We need to be told *how* God unites two substances. These Cartesians even say that God is the immediate cause of all the motions of the body (p. 867).

Tournemine says that Leibniz has exposed the weakness of the notion of occasional causes by his analogy of two synchronous clocks. The occasionalist has the clock-maker adjusting the wheels and weights of both clocks regularly, a sign of poorly made clocks. Tournemine thinks Leibniz's account of the union better; it gives God a more dignified role. God by means of his omniscience is able to know everything that will ever occur in or by means of the body; he also selects a specific individual soul for each body. God also knows in advance the soul's perceptions, volitions, and thoughts. The individuality of each soul is thus made to fit the individuality of each body (pp. 872–3). Tournemine offers one half of a system of influence, an influence of soul on body. The soul, he says, acts on the body by a natural force, a force that is natural, essential, and fitted to that soul. The action of the soul on body does not come from the

---

[21] The official name of the journal was *Mémoires pour l'histoire des sciences et des beaux arts*. It was usually known as the *Journal de Trévoux*, or sometimes as *Mémoires de Trévoux*.

knowledge or *volition* of the soul (thereby avoiding part of the difficulty of explaining how willing or knowing could move the body); it is a natural feature of each soul. The union is characterized as 'a union of property ("propriété"), of possession, the soul appropriates the body by that action' (p. 873). This particular body is the body of this particular soul because that body 'has an essential need of that soul in order to be supported in situations advantageous to human functions' (p. 874). Tournemine's point is that 'it is not only because the soul acts on this body that it is united with it; it is because the soul's action on the body is, on the one hand, so essential to the body that without it the body would not be a human body; on the other hand, that soul is so proper to that body that no other would be able to produce that action by natural forces'. The union is one of *appropriation* and *possession*. Tournemine suggests that this account gives meaning to Augustine's definition of man as 'a soul which has a body'.

Various objections were made against Tournemine's union of appropriation and possession. To the objection that motion or the faculty of moving is not part of the concept of soul, he replies that experience tells us that the soul does act on the body, just as experience informs us that we think and will. To the objection that the soul can only act via the will, he replies that while God acts freely, the soul moves its body necessarily. God's will and power are the same, but in finite creatures they are different. Even some theologians distinguish between God's decree and the power that carries it out. In October 1703, the Abbé Languet de Montigny published a series of objections. The journal printed these followed by Tournemine's replies.[22] The abbé cites Leibniz for support of the claim that a mind is not able to act immediately on a body, since the two are of such different natures (p. 1841). The implication is that the action cannot work the other way either, at least not immediately. It is not clear from the abbé's article just what the mediating factors are, but they are probably, as they are for Tournemine, the nerves and animal spirits. The abbé presses Tournemine to recognize that there are some passions which the body does communicate to the soul. The body also transmits the motions of external objects to the soul and the soul can stir motion in the brain. The abbé seems close to accepting physical influence.

[22] Art. 176, 'Lettre de Mr. L'Abbé Languet de Montigny aumonier de Madame la Duchesse de Bourgogne au P. Tournemine Jesuite', pp. 1840–54. Tournemine's replies follow in art. 177, pp. 1856–70.

In his replies, Tournemine maintains that the action between soul and body goes from the former to the latter, from superior to inferior (p. 1860). Bodies can only act by impulse, which is not a mode applicable to souls. Souls can act in two ways, by thinking and by willing. In moving bodies, the soul does so without itself being moved; but for Tournemine, moving the body means moving the animal spirits, those rarified bodies of the physiology. He compares the spring of machines to the soul as the 'spring' or driving mechanism of the body (pp. 1863–4). The precise nature of the soul's action on the animal spirits is left obscure. Tournemine also denies to the abbé that he ever said the soul applies the sense organs to external objects. External objects can activate the animal spirits in the nerves of the body and thus get impressions transmitted to the soul which in turn calls forth, in ways left unexplained, thoughts and ideas.

LEIBNIZ AND THE *JOURNAL DES SÇAVANS*

Leibniz was a frequent contributor to this important Paris journal, writing mostly on science and mathematics. In July 1695, he sent the journal what he referred to as 'this system', a system which he said had been developed and refined by exchanges with theologians and philosophers. He mentions he has been told that Arnauld has found some parts of this system paradoxical.[23] The basis of his system is a concept of particulars, of what he calls 'true unities' or 'formal atoms'. This concept in turn is related to his conviction that extended matter by itself is inadequate to account for phenomena and the laws of nature (p. 454). In addition to extension, the concept of *force* is required. Leibniz considered the combination of force and true unities as an updated version of the much maligned scholastic substantial forms, or of Aristotle's 'first entelechies'. He calls these unities 'primitive forces' or 'formal atoms', explaining that they 'contain not only the *actuality* or the *completion* of possibility but an original *activity* as well'. He also used the term 'souls' for these primitive forces, a term which can easily mislead if we fail to realize that rational souls or minds are only one kind of formal unities. The notion of vegetative, sensitive, and rational souls had its origins in

[23] The article appeared on 4 July 1695 (pp. 455–62), with the title, 'Sistême nouveau de la nature & de la communication des substances, aussi bien que de l'union qu'il y a entre l'ame & le corps'. For this and, unless noted, all other references to Leibniz, I am using the English translation in Leroy E. Loemker's edition of *Philosophical Papers and Letters* (Dordrecht: Reidel, 2nd edn., 1970), 453–60.

Aristotle and scholastic writings on organic substances, but Leibniz takes the notion to apply to matter as well. It might be better to say that all matter, whether inorganic or organic, is active. To say, as John Toland and Robert Clayton were to say later, that all is alive, does not quite catch Leibniz's meaning.[24] Activity takes different forms in matter, in organic animal machines, and in minds or rational souls. 'Minds . . . have special laws which place them beyond the revolutions of matter' (p. 455).

Leibniz criticized those philosophers who confused natural with artificial machines. He may have had Descartes in mind, but he explicitly cites Fontenelle, *Entretiens sur la pluralité des mondes* (1686). 'A natural machine remains a machine in its smallest parts, and what is more, it always remains the same machine that it has been' through various transformations (p. 456). The kind-difference between artificial and natural machines such as humans is that 'by means of the soul or form there is a true unity corresponding to what is called "I" in us'. The difficulty is to account for what appears to be an interaction between this soul and its organic body. Leibniz thinks that Descartes gave up trying to account for such interaction. The occasionalist disciples of Descartes concluded that 'we sense the qualities of bodies because God causes thoughts to arise in our soul on the occasion of material movements and that when our soul in its turn wishes to move the body, God moves the body for it' (p. 457). Leibniz agrees with the occasionalist that 'there is no real influence of one created substance upon another and that all things, with all their reality, are continually produced by the power of God', but he does not like the appeal to God in order to solve difficulties, especially if God has to be invoked on every occasion of awareness or of the movement of limbs: 'In philosophy we must try to give a reason which will show how things are brought about by the Divine Wisdom in conformity with the particular concept of the subject in question' (p. 457).

In describing his alternative explanation, Leibniz says that he was surprised at his solution when he first articulated it. Responsibility is still traced to God, but only at the creation: God has originally created the soul, and every other real unity in such a way that 'everything in it must arise from its own nature by a perfect *spontaneity*

[24] For a discussion of Toland and Clayton, see my *Thinking Matter: Materialism in Eighteenth-Century Britain* (Minneapolis, Minn.: University of Minnesota Press; Oxford: Basil Blackwell, 1984), 97–8, 101–2.

with regard to itself, yet by a perfect *conformity* to things without' (p. 457). Internal sensations are phenomena which follow upon external objects affecting the body and brain, but they arise in the soul 'through its own original constitution'. That constitution is the soul's *representative* nature which is 'capable of expressing entities outside of itself in agreement with its organs—this nature having been given it from its creation and being constitutive of its individual character'. Those perceptions or expressions of external objects 'reach the soul at the proper time by virtue of its own laws, as in a world apart, and as if there existed nothing but God and itself' (p. 457). Leibniz does not want to deny an external world; he only means to emphasize that perceptual awareness is not caused by species coming from objects to sense organs, as the system of physical influence among the scholastics said. The sequences of perceptions produced by the soul 'correspond naturally to the sequence of changes in the universe'.

Leibniz called his explanation the 'hypothesis of agreement'. Commenting later to Basnage de Beauval on his *Journal des sçavans* article, he used the clock metaphor or analogy which so many critics cited.[25] The agreement of the two clocks can happen in three ways: by a natural influence, by having a skilled craftsman constantly adjusting them, or by so constructing the clocks that both will never need any adjustments (pp. 459–60). Leibniz says the way of influence is what 'common philosophy' asserts. Since it is impossible 'to conceive of material particles or of species or immaterial qualities which can pass from one of these substances' to the other, the system of physical influence must be rejected. The second solution of periodic adjustments by God requires a *deus ex machina* in natural events, which does not do justice to God. Thus, the third hypothesis, which Leibniz now calls *the way of pre-established harmony*, is the only acceptable explanation.

In his correspondence with Arnauld, Leibniz restated and elaborated some of the features of his explanation. In a long letter of 16 July 1686, he names his account 'the *hypothesis of concomitance or of the correspondence of substances with each other*'.[26] Physical influence is there described as the *hypothesis of impressions*. The notion of expression for the perception of rational souls is defined in a 9 October 1687 letter to Arnauld: 'One thing expresses another, in

---

[25] In a communication published in *Histoire des ouvrages des savans* (Feb. 1696).
[26] In *Philosophical Papers*, p. 338.

my usage, when there is a constant and regular relation between what can be said about one and about the other.'[27] Natural perception, animal feeling, and intellectual knowledge are all species of expression. In an earlier 1678 paper on 'What is an Idea', Leibniz identified various kinds of expression:

the model of a machine expresses the machine itself, the projective delineation on a plane expresses a solid, speech expresses thoughts and truths, characters express numbers, and an algebraic equation expresses a circle or some other figure. What is common to all these expressions is that we can pass from a consideration of the relations in the expression to a knowledge of the corresponding properties of the thing expressed. Hence it is clearly not necessary for that which expresses to be similar to the thing expressed, if only a certain analogy is maintained between the relations.[28]

Consciousness or thought accompanies representation in the rational soul. The topic under discussion in the October 1687 letter was pain: how is it that the soul feels a pain correlated with a blow or a pinprick (p. 340)? Awareness of bodily states is no more possible on Leibniz's hypothesis than is awareness of external objects, but in both cases the sequencing of bodily states and perceptual states is synchronized, the latter expressing or representing the former. Each of the sequences (of the soul, the body, the universe) belongs to a separate world, but the correlation is not contingent. Moreover, the representative function of the soul informs the soul about body and the world. Trans-world causation is ruled out. There is some suggestion of causal connections internal to each kind of sequence. The representative function is close to a cognitive connection between conscious soul and its body and external objects. In the same 1678 paper cited above, Leibniz speaks of the power of thinking impressed upon the mind 'so that it can by its own operations derive what corresponds perfectly to the nature of things'.[29] 'Derive' sounds like a cognitive operation.

In his criticism of the *Journal des sçavans* article, Pierre Bayle had argued that Leibniz's separation of body and soul, each with its sequences of events, amounted to saying that the soul would feel pain even if there was no blow or pinprick; thereby, although Bayle did not explicitly say so, the way was open for some form of idealism.[30] Bayle was arguing that the behaviour of the dog (the example

---

[27] Ibid. 339.   [28] Ibid. 207.   [29] Ibid. 208.
[30] See Bayle's *Dictionnaire historique et critique*, article on Rorarius, Note H: 'je ne

he was using) and its 'spontaneous' feelings cannot be as disconnected as Leibniz seems to make them. In his reply, Leibniz
points out that his account requires that each soul represents what
does occur in its body or in the world.[31] Souls do not just have ideas
or perceptions with formal reality (to use Descartes's language): they
have objective reality as well by representing and expressing what
exists and occurs in the body and in the physical world. Leibniz is
rejecting any *causal* connection between thoughts and things, but
accepting a *cognitive* relation. The difference between Leibniz and
Descartes on the cognition of objects is that for Leibniz there is no
triggering mechanism in the body which stimulates the cognitive
reaction, as there is for Descartes. Descartes's soul responds to
certain motions in the brain in a cognitive way because those
motions have a dual reality: they are physical but also *significatory*.[32]
Just as, Leibniz says, 'my hand does not move because I will it, for I
might well will a mountain to move', my hand moves because I could
not 'successfully will its motion except at the exact moment when the
muscles of the hand make the contractions necessary to that end'.[33]
In a similar way, I will not have perceptions of trees and houses unless
there are specific nerve and brain events in my body and specific
phenomena in the world. It is the fact that God has constructed soul,
body, and world in such a way that these conditions are met, which
made Leibniz's system seem to his readers to go against what we do
take to be causal connections between awareness and objects. The
clock analogy used by Leibniz did not help to dissipate his readers'
confusions of causal with cognitive events.

In Basnage's journal *Histoire des ouvrages des savans*, July 1698
issue, Leibniz points out that 'I have compared the soul with a clock
only with regard to the regulated precision of its changes, which is
only imperfect in the best clocks, but which is perfect in the works of
God'.[34] Whereas, for the occasionalists, the changes in the soul's
thoughts or actions are controlled by a force outside its nature (i.e.

sçaurois comprendre l'enchainement d'actions internes & spontanées, qui feroit que
l'ame d'un chien sentiroit de la doleur immédiatement après avoir senti de la joie,
quand même elle seroit seule dans l'Univers.'
   [31] *Philosophical Papers*, p. 493.
   [32] For a development of Descartes's theory of perception, see my *Perceptual
Acquaintance, from Descartes to Reid* (Minneapolis, Minn.: University of Minnesota
Press; Oxford: Basil Blackwell, 1984), ch. I.
   [33] *Philosophical Papers*, pp. 341–2.
   [34] Ibid. 495.

God), on Leibniz's account these changes are a function of the *natures* of soul and body. 'It is not enough to say that God has made a general law, for besides the decree there is also necessary a natural means of carrying it out, that is, all that happens must also be explained through the nature which God gives to things.' Leibniz also spoke of the soul as 'a most exact immaterial automaton', a characterization giving rise to those fears which run throughout the eighteenth century in Britain and France, the fears of *l'homme machine*.

Bayle illustrated these fears with his suggestion that Leibniz had made the soul like a ship which reaches port all by itself without any guidance by a pilot.[35] Leibniz's reply to this interpretation of his system contains some important clarifications. First of all, the 'faculty' of the ship to move should not be seen as one of those scholastic qualities, e.g. heaviness as the faculty which draws bodies toward the centre. If Bayle means 'a faculty of the ship which can be explained by the laws of mechanics and by internal forces as well as by external circumstances', then the charge that Bayle makes (that such a ship is impossible) falls to the ground. When the ship is viewed as having a guidance system internal to its structure (as the soul's actions stem from internal forces), it is possible to understand how a skilful craftsman could build such an automatic machine. 'There is no doubt whatever that a man could make a machine capable of walking about for some time through a city and turning exactly at the corners of certain streets. A spirit incomparably more perfect, though still finite, could also foresee and avoid an incomparably greater number of obstacles' (p. 575). Leibniz goes even further. If the world were, as the Epicureans and others say, composed of atoms moving in accordance with the laws of mechanics, it would be relatively easy for a clever artisan not only to 'construct a ship capable of sailing by itself to a designated port, by giving it the needed route, direction, and force at the start', but

---

[35] Bayle, *Dictionnaire*, under 'Rorarius', Note L: 'Figurez vous un vaisseau qui sans avoir aucun sentiment ni aucune connoissance, & sans être dirigé par aucun être ou créé ou incréé, ait la vertue de se mouvoir de lui-même si à propos qu'il ait toûjours le vent favorable, qu'il évite les courans, & les écueils, qu'il jette l'ancre où le faut, qu'il se retire dans un havre précisément lors que cela est nécessaire; suposez qu'un tel vaisseau vogue de cette façon plusieurs années de suite, toûjours tourné & situé comme il le faut être en égard aux changemens de l'air & aux diférentes situations des mers & des terres, vous conviendrez que l'infinité de Dieu n'est pas trop grande pour communiquer à un vaisseau une telle faculté & vous direz même que la nature de vaisseau n'est pas capable de recevoir de Dieu cette vertu-là.'

such an artisan could 'also form a body capable of counterfeiting a man' (p. 575).

The world is not, on Leibniz's account, composed of atoms 'but is rather like a machine composed in each of its parts of a truly infinite number of forces'. The world was made by an infinite spirit. In this world,

everything is so controlled and bound together that these infallible machines of nature, which are comparable to ships that would arrive at port by themselves in spite of all obstacles and storms, ought not to be considered any stranger than a rocket which glides along a string or a liquid which runs through a tube. (p. 576)[36]

The combination of the interconnectedness of all components with the notion of the internal structure of each part leads Leibniz to an epistemic claim: 'a sufficiently penetrating spirit could ... see and foresee in each corpuscle everything which has happened and will happen in that corpuscle and everything which has happened and will happen everywhere both within and outside of the corpuscle.' When speaking about the body, Leibniz has no objection to talking of an automaton, so long as we recognize that the body works by internal principles; it is not a puppet worked from the outside. The same is true of the soul, except that it is an immaterial automaton with an immaterial 'mechanism' fitted to its nature. One important difference between these two automata is that the spiritual one has a consciousness of the 'I', the 'ego', 'which perceives the things occurring in the body' (pp. 577–8).[37] The word 'perceives' here should not be taken as if the soul is a spectator of events in the body; rather, it has the cognitive sense of 'represents the events in the body'. Everything occurs in the soul 'as if the evil doctrine of those who believe, with Epicurus and Hobbes, that the soul is material were true, or as if man himself were only a body or an automaton' (p. 578). Leibniz's system combines, he says, what is good in 'the greatest materialists and the greatest idealists' (p. 598).

[36] Cf. Preface to his *Theodicy*: 'Moreover, as God orders all things at once beforehand, the accuracy of the path of this vessel would be no more strange than that of a fuse passing along a cord in fireworks, since the whole disposition of things preserves a perfect harmony between them by means of their influence one upon the other.'

[37] In his *Theodicy*, Leibniz uses the phrase 'spiritual automaton' ('Essays', pt. I, § 52). There he also speaks of a union between soul and body, a 'metaphysical' union which makes a person ('Preliminary Dissertation', § 55; see also 'Essays', pt. I, § 59).

CONCLUSION

The interplay of materialism and idealism which is exemplified in Leibniz's system reflects the concern of many in the eighteenth century. The tendency towards idealism (sometimes called 'egoism') came from the difficulties, if not impossibilities, that were attendant upon the attempts to understand how *physical* causal processes could be responsible for *cognitive* awareness. Those who did believe, as most ordinary people do, that physical and physiological processes play some causal role in perceptual awareness never did reach a satisfactory explanation of how those causes produce perception. Most writers who worked with some version of physical influence were content to trace the physical antecedents of perception to some area of the brain, saying that the mind becomes aware of or has ideas or perceptions when the brain receives specific motions and impressions. What the connection was between brain states and perceptual awareness (between body and mind) was left blank, except in some few writers, beginning with Descartes, who talked of certain motions in nerves and brain being *signs*, not just physical events, motion-signs which the mind interprets. Sign and interpretation belong to the same category of meaning and signification. Ideas for Descartes had a dual reality, as modes of mind and as the cognitive existence of objects in the mind. Similarly, certain physical motions in nerves and brain also had for Descartes a dual reality: physical and significatory.

Even with Descartes, this latter duality receives scant attention and little elaboration or development. For the most part, on the hypothesis of physical influence, the physical–cognitive relation was said to be beyond our comprehension. Everyone, even those who rejected physical influence, recognized the close correspondence between bodily physiology and perceptual awareness; but in the absence of characterizing correspondence as dependent and causal, it was easy for others to settle for correspondence as correlation only. The question then was, how to account for that correlation? The difference between occasionalist and pre-established harmony hypotheses lay in the former assigning to God the task of maintaining the correspondence at every moment, and the latter giving to the *natures* of body and soul the internal principles and forces which bring about the tandem sequences of events. Leibniz retains the notion of interpretation and representation found in Descartes but rejects any attempt to link the interpretation with the interpreted other than as the cognitive expression of events in the body and the world. Those critics who saw idealism in the causal separation of mind and body missed the important fact that cognition contains information about the body and external objects. The mind's sequences of perceptions may seem disconnected from the world, and may even be characterized, as Leibniz himself did, as if there were no body or world. Nevertheless, Leibniz insisted that his system contains the explicit feature that most sequences of perceptions would not occur if there were in fact no specific sequences of events in the body and the world. Illusions and other forms of misperceptions (confused ideas) pose a problem of detail only.

Leibniz's characterization of the soul as an immaterial automaton was intended to indicate the self-containedness of the soul, to stress the causal independence of the soul from the body. The term 'immaterial' was traditional but 'automaton' was radical, especially in the context of the materialist scare in Britain and France. There were several strands in what was perceived by the traditionalists as a move towards materializing the soul, or as reducing thinking to brain events. The failure to define the self in terms of a soul (e.g. with Locke) was seen as making the soul an accident or property, or, at least, as concentrating upon the faculties rather than upon their substance. The location of the causes of awareness in bodily processes, the causal theory of perception (e.g. again as with Locke) violated the deep-seated belief that there could be no causal influence from one kind of substance to another kind of substance. With these two features combined, as they were in Locke's *Essay concerning Human Understanding*, Locke's suggestion of the possibility of thought being a property of the brain became threatening. Man as a corporeal automaton took his place among Vaucanson's mechanical devices. The fact that Locke disclaimed the actuality of thought being a property of the brain did not calm the fears. The echoes of one-substance man (thinking matter) are in the background of the reactions to Leibniz's phrase 'immaterial automaton'.

The appearance of Locke's name and doctrines in the midst of the running debate over the three systems in the pages of the *Journal helvétique*, the explicit mention of his suggestion about *matière pensante* in several of those articles, reflect a much wider involvement of Locke's name and doctrines in the radical literature in France. We shall see in subsequent chapters that this more extensive involvement revolved around his suggestion about thinking matter as well as his causal theory of perception. The latter placed him among the defenders of the system of physical influence.

2

The French Connection

LOCKE wanted to defend the intelligibility, not the actuality, of matter of a certain complexity and organization having dual properties, those usually ascribed to body and mind or, in a more traditional language, body and soul. After all, according to the view Locke shared with Robert Boyle, God did add motion to matter, motion not being a natural property of matter. Moreover, Newton had recently shown the importance of gravitation in the behaviour of all bodies (especially planetary ones); and gravity, not being natural to body, had to be added by God. When Bishop Stillingfleet drew Locke out on this suggestion, Locke sketched a possible Creation scenario where God creates bare substance and adds various qualities and powers to it, e.g. motion, attraction and repulsion, sense, life. God could, Locke suggested, have added the property of thought to biological matter having these other properties. At the same time, Locke makes it clear that he does not think any matter does think, certainly not corpuscular matter which everyone agreed was dumb and inactive.

While I do not find the text of Locke at all ambiguous on the question of matter thinking, some of his readers then and now suspect a hidden agenda, where Locke was moving in the direction of a materialism which said some matter does think. There was a storm of protests, reactions, and support of some few who did try to develop such a view in eighteenth-century Britain. By means of translations of his various books, reviews and extracts of them in French-language journals, and, most importantly, by Voltaire's letter on Locke (Letter XIII in his *Letters concerning the English Nation*, 1733; French edn., 1734) which highlighted the suggestion of thinking matter and located Locke in the context of such deistical and materialist writers as Collins, Toland, and Spinoza, attention was called in France to Locke's possible materialist tendencies. Bayle cited and discussed the exchange with Stillingfleet on that topic, it appeared in a long footnote to Coste's second French edition of the *Essay*, and, more significantly, it appeared in the body of an important clandestine tract, *L'Âme matérielle*.[1]

VOLTAIRE'S LETTER XIII

The letter on Locke in Voltaire's *Letters concerning the English Nation*[2] was placed just after one on Bacon and ahead of those on Descartes and Newton. Three letters are devoted to aspects of Newton's thought: attraction, infinites in geometry, and optics. As Henri Duranton notes, by 1733 Voltaire was a prominent person; reactions to his work were mixed.[3] His *Zaïre* had been performed in August of 1732, his *Le Temple du goût* had created a scandal. Rumours from England began to spread: 'Le bruit court aussi avec insistance de certaines *Lettres anglaises* dont on ne sait pas encore grand chose, mais dont les initiés content merveilles.'[4] Notices in some of the French-language journals began to appear, announcing the imminent publication of those letters.

With all this advance notice and curiosity about a new publication from Voltaire, the letters were bound to be read by a wide public, looking for scandalous and unorthodox materials. The Letter XIII did not disappoint. It opens with warm praise for Locke as a judicious and methodical genius, characterizing him also as an acute logician. There then follow a number of paragraphs summarizing the accounts of the nature of the soul given by such writers, as Anaxagoras, Diogenes, Epicurus, Plato, Aristotle, the Church Fathers, Descartes, Malebranche. Voltaire then comments:

Such a Multitude of Reasoners having written the Romance of the Soul, a Sage at last arose, who gave, with an Air of the greatest Modesty, the History of it. Mr. *Locke* has display'd the human Soul, in the same Manner as an excellent Anatomist explains the Springs of the human Body. (p. 98)

[1] Alain Niderst has edited this work, identifying the sources for its survey of ancient and modern writings: *L'Âme matérielle (œuvre anonyme)* (Paris: Nizet, 1969).
[2] The French original appeared one year later: *Lettres écrites de Londres sur les Anglois, et autres sujets, par M. D. V**** (1734). Later French edns. carry the title *Lettres philosophiques*. The 2 texts are virtually identical, but while the English version has a 6-page preface, the preface in the French version is only 2 pages long.
[3] Henri Duranton, 'Les Circuits de la vie littéraire au XVIIIe siècle: Voltaire et l'opinion publique en 1733', in *Le Journalisme d'ancien régime: Table ronde, CNRS, 12–13 juin 1981* (Lyons: Presses universitaires de Lyon, 1982), 101–15.
[4] Ibid. 102.

Voltaire continued by expressing agreement with Locke that he does not always think, Locke having rejected the Cartesian insistence that the soul does always think. Voltaire also refers to Locke's rejection of innate ideas, and he gives a quick sketch of how Locke observed children as a way of describing how we acquire ideas and knowledge. Remarking that Locke called attention in Book 4 to the limitations of knowledge, Voltaire then cites the passage from *Essay*, 4. 3. 6, where Locke says, 'We shall, perhaps, never be capable of knowing, whether a Being, purely material, thinks or not' (p. 100).[5] Voltaire comments that this assertion by Locke,

was, by more Divines than one, look'd upon as a scandalous Declaration that the Soul is material and mortal. Some *Englishmen*, devout after their Way, sounded an Alarm. The Superstitious are the same in Society as Cowards in an Army; they themselves are seiz'd with a panic Fear, and communicate it to others. 'Twas loudly exclaim'd, that Mr. *Locke* intended to destroy Religion; nevertheless, Religion had nothing to do in the Affair, it being a Question purely Philosophical, altogether independent on Faith and Revelation. (p. 101)[6]

Voltaire was aware of the extensive reaction in England to Locke's suggestion. He was correct also in his remark about the issue for Locke being philosophical, not a challenge to faith and revelation, although that was not how it was interpreted. Locke made that suggestion as a conceptual point related to the limitations of our knowledge of soul and body, but his British readers did not examine the suggestion, as Voltaire urged, 'calmly and impartially'. Many French readers of Locke, and of Locke filtered through Voltaire, reacted similarly. Voltaire did not calm the passions of his readers when he indicated agreement with Locke against Stilling-fleet's attack on this point. Nor did passions subside when Voltaire said of the soul that it is 'a Clock which is given us to regulate, but the Artist has not told us what Materials the Spring of his Clock is

---

[5] In his edn. of the *Lettres philosophiques* (3rd edn., Paris: Hachette, 1924), Gustave Lanson gives this reference incorrectly as 4. 3. 22.

[6] Voltaire argues, perhaps in his own defence, that philosophical opinions never create social unrest and are not a danger to religion. His final paragraph in the 1733 and 1734 edns. of the *Lettres* (there were later reprints with additions) could have done little to deflect outrage: 'Neither Montaigne, Locke, Bayle, Spinoza, Hobbes, the Lord Shaftesbury, Collins, nor Toland lighted up the Firebrand of Discord in their Countries; this has generally been the Work of Divines, who being at first puff'd up with the Ambition of becoming Chiefs of a Sect, soon grew desirous of being at the Head of a Party.'

compos'd' (p. 103). Even more emphatically, Voltaire declares in favour of one substance only: 'I am a Body, and, I think, that's all I know of the Matter.'

Not only was the appearance of Voltaire's *Letters* anticipated in the French journals, it was given reviews after its publication. The Abbé Prévost's *Le Pour et contre* devoted three articles to it in 1733. In the last of these articles, there is a brief mention of the letters on Locke and Newton but no mention of thinking matter.[7] The *Bibliothèque britannique* has two articles on the *Letters*; the second one gives three pages and a note to Locke.[8] Locke's *Essay* is characterized as 'une Histoire, et une Histoire excellente'. The author of this review notes Locke's rejection of thought as essential to the soul (hence, the soul does not always think) and Voltaire's agreement with Locke on this and on the rejection of innate ideas. On Locke's suggestion about the possibility of matter thinking, the reviewer remarks that this is not entirely a new suggestion, although it is 'une proposition qui a fait du bruit'. The brief account of this possibility is given in neutral terms, without any signs of rejection or animosity. Perhaps the reviewer takes refuge in the notion, which he credits to Locke, that because our knowledge is limited we must have recourse to God for first principles. The reviewer adds a footnote saying that Voltaire has not been entirely fair to Locke, for a reading of the chapter in the *Essay* on faith and reason shows that Locke does not belong in the company of those men listed in Voltaire's final paragraph (Bayle, Spinoza, Hobbes, Collins, Toland), a list frequently cited as deists, free thinkers ('esprits-forts' in France), and materialists. Thus for this journal, Locke was not seen as a threat to religion and his suggestion about thinking matter *is* taken calmly and impartially.[9]

[7] Arts. 11, 12, and 13 in vol. 1 (1733), 241–9, 273–88, and 291–309. Prévost's journal came to 20 vols. and ran from 1733 to 1740. In a letter to Charles Étienne Jordan, Voltaire complains of Prévost's criticisms, saying that 'the reference to his discussion of Locke and Newton has hurt him most' (Besterman's summary, see Letter D662 in *The Complete Works of Voltaire*, lxxxvi (1969), vol. ii of the correspondence ed. T. Besterman).

[8] *Bibliothèque britannique, ou Histoire des ouvrages des savans de la Grande-Bretagne*, 2, arts. II and VI (1733), 16–35, 104–37. Letter XIII is discussed in art. VI. This journal was edited by Pierre Desmaizeaux and Jean-Frédéric Bernard from the Hague. It ran to 25 vols. (1733–47). For useful information on this and other 18th-century French-language journals, see Marianne Couperus (ed.), *L'Étude des périodiques anciens* (Paris: Nizet, 1972).

[9] The *Bibliothèque britannique* review of the 2nd edn. of the *Letters* (17 (1741), 251–60) makes no mention of Locke. That article is concerned mainly with the piece on Pascal added in the new edn.

Locke was similarly protected from Voltaire's more radical image (although Locke's doctrines are criticized) by an anonymous article in the *Bibliothèque françoise* for 1735.[10] The author was David R. Boullier.[11] The article was headed: 'Réflexions sur quelques principes de la philosophie de Mr. Locke, à l'occasion des "Lettres philosophiques" de Mr. Voltaire'. Boullier remarks that these letters are so well known that there is no need to give any extracts from them. He thinks that his remarks will show that Voltaire was not a good philosopher; he should have stuck to being a poet. The letters do not merit all the noise they have caused. There is some French pride in Boullier's objection to Voltaire's placing Locke above Descartes and Malebranche, especially when that ranking is based on such claims of Locke as that we are ignorant of the nature of the soul, that the soul does not always think, that it might be material, and that we cannot say whether matter might not think (p. 193). Locke's account of the origin of ideas has some value, but it fails to identify the real efficient cause of them (p. 196).

Voltaire had derisively referred to Father Malebranche's 'sublime

[10] The article appears in vol. 20 (1735), 189–214, although it is dated at the end 18 Dec. 1734. This journal ran from 1723 to 1746, carried the subtitle of 'Histoire littéraire de la France', and was published at Amsterdam. The editors were Denis-François Camusat (1695–1732), Jean-Frédéric Bernard (1690–1752), Claude-Pierre Goujet (1697–1767), H. du Sauzet, François Garnet (1692–1741), and Bel. This is the list given in Jean Sgard's 'Table chronologique des périodiques de langue française publié avant la Révolution', in Couperus, *L'Étude des périodiques anciens*. The latter may be Jean-Jacques Bel (1693–1738). A. Cioranescu (*Bibliographie de la littérature française du dix-huitième siècle* (Paris: Éditions du CNRS, 1969)) does not list Bel with the other editors.

[11] This article was reprinted four times between 1741 and 1759. In his *Lettres sur les vrais principes de la religion, où l'on examine le livre de 'La Religion essentielle à l'homme'* [by Matthew Tindal], *avec la défense des 'Pensées' de Pascal contre la critique de Voltaire, et trois lettres relatives à la philosophie de ce poète* (2 vols., 1741), the article, together with two others on Locke and Voltaire, appears in vol. ii (pp. 320–422). It is there dated 18 Dec. 1734. The second letter refers to Voltaire as 'Le nouveau Disciple de Locke' (p. 392). The same three letters appear in Boullier's *Lettres critiques sur les Lettres philosophiques de Mr. de Voltaire, par rapport à notre âme, à sa spiritualité et à son immortalité, avec la défense des Pensées de Pascal contre la critique du même Voltaire* (1753). A note to the first letter in this reprint reminds the reader that it appeared earlier in a journal. The three letters are printed yet again in his *Apologie de la métaphysique* (1753). They are reprinted a fourth time in the collection *Guerre littéraire* (1759). The 1741 work was reviewed in the *Bibliothèque raisonnée* for July–Sept. 1741 (27, pp. 248–66). The reviewer thinks that Boullier wants to establish deism on the ruins of revealed religion. On the question of 'can matter think?', he says that he finds it difficult to decide, especially when Locke and Voltaire have written about it. For a listing of other works by Boullier (including his well-known 2-vol. *Essai philosophique sur l'âme des bêtes*, 1728), see A. Cioranescu, *Bibliographie de la littérature française*.

Illusions', among them his acceptance of innate ideas (*Letters*, p. 98). Boullier took delight at pointing out the misreading of Malebranche by Voltaire, for 'Dire que vous voyons tout en Dieu, c'est donc nier les idées innées' (p. 195). Voltaire had attributed contradictory doctrines to Malebranche and was unaware of the contradiction or the falsity of saying Malebranche accepted innate ideas. On the topic of the soul always thinking, Boullier argues that this is not resolvable by experience. Everyday I have an 'infinity of thoughts' which I do not remember. Moreover, 'I am never certain of not having thought at this or that moment', nor can I always recall what occupied my mind at some particular time (p. 198). Our mind, he says, 'is the rendez-vous of a thousand quiet [*legères*] thoughts which are nearly imperceptible, which follow each other rapidly, and which move like lightning'. Furthermore, since 'it is clear that the least sensation is a thought, because it contains the awareness of the subject who thinks' (p. 199), the soul must always think since it always has some sensation or other. The close union of soul and body also requires the soul to perceive, at least confusedly, whatever occurs in the body. Thought in this sense is not 'a particular act but something permanent which connects the different modifications of the soul substance'.

The main feature in Locke to which Voltaire was attracted, Boullier claims, is his 'discovery' that we are unable to know whether a purely material being thinks or not. Voltaire, Boullier remarks, has received this suggestion as a revelation, as if coming from an oracle; he probably has the suggestion engraved in gold over his mantel. While Locke was a virtuous man, he was not infallible, he does sometimes assert false and dangerous doctrines. Libertines like what he says about matter and the soul (p. 201). Boullier mentions other discussions of this topic which deny the possibility of matter thinking, e.g. by Abbé de Dangeau, Bayle, Clarke, Collins, Bishop Stillingfleet. He says that, in England, Clarke is beginning to be placed above Locke (reflecting Boullier's own ranking). In Letter VII, 'On the Socinians, or Arians, or Antitrinitarians', Voltaire described Clarke as 'the most sanguine stickler for Arianism', going on to characterize him, in a way that angered Boullier, 'as a man who was rigidly virtuous, and of a mild disposition; [he] is more fond of his tenets than desirous of propagating them, and absorb'd so entirely in problems and calculations, that he is a mere reasoning machine' (*Letters*, p. 48). That last phrase ('une vraye machine à 'raisonnemens' in the French version used by Boullier) really angered Boullier, drawing from him the taunt that Voltaire was '*un moulin à vers*'.

For Boullier, it is obvious that the soul is *naturally* immortal and that matter cannot think (p. 203). We know with certitude, he says, that matter is a substance extended, and divisible. We see that these properties exclude all others. We know our own soul by feeling ('sentiment') and by awareness ('conscience'). In knowing myself, I know with certitude that the *I* is a substance simple, indivisible, active (p. 210). From this self-knowledge, 'I conclude or infer that the *I* which I call my soul, is not a body.' He does not think we need to have a knowledge of the *nature* of substance in order to reach these conclusions. 'Pour assurer hardiment tout cela, on n'a besoin de connoitre à fond ni l'esprit ni la matière; il suffit de se sentir soi-meme, et de se rendre attentif à ce qui s'offre à notre pensée quand on prononce le mot de *matière* ou de *Corps*' (p. 210). Boullier concludes his discussion by saying Locke is badly represented by Voltaire because he is made to sound very Pyrrhonian, but Pyrrhonism is far from Locke's thought (p. 213).

VOLTAIRE AND FATHER TOURNEMINE

Another attack on Letter XIII appeared in the October 1735 issue of *Mémoires pour l'histoire des sciences et des beaux arts*, frequently referred to as the *Journal de Trévoux*. The author of this attack was Father Tournemine, one of the editors and a frequent contributor to this journal as well as a correspondent of Voltaire. In fact, Article XCIX in that issue, 'Lettre de P. Tournemine de la Compagnie de Jesus, à M. de *** sur l'immatérialité de l'ame, & les sources de l'incrédulité', was a public response to questions raised by Voltaire in earlier private letters to Tournemine.

While preparing the *Letters* for the French edition, Voltaire remarked to Jean-Baptiste Nicolas Formont that he must tone down what he wrote 'à l'occasion de m. Locke, parce qu'après tout je veux vivre en France, et il ne m'est pas permis d'etre aussi philosophe qu'un Anglois. Il me faut déguiser à Paris ce que je ne pourrai dire trop fortement à Londres.'[12] It is important to note that, in this same letter, Voltaire tells Formont that he is rereading Newton to be sure

[12] Letter D542 in *Complete Works*, lxxxvi. Besterman dates this letter around 6 Dec. 1732.

he makes no mistakes in his account.[13] One of the more important features in Voltaire's correspondence is the linking he makes between Newton's account of gravitation and Locke's suggestion of thinking matter. This was a connection also present in the British debate.

In a somewhat later letter to Formont (Besterman dates it around 15 Dec. 1732), Voltaire says about the letter on Locke: 'La seule matière philosophique que j'y traite est la petite bagatelle de l'imma-térialité de l'ame', adding rather cryptically, 'mais la chose est trop de conséquence pour la traiter sérieusement' (Letter D545). Writing to Nicolas Claude Thieriot in February 1733, Voltaire says that the Abbé Rotelin had assured him that he would give his approval for all the letters *except* the one on Locke, so that 'petite bagatelle' was sufficient to worry the authorities (Letter D570). Voltaire claimed not to understand this exception, which is surprising in the light of his earlier comments about toning that letter down. He may have been serious in his remark to Thieriot for, as he said to Formont in a letter of 26 July 1733: 'Qui osera dire *qu'il est impossible que la matière puisse penser*' (Letter D637).

In a number of letters, Voltaire makes the point that, as he said to Charles Marie de la Condamine in June 1734, his letter on Locke reduces to this one point: '*la raison humaine ne sauroit démontrer qu'il soit impossible à dieu d'ajouter la pensée à la matière*' (Letter D759). He railed against the censors of his *Lettres philo-sophiques*, charging them with not being good philosophers and with having only a mediocre understanding of Newton and Locke. Many French readers were reluctant to accept Newton's term 'attraction', seeing it as referring to an occult quality. Tournemine read it that way, as we shall see. In the letter to Condamine, Voltaire laments: 'Si M. Neuton ne s'étoit pas servi du moi d'attraction dans son admirable filosophie, toute notre académie auroit ouvert les yeux à la lumière, mais il a eu le malheur de se servir à Londres d'un mot auquel on auroit attaché une idée ridicule à Paris.' Voltaire feels that he too is being judged on the words he uses: 'S'il est permis de comparer les petites choses aux grandes, j'ose dire qu'on a jugé mes idées sur des mots. Si je n'avois pas éguaié la matière, personne n'eut été scandalisé, mais aussy personne ne m'auroit lu.'

---

[13] In a letter in 1734, Voltaire says he has been rereading Locke (D764), and in a letter to Thieriot in 1735 he says he and Algarotti (the Italian translator of Newton) have been reading Newton and Locke, as well as some plays, 'non sans vin de champagne, et sans excellente chère' (D935).

In two letters to Tournemine around June and August of 1735, Voltaire addresses both the misreading of Newton's principle of gravitation as an occult quality, and the rejection of the claim made by Locke and Voltaire that it is not impossible that God could make matter think. In the June letter (D877), he asks Tournemine whether those philosophers he knows (i.e. his fellow Jesuits) who have studied Newton really deny that there is in matter a principle of gravitation which acts 'en raison directe des masses, & en raison renversée du carré des distances'. Voltaire points out that in order to accept that principle, we do not need to know the nature of gravitation; it is impossible for us to know the nature of any first principle. But gravitation can be measured, we can base calculations on it; thus, it operates in the world. It is just as certain that matter gravitates according to the laws of centripetal forces, as it is that the three angles of a triangle are equal to two right angles. That was his first question for Tournemine: do he and his friends really deny gravitation?

His second question concerns the proposition, '*Nous ne pouvons pas assurer qu'il soit impossible à dieu de communiquer la pensée à la matière*'. He says that those who condemn him for saying it *is* possible charge him with making the soul mortal. He points out that to say the soul is matter is very far from saying it is mortal, or that it perishes. Even matter itself does not perish: 'Son étendue, son impénétrabilité, sa nécessité d'etre configurée & d'etre dans l'espace, tout cela & mille autres choses lui demeurent après notre mort.' Why would the soul not remain, even if it were material? He then runs through the inadequate knowledge that we have about matter: we only know it from some of its qualities. Even those qualities are known imperfectly. Therefore, how can I be assured that God does not have the power to give thought to matter? He agrees that God cannot do what implies a contradiction, but he fails to see that 'matière pensante' implies a contradiction. He insists, as he had in other letters, that he does not assert that thought is material. His knowledge falls short of knowing the nature of thought or mind. The only point he wants to make is that it is as possible for God to give thought to extended matter as it is to join together an extended and an immaterial being.

Voltaire next turns to the argument over the souls of animals. This is a feature of Voltaire's letter that especially upset Tournemine. Voltaire's point was that, even if we grant with the Cartesians that animals are machines, it is far more difficult for us to deny that God could add thought to those machines. When Tournemine dealt with this example, he simply pleaded ignorance of the nature of animals and stoutly asserted that the human machine has a soul attached. Voltaire has an effective argument with this example, for, as Boullier argued in 1728, there are many similarities between animal organs and behaviour and our own.[14] Voltaire thinks Tournemine will have a difficult time denying God the possibility of adding thought to animal machines (if they are in fact only machines), and he suggests that that leaves open the possibility in our case too.

Tournemine's reply to this June letter has not survived, but it must have been unsatisfactory since Voltaire runs over much the same ground (and, in doing so, reveals something of Tournemine's replies) in his August letter (D901).[15] Putting the first question again, about gravitation, Voltaire had to correct Tournemine's understanding of gravity. Apparently, Tournemine and his friends interpreted Newton as saying bodies push other bodies, but the question is, is there 'a tendency, a gravitation, an attraction from the centre of each body', even over great distances. Voltaire chastises Tournemine and his friends who have refused to read Newton carefully, or to dispense with their own biases. Even what Newton said on motion has not been understood: 'il ne s'agit pas ici du mouvement ordinaire des corps, mais du principe inhérent dans la matière, qui fait que chaque partie de la matière est attirée & attire en raison directe de la masse', etc. To say such a principle is *inherent* in body is not the same as saying it is *essential* to body. This was a distinction present throughout the British debate but wasted on Tournemine. Were God to give thought to matter, Voltaire implies, it would be made inherent but not essential, just as with motion.

Voltaire then turns to a strange argument which Tournemine must have used (he repeats it in his *Journal de Trévoux* article). Tournemine had argued that God could not communicate the gift of thought to matter in the way in which he communicated attraction and motion because we see objects whole—'indivisibly' is the term used by Tournemine. This seems to be a curious form of the standard

---

[14] Boullier, *Essai philosophique sur l'âme des bêtes*.
[15] I am of course relying upon Besterman's dating of Voltaire's letters, some of which are not dated. Similarly, with his suggestion of the lost Tournemine letter, his reply to the June Voltaire letter. The Aug. letter reads very much like a reply to Tournemine's published letter in the *Journal de Trévoux*, which probably only means that Tournemine simply repeated himself.

argument in this thinking-matter debate: matter is divisible, the soul or mind is not. Voltaire repeats the argument used by Tournemine: 'il faudrait que le corps organisé aperçut tout le pain; or la partie A du pain ne frappe que la partie A du cerveau, la partie B que la partie B, & nulle partie du cerveau ne peut recevoir tout l'objet'. Voltaire simply does not see any way that this conclusion could be drawn: Tournemine cannot prove that God has not been able to give to an organized body the faculty of receiving at once the impression of the whole object. Such a faculty could be given to the brain.

There are several more of Tournemine's objections discussed by Voltaire in this August letter, e.g. that the words 'je' and 'moi' imply immateriality, that only an immaterial being could have the idea of immateriality, that the very suggestion of the possibility of matter's thinking gives aid and support to the free thinkers. Voltaire ends this letter by recommending to Tournemine that he read Locke's *Essay* on the extent of human knowledge.

Whether it was the June or August letter (or both) that sparked Tournemine into going public with his reply, the article in the October 1735 issue of the *Journal de Trévoux* is structured around the questions raised in the June letter.[16] After an opening in which he professes his faith in 'l'Eglise Romaine' and prides himself on being orthodox and conservative, Tournemine takes up Voltaire's second question first, the one about our knowledge not ruling out the possibility that God could give thought to matter. The main objection that he uses in various forms is that thought as a property of matter is an obvious absurdity, since matter has parts and is divisible, divisibility being essential to matter. A being comprised of parts is not able to think. He supports this claim with his example about perceiving the whole of an object and seeing objects 'indivisibly'. He probably had some sort of physiology in mind when he speaks of part A of the object striking part A of the brain, etc. Were the brain able to think, it would both have parts (as a body) and not have parts (as that which thinks).

Tournemine confesses that this argument is less a reasoning than a feeling, but it is a feeling drawn from the very foundation of our being, expressed by the first-person pronouns. Moreover, only an immaterial being could form the idea of an immaterial soul and apply it to its own existence. There is no difficulty in conceiving that a mind or soul is attached to matter, depends on it, experiences pains

[16] This letter is reprinted in the *Complete Works*, lxxxvii, as D913.

and pleasures in it. He does not understand the nature of Locke's limitation of knowledge to experienced properties; his metaphysics and religion assures him that the union of mind and body is possible, that matter is divisible, that mind or soul is not divisible. Underlying his inability to appreciate Locke's suggestion is a moral fear, the same fear that motivated many of Locke's critics in Britain: the support given the free thinkers and libertines. He even gives two testimonials from 'esprits-forts' who have since been persuaded of the evils of their lives and have now returned to religion.

The assurance that Voltaire gave that neither he nor Locke said (or meant to say) that matter does in fact think had little effect on Tournemine. The comparison with Newton's account of gravitation and motion (two properties not essential to matter but made inherent by God) fails to convince him of the intelligibility of Locke's suggestion. He really thinks gravitation is nothing more than an occult quality: 'Quelle différence en effet entre une qualité attractive, & les qualités inflammatoires, réfrigerantes, digestives?' But even if he were to accept Voltaire's account of gravitation and motion, he would remain unconvinced about thought: 'de la gravitation à la pensée il y a une distance immense, une difference infinie'. He does make one interesting point, although it stems from his confusion about the difference between *essential* and *inherent*. He takes an inherent property to be distinct from the substance to which it belongs. Any property of matter which is not essential to matter, not part of its nature, is not material. Thus he says: 'M. Loke, vous, Monsieur, & tout Philosophe, se trouve enfin reduit à n'attribuer la pensée qu'à un principe distingué de la matière'. He thinks this puts Locke and Voltaire close to the standard view that God has united a thinking substance to matter.

In November 1735, Voltaire comments to another of his correspondents (Pierre Joseph Thoulier d'Olivet) that Tournemine 'dispute bien mal contre m^r Loke, et parle de Newton comme un aveugle des couleurs' (Letter D950). He is afraid that if philosophers read this article they will be astonished and form a bad opinion of the French. In December of that year, Voltaire writes to Formont and runs through again some of his arguments supporting Locke's suggestion (Letter D960). He tells Formont that while we do not understand how matter thinks, neither can we understand how a thinking substance can be united to matter. Both are equally incomprehensible. Nevertheless, one must be true. We have to go with probabilities, not demonstrations. He cites the axiom, '*les memes effets doivent etre attribués à la meme cause*' and remarks that the same effects are found in beasts and men: they feel, think, and have ideas. He does not say we *know* that animals feel and think, but he takes it as probable. He thinks it is very probable that 'la nature a donné des pensées à des cerveaux, comme la végétation à des arbres; que nous pensons par le cerveau, de meme que nous marchons avec le pied'. This is, he says, what our reason would allow us to think, if 'la foi divine ne nous assurait pas du contraire'. He then departs from the cautious way in which he has always stated Locke's suggestion (that for all we know, God may, etc.) and says outright that 'c'est ce que pensait Locke, et ce qu'il n'a pas osé dire'.

In the same month, Voltaire writes Tournemine a very long letter about his public reply (Letter D963). He reverts to the cautious formulation. The question is whether Locke had reason in examining the human understanding, without relation to faith, to say that '*il est possible à dieu de donner la pensée à la matière*'. He even says that Locke rejects the claim that matter does think. The letter continues as a full-scale reply to Tournemine, but for the most part it is a repeat of the August letter. One point is worth noticing. When Tournemine says that 'esprits-forts' take up Locke's idea and link it with having inadequate knowledge of right and wrong, Voltaire says this remark is out of order. There is no necessary connection between Locke's suggestion and immorality. 'Locke, le plus sage & le plus vertueux de tous les hommes, était bien loin d'avancer une impiété aussi absurde & aussi horrible.' Later in this letter, he returns to the same point. 'Je ne sais pas, en vérité, à propos de quoi vous parlez de libertinage, de passions, & de désordres, quand il s'agit d'une question philosophique de Locke, dans laquelle son profond respect pour la divinité lui fait dire simplement qu'il n'en sait pas assez *pour oser borner la puissance de l'etre supreme*.'[17]

'LETTRE SUR LOCKE'

The notice in *Le Pour et contre* of the *Lettres philosophiques* remarked that the French originals had circulated in manuscript for

[17] After Voltaire began corresponding with Frederick, the Crown Prince of Prussia, he sent Frederick a copy of this letter. Earlier letters between Voltaire and Frederick had talked of Locke, and the prince was reading Locke. In a letter of Dec. 1736 to Voltaire, Frederick says that he has read Voltaire's letter (i.e. D963), and that he has been convinced by Voltaire's 'dissertation sur l'ame'.

some time. What in fact circulated that way, what was part of the clandestine literature, was a version of the letter on Locke. That version was known as 'Lettre sur Locke' or sometimes as 'Lettre sur l'âme'. Lanson has reprinted that early version in his edition of the *Lettres philosophiques*.[18] It was also, Lanson tells us, reprinted as 'XXVI Lettre sur l'âme' in a 1738 collection (and in later editions still) of short essays by several writers.[19] Lanson argues that the *Lettres philosophiques* were written between 1727 and 1728. Duranton cites a notice appearing in the *Mercure suisse* saying they were written in 1727.[20] The preface to the French edition says the letters 'furent écrites de Londres depuis 1728 jusqu'à 1730'. Lanson also says that the 'Lettre sur Locke' forms the basis for the entry 'Âme' in Voltaire's *Dictionnaire philosophique*.[21]

In the manuscript version, all the essential material from and about Locke found in the 1733 and 1734 English and French

[18] In Lanson's edn. of the *Lettres philosophiques*, i. 190–203. The manuscript of this version can be found in the Bibliothèque de l'Arsenal, MS 2557. For other remarks on this MS, as well as for very helpful accounts of the clandestine literature, see Olivier Bloch (ed.), *Le Matérialisme du XVIIIe siècle et la littérature clandestine* (Paris: J. Vrin, 1982), especially Ann Thomson's 'Qu'est-ce qu'un manuscrit clandestin?' and 'La Mettrie et la littérature clandestine'.

[19] Lanson's edn., i. 190. Lanson gives the title of this 1738 work as *Lettre de M. de V** avec plusieurs pièces de différents auteurs*. The half-title is: 'Lettre philosophique par Mr. de V** Lettre sur l'âme'. Lanson lists many reprints of this work: 1747, 1756, 1775, 1776. I have a 1774 edn., *Lettre philosophique, par M. de V**, avec plusieurs pieces galantes et nouvelles, de différents auteurs*, Nouvelle Edition, revue & corrigée. There are various minor changes in these edns., but Locke's name is prominent in them all. Raymond Naves thinks this version is not that of the 'Lettre sur Locke', but a text 'peut-être contemporaine de *Lettre Anglaise* mais qui ne saurait être considerée comme une *Lettre Anglaise* authentique'. See his edn. of *Lettres philosophiques* (Paris: Garnier, 1988), 223. Naves points out that the 'Lettre sur Locke', as printed in 1738, was incorporated into Voltaire's *Dictionnaire* after the Kehl edn. See e.g. vol. xvii of the *Œuvres complètes* (Paris: Garnier, 1878), entry for 'Âme', §VIII. A comparison between the 'Lettre sur Locke' as printed by Lanson, the 1738 version in the later edns. of the *Dictionnaire*, and the 1774 *Lettre philosophique* reveals all three versions to be virtually identical, except for a few different words and phrases and many different paragraph breaks in the 1774 version. The 1738 version in the 1878 edition of the *Dictionnaire* does, however, omit the important paragraph listing Montaigne, Locke, Bayle, etc. as those not responsible for discord.

[20] Duranton, 'Les Circuits de la vie littéraire', p. 103.

[21] Lanson's edn., i. 190. There is very little Locke material from Letter XIII in Voltaire's article on 'Âme' in his *Dictionnaire*, except in some late edns., after 1770. For a discussion of the 1770 addition, and other material on Locke in Voltaire's writings, see below, ch. 8, pp. 201–5. The entry under 'Âme' in the Diderot and d'Alembert *Encyclopédie* (1751–65) does have, as direct quotation, that portion of Letter XIII which comments on the row raised in England by Locke's suggestion. The *Encyclopédie* article 'Locke' also gives a passing reference to that suggestion, but the article plays down the radical consequences that others saw in it.

versions is there. In the early version, Voltaire is ostensibly a bit more cautious about his own position on the issues, presenting what he terms 'un petit précis de Mr. Locke que je censurerois si j'étois Théologien, et que j'adopte pour un moment comme pure hypothese, comme conjecture de simple philosophie'.[22] Nevertheless, the 'conjecture' about matter thinking is elaborated without much qualification: 'Je penserai que Dieu a donné des portions d'intelligence [à] de portions de matière organisées pour penser: je croirai que la matière a pensé à proportion de la finesse de ses sens, que ce sont eux qui sont les portes et la mesure de nos idées.'[23] The paragraph which places Locke with Spinoza, Hobbes, and Toland is also in this early version.

Thus Locke's suggestion of thinking matter became part of the clandestine writings under the important name of Voltaire. Lanson thinks that 'la lettre sur Locke eut, avec les Remarques sur Pascal, un part prépondérant dans la persécution que l'ouvrage essuya'.[24] It may not have been only Voltaire who suffered because of views he shared with Locke. In Voltaire's case, of course, he gave the authorities many reasons for attack. The editor of a short-lived bi-weekly paper, J.-B. de la Varenne, printed the 'Lettre sur Locke' in two issues of his *Observateur polygraphique*.[25] In her excellent study of La Varenne, M. C. Couperus quotes from one of his contemporaries, François Bruys, saying that it was these two issues devoted to the 'Lettre sur Locke' that caused the authorities to close down the *Observateur polygraphique*.[26]

It was the same manuscript version of Voltaire's Letter XIII which

---

[22] Lanson's edn., i. 192.

[23] Ibid. i. 197–8.

[24] Ibid. i. 177. The *Lettres philosophiques* were condemned 'to be torn and burnt by the public executioner as scandalous and contrary to religion, morality and the respect due to the authorities'. (See Letter D758, Note 1.)

[25] The issues for 8 and 18 June 1736. See M. C. Couperus's study, *Un périodique français en Hollande* (The Hague: Mouton, 1971), 63.

[26] *Un périodique français*, p. 63. Bruys said in his *Mémoire*: 'deux lettres impies sur la nature de l'ame, insérées dans cette feuille, ont obligé la Cour de Hollande de servir contre ce nouveau monstre littéraire, qui semblait braver la justice de Dieu et la sévérité du magistrat.' Lanson points out that La Barre de Beaumarchais reprinted these two letters in the 2nd edn. of his *Amusemens littéraires, ou Correspondance politique, historique, philosophique, critique & galante* (3 vols., 1740) (*Lettres philosophiques*, Lanson's edn., i. 191). Couperus thinks La Barre escaped a fate similar to La Varenne's because 'il avait pris la précaution de faire suivre les lettres de Voltaire d'une réfutation'. In his *Lettres sur les vrais principes de la religion*, Boullier cites the printing of the 'Lettre sur Locke' in the *Amusemens littéraires*, saying that Voltaire was the author.

stimulated a strong reaction from a German writer, Reinbeck. The French translation of Reinbeck's book carries the title *Réflexions philosophiques sur l'immatérialité de l'âme raisonnable* (1744).[27] The Epistle to the reader is signed by Formey, the translator. Either Formey or a third person added an explanatory preface. The author of that preface says that what stirred Reinbeck into action was 'une Lettre Philosophique, où l'Auteur tache de soutenir que c'est la Matière qui pense'. Remarking that this letter had circulated in manuscript, he also calls attention to the 1736 printing in the *Observateur polygraphique*. Pages 266–323 in the main text are devoted to replying to Voltaire's letter on Locke. Locke is mentioned in the reply but Reinbeck's attention is mainly directed against the arguments of the letter. In general, he argues that appeals to the power of God do not tell us what is actually possible in our world. For that, we need to consider the nature of thought and the nature of matter; then we will see that they are incompatible.

In presenting his own views, Reinbeck follows the tradition in defining the soul as a substance which has the faculty of forming certain representations and of producing in itself desires and passions. This faculty is an active one. He notes that those who say the soul is material do not say that thought (which he, echoing Leibniz and Wolff, characterizes as the ability to form representations) is in every part of matter, only in 'une certaine espèce' of matter (p. 7). There is some interesting discussion of ideas, reasoning, and the nature of the rational soul. Significantly, in the light of the fears people had of turning man into an automaton, he also makes some explicit comparisons between the soul and machines ('une Machine Automate') such as watches and clocks. In a self-moving machine such as a watch, the source of the movement is internal, but the machine follows the laws of mechanics and cannot deviate from them. The soul can change and alter its operations. Matter and body can act only through motion. Reinbeck gives a very

---

[27] The work carried the subtitle: 'Avec quelques remarques sur la lettre dans laquelle on soutient que la matière pense'. The German original was published in 1740, *Philosophische Gedancken über die vernünfftige Seele und derselben Unsterblichkeit*. Couperus suggests this may have been the theologian Johann Gustav Reinbeck who died in 1741. See Couperus, *Un périodique français*, p. 63 n. 83. This identity is confirmed by a reference to Reinbeck's 1740 work in Jean Formey's *La Belle Wolfienne* (1741), i. 128–9. A review in the *Journal littéraire d'Allemagne, de Suisse et du nord* for 1743 of a collection of Reinbeck's sermons translated into French gives his birth date as 1682. In that review, the *Réflexions philosophiques* is cited and briefly discussed. A list of Reinbeck's writings is given on pp. 144–6.

careful and detailed account of the body and how it moves, detailing what those who say some matter thinks say about body. His point is to show some of the things that the soul can do which body cannot. His arguments are not emotional responses, even though the reviewer of the book in the *Bibliothèque raisonnée* (as we shall see) thinks he reasons badly. He does use one of the standard responses found in many writers in Britain, the *reductio* of asking, can thought be shaped or have a length? (p. 45)—a response which the *Bibliothèque raisonnée* mocks.

The terms of Locke's suggestion are clearly evident in Reinbeck's book. The French translation was the subject of a long article in the journal I have just mentioned, in 1744.[28] After presenting Reinbeck's general account of the soul as a rational, self-active substance, the reviewer remarks that it is not immediately obvious, as Reinbeck claims, that the action of the soul is not like the actions of a '*Machine Automate*' (p. 140). The author agrees that the action of such machines as watches and clocks (or of Vaucanson's automata) differs from the action of souls, but he says that no one has as yet shown us that our soul is not 'une sorte de Machine infiniment plus parfaite que celles-là, et qu'aucune de celles que vous connoissez' (p. 141). How can we, he goes on to say, so confidently assert that God has not been able and even wanted to give to the machines he makes 'des facultés que ne sauroient jamais avoir les Machines faites par des hommes' (p. 142). The writer neither asserts nor denies this suggestion, but he sees no contradiction in it. Reinbeck, he says, only compares man to very imperfect machines, those made by man. If we were able to demonstrate that a machine could think, that action would not compare with the action of Reinbeck's clocks. So the question remains: 'is matter able to think?'

Reinbeck offers a number of arguments for the conclusion that no motion, external or internal to the body, can cause thought. The reviewer finds all these arguments faulty and superficial (p. 144). He charges Reinbeck with confusing the effect with the cause: 'Dire que le mouvement est nécessaire à un Etre pensant, n'est pas dire que le mouvement soit la pensée.' (p. 147). All sorts of organic bodies in nature—plants, animals—produce amazing effects via motion of fluids and action of nerves, but those motions are not the same as the

---

[28] *Bibliothèque raisonnée des ouvrages des savans de l'Europe*, 33 (July–Sept. 1744), 134–55. The main editors of this journal were Barbeyrac, Armand Boisbeleau de La Chapelle (1676–1746), and Pierre Desmaizeaux (1673–1745).

effects produced. All the greatest philosophers agree, the reviewer says, that we cannot know the powers of matter, especially when that power resides in organs so complex, so fine and delicate, as those of living organisms. We cannot form the least idea of their structure or arrangement. Therefore, 'Disons donc que la pensée est le produit, non du mouvement seul ou de sa force, mais du mouvement joint à d'autres causes qui ont leur principe dans la structure admirable d'un Organe qui nous est inconnu' (p. 147). Nature most often acts in secret. He agrees that no one has explained how, in what way, matter might be able to think, but equally the opposition has not been able to show that matter could not think (p. 148). The reviewer several times makes the point which was made by Locke and other writers in Britain, that the suggestion is not that brute, inactive matter might think, but rather that a body of a particular organization and complexity ('fitly disposed', was Locke's phrase) of which God is the author might, and only he would know how it worked (p. 149).

The reviewer reminds his readers that Reinbeck attacks both those who think they have shown that some matter does think, and those who only argue for its possibility. The reviewer only wants to defend the latter, but that very defence places him on the side of Locke. Perhaps this fact explains the sober way in which this same journal examined Voltaire's use of Locke's suggestion. The reviewer also argues like Locke in saying that, even were the soul material, that would not rule out its being immortal. Very reminiscent of a remark Locke also makes, the reviewer ends by commenting that Reinbeck's fears are misplaced, his fears that if the soul were material (and hence if some matter did think), the soul would be mortal. God will take care of our soul whether it be material or immaterial: 'Son essence est un mystère impénétrable, aussi bien pour le plus grand Philosophe que pour le plus stupide des Hommes. L'Ecriture ne nous a rien revelé là-dessus, elle nous enseigne seulement qu'elle est immortelle ...' (p. 155). The fears of 'mortalism' (that the soul is not immortal) also motivated many writers in England who rejected the possibility of 'matière pensante'.

L'ÂME MATÉRIELLE AND OTHER RADICAL WRITINGS

In her article in the Bloch collection, Ann Thomson calls attention to the fact that when La Mettrie refers to Voltaire's Letter XIII, it is to the clandestine version 'Lettre sur Locke'.[29] The reference is to that paragraph where Voltaire lists Locke along with such writers as Bayle, Spinoza, Hobbes, Toland.[30] Thomson also remarks that the 'Lettre sur Locke' not only was used by La Mettrie, it also influenced 'la pensée clandestine'. The early version of Letter XIII was just one of a long list of radical tracts that have come to be known as 'Des traités clandestins'.[31] Most of these tracts were anonymous though the authors of many can now be established. Some of the items on the list of clandestine tracts were better known than others, some were more widely circulated, and some were more radical in their attacks on and rejection of religion. Many of these reflect in some form the moves towards materializing the soul, as did the 'Lettre sur Locke'.

One of the more important of these materialist tracts was known as *L'Âme matérielle*. This was in fact a compilation, a patchwork of passages taken from a wide range of writers, passages not often identified in the tract itself but recently nicely identified and presented on opposite pages in Alain Niderst's edition of this work.[32] Bayle is frequently the source of passages, Hobbes is also used, Lucretius, various Cartesians, many long passages from Dilly's work *Traité de l'ame et de la connoissance des bêtes* (1691), Bernier's abridgement of Gassendi, and some ancient writers.

[29] 'La Mettrie et la littérature clandestine', in Bloch, *Le Matérialisme*, pp. 238–9.

[30] See her edn. of La Mettrie's 'Discours préliminaire', *Materialism and Society in the Mid-Eighteenth Century: La Mettrie's 'Discours préliminaire'* (Geneva: Droz, 1981), 130–1; cf. 225. A similar passage is found in the conclusion to La Mettrie's *Histoire naturelle de l'âme*. In the edns. of 1745 and 1747, but not in the version that appeared in the *Œuvres philosophiques* of 1751, there is a long passage which includes those remarks of Voltaire about it not being philosophers who spread discord, but religious defenders. The philosophers cited by La Mettrie do not include all those listed by Voltaire, but Locke, Bayle, and Spinoza are there. (See above, n. 6, for the full passage in Voltaire's Letter XIII.) It is clear, however, that La Mettrie is following the 'Lettre sur Locke' version, which varies a bit from that of Letter XIII. For the scholarly editing of this work of La Mettrie, with the details on the texts of these three versions, see Theo Verbeek's critical edn. *Le Traité de l'âme de La Mettrie* (2 vols., Utrecht: OMI-Grafisch Bedrijf, 1988). The passage which is in the first two versions is found in vol. i, on pp. 217–18. In the text of all three versions, there is a footnote to Voltaire's Letter XIII and the remark, 'I am a body and I think'.

[31] For a recent listing of these manuscripts, with their locations, see Miguel Benitez's 'Liste et localisation des traités clandestins', in Bloch, *Le Matérialisme*, pp. 17–25. There are 130 such tracts listed. For a useful characterization of a clandestine manuscript, see Ann Thomson's 'Qu'est-ce qu'un manuscrit clandestin?', ibid. There is a summary of the contents of 19 of these tracts in Pierre Clair's 'Libertinage et incrédules (1665–1715)', in *Recherches sur le XVIIe siècle*, 6 (1983), 1–294.

[32] See n. 1 above.

Malebranche is extensively used for the detailed physiology in his *De la recherche de la vérité*. As Niderst remarks, the author of *L'Âme matérielle* 'transforme cette physiologie en un franc matérialisme'.[33]

Among the authors whose works are incorporated into this tract we also find Locke. Almost six pages are inserted from Locke's reply to Stillingfleet's attack on the 4. 3. 6 *Essay* passage, Locke's suggestion about thinking matter. Niderst reminds us that these passages had also appeared in Coste's second edition of the French translation of the *Essay* in 1729, and that the *Nouvelles de la république des lettres* carried them in 1699.[34] In his reply to Stillingfleet, Locke went into some detail explaining what would be involved if God were to add thought, just as he had added motion, to matter. He makes suggestions on how the Creation might have proceeded and explains how the adding of thought to matter would not be inconsistent with the nature of matter. These passages lend much more weight to the claim that Locke took his suggestion seriously, than does his discussion in the *Essay*. Thus, with Locke's name being associated with thinking matter in Voltaire's 'Lettre sur Locke' and with these passages appearing in this radical tract, along with passages from Hobbes, Bayle, and others, Locke's name and doctrines were placed at the heart of the clandestine literature in the early part of the eighteenth century in France.

Locke's name appears in one other clandestine tract, 'Réflexions sur l'argument de M. Pascal et de M. Locke concernant la possibilité d'une vie à venir', sometimes attributed to Fontenelle. This item was published in a collection, *Nouvelles Libertés de penser* (1743), along with several essays on the soul, and one, 'Traité de la liberté', which *is* by Fontenelle.[35] This last-named tract makes heavy use of physiology and the tight dependence of thought and action on the physiology of the body. The essay on Pascal and Locke is mostly about

[33] *L'Âme matérielle*, p. 13.
[34] The *Nouvelles de la république des lettres* (a journal ed. by Jacques Bernard) devoted two long articles to Locke's *Reply to the Right Reverend the Lord Bishop of Worcester's Answer to His Second Letter*. See the issues for Oct. 1699, art. I, pp. 363–85, and Nov. 1699, art. I, pp. 483–513. The specific replies to Stillingfleet's attack on the thinking-matter suggestion are in the Nov. article, pp. 496–511. Extracts, translated into French, occupy pp. 498–506.
[35] See 'Matérialisme et déterminisme dans le Traité de la liberté de Fontenelle', by C. Romeo, in Bloch, *Le Matérialisme*, pp. 101 ff. In his *Discours philosophiques: Le Premier sur les causes finales, le second sur l'inertie de la matière; et le troisième sur la liberté des actions humaines* (1759), Boullier discusses and analyses this treatise on liberty.

Pascal, but Locke is cited on the need to have faith agree with reason. Jean Baptiste de Mirabaud, whose work on the origin of the world and on the nature of the soul often reads like Locke and the British formulation of thinking matter, also knew Locke's writings.[36] A radical writer whom Antoine-Martin Roche ranks among Locke's disciples, the Marquis d'Argens, praises Locke, cites him frequently, and borrows many of his doctrines.[37]

CONCLUSION

The association of Locke with materialism, irreligion, and free thinking (the frequent French epithet was 'les prétendus esprits-forts') comes from several different features of his thought. One writer saw materialism in his acceptance of the chain of being, because the continuity of being, from God to matter, suggested to this author that all is material.[38] That same article discusses a prospectus for a book in which Locke is linked with Bayle as two of the most prominent writers responsible for the irreligion of the day. The author of this proposed work admits that Locke was a great metaphysician, but charges him with abusing his talents by advancing new opinions, such as thinking matter, which undermine faith and religion, leading to infidelity and atheism. The marginal comment of the editor of this journal, 'Bayle et Locke fort maltraitez', hardly counteracts the charge. In a later article in the same journal, there is a discussion of passions and feelings, where Locke is said to oppose any *natural* passions.[39] This interpretation seems to come from the talk of the *tabula rasa*. An unnamed English writer, a 'disciple of Locke' who agrees with him, is cited. The suggestion of the article is that the attempt to establish a *natural* religion (which was also seen as evil) is incompatible with the rejection of natural passions; but the main point of the article is to claim that those who seek to establish natural religion also favour materialism. Such people are said to attack the existence of the soul 'et de toutes sortes de substances immaterielles'.

[36] The title of Mirabaud's work is *Le Monde, son origine et son antiquité* (1751). For a discussion, see 'Érudition et philosophie: Mirabaud et l'antiquité', by P. Rétat, in Bloch, *Le Matérialisme*, p. 99 n. 6. See also ch. 3 below.

[37] See Argens, *La Philosophie du bon-sens* (1737). For Roche, see his *Traité de la nature de l'âme, et de l'origine de ses connoissances, contre le système de Mr. Locke et de ses partisans* (2 vols., 1759).

[38] See *Le Pour et contre*, 3 (1734), art. 38, p. 186.

[39] Ibid. 4 (1734), art. 55, pp. 224, 227–8.

A letter to the editor printed in vol. 7, art. 105 (1735), 343, in this same journal reinforces the interpretation of this article. Charging that these writers treat natural religion in the same terms as revealed religion, the author of this letter comments: 'Il n'y a rien de si absurde et de si extravagant qui n'ait été avancé ou cru par les pretendus Esprits-forts de tous les siècles.' The writer of the earlier article ends by listing the enemies of religion: Locke, Collins, Toland, Tindal, Wollaston, Woolston, citing Locke's 'celebrated passage' on thinking matter.

This linking of Locke with writers such as Collins and Toland reflects that paragraph in Voltaire's Letter XIII with its very similar listing. That the association of Locke with such writers had reached something like a canonical status by the mid-eighteenth century is suggested by Tabaraud's two-volume study *Histoire critique du philosophisme anglais, depuis son origine jusqu'à son introduction en France* (1806). Tabaraud's term 'philosophisme' designates irreligion: deism, atheism, and materialism. The writers he studies remind us again of Voltaire's list: Hobbes, Blount, Locke, Collins, Tindal, Toland, Wollaston, Shaftesbury, Mandeville. While Tabaraud admits that Locke may not quite belong in this list, he places him in his study because of his doubts about the soul's immateriality and consequently its immortality. 'Locke jeta dans sa philosophie des germes de matérialisme et d'immoralité que ses disciples cultivèrent avec un succès malheureusement trop funeste' (i. 49–50).[40] The chapter on Locke (i. 223–387) contains much discussion of thinking matter, some on Locke's religion, and his account of liberty and freedom. The final chapter of his study is on 'l'introduction du Philosophisme anglais en France'; he devotes most of the discussion to Voltaire, especially his letter on Locke.

[40] An 18th-century historian, the Abbé Daniel le Masson des Granges (*Le Philosophe moderne, ou L'Incrédule condamné au tribunal de sa raison*, 1759), gives a list of modern deists and unbelievers: Spinoza, Vanini, Socinus, Bayle, Hobbes, Toland, Collins. He then adds: '& peut etre encore un Locke, que nos Incrédules puissent citer en leur faveur'.

3

French Materialist Disciples

TABARAUD may not belong among the first rank of historians, but his accounts of Locke and Voltaire are sound. That Tabaraud was not alone in locating Locke and his doctrines among the deists, free thinkers, and materialists is confirmed by three occasionalist critics of Locke. A famous medical doctor who wrote on metaphysics and theology as well as on physiology and diseases, Jean Astruc, attacked Locke along with Fontenelle and Mirabaud, in his *Dissertation sur l'immatérialité et l'immortalité de l'âme* (1755). Astruc saw Locke as providing the conceptual foundation for the 'esprits-forts' with his conjecture about thinking matter. Gerdil wrote an extended attack on this same subject, *L'Immatérialité de l'âme démontrée contre M. Locke* (1747). Roche identified and attacked Locke along with those he described as 'partisans' or 'disciples' of Locke, in his *Traité de la nature de l'âme* (1759). While the term 'disciples' may be too strong, suggesting a more conscious intention to follow Locke than may be true of the writers given that label by these three occasionalists, the charge is nevertheless very revealing about the extent to which Locke's doctrines had become intertwined with heterodoxy in France. To a large extent, the attacks of these three reflect the debate between occasionalism (and perhaps pre-established harmony) and physical influence, with Locke always associated with the latter.

GIACINTO SIGISMONDO GERDIL

It is indicative of the status of Locke's suggestion that Cardinal Giacinto Sigismondo Gerdil refers to Locke's 'fameux doute sur l'immaterialité de l'Ame'.[1] Gerdil's critique of Locke is, of the three

---

[1] *L'Immatérialité de l'âme démontrée contre M. Locke, par les mêmes principes par lesquels ce philosophe démontre l'existence & l'immatérialité de Dieu, avec des nouvelles preuves de l'immatérialité de Dieu et de l'Âme, tirées de l'Ecriture, des Peres & de la raison* (1747), 124. Gerdil was Professor of Philosophy at the Royal College of Casal, Italy. He published a year later another attack on Locke, *Défense du sentiment*

I am discussing, the most judicious and best reasoned. The so-called 'new proofs' in the title of his book are hardly new, since they are all found in many of the tracts in Britain. His discussion is wide-ranging: it includes the physiology of the body, the nature of space, as well as the nature of the soul. One unique feature of Gerdil's discussion is his account of Locke on the motion of the soul. Locke, along with a number of other writers in Britain, including those who stoutly defended immaterialism, had ascribed extension to space and to souls, although some were quick to point out that souls were not extended in the same way as bodies. Locke's talk of motion as a property of immaterial things (motivity was the term he used to distinguish that motion from the mobility of body) occurs in a passage very similar to one in Descartes's 'Regulae ad directionem ingenii' (1701).[2] Gerdil finds it impossible even to conceive of a thought or a volition being located in a place, as it would have to be were the soul located (p. 47). There is for Gerdil only one way in which something can occupy a place and that is corporeally, the way an extended, hard body does. Like most traditional metaphysicians at that time, he insists on sharp differences between thought and extension, material and immaterial substances. Something is either extended or not extended, divisible or indivisible, located in space or non-spatial. To cross these categories—even for God to do so— would require a change in the perfections or essences of extended or non-extended substance.

En effet si les objets materiels n'étoient pas simplement des occasions, mais des causes proprement efficientes des idées, & des sensations, qu'ils excitent en nous par le mouvement; il faudroit, que la matière, & le mouvement eussent en eux-mêmes, ou actuellement, ou dans un plus haut degré toute la perfection des idées, & des sensations, ce qu'on ne peut supposer sans absurdité. (pp. 11–12)

A consequence of the impossibility of transferring the essence or perfection of one kind of substance to another (e.g. thought to body) is that there can be no interaction between different substances. Thus for Gerdil, 'il s'ensuit nécessairement, que des objets purement

---

du P. Malebranche sur la nature & l'origine des idées, contre l'examen de Mr. Locke (1748). Each of these books is over 250 pages long.
  [2] The passage in Locke's *Essay* is 2. 21. 73. For a similar list in Descartes, see his 'Regulae', 12. I have discussed these lists in 'Méthode et métaphysique dans la philosophie de John Locke', in *Revue philosophique*, 163 (1973), 171–85. Gerdil's discussion of the motion of the soul is found on pp. 44–51 of *L'Immatérialité de l'âme*.

materiels ne peuvent jamais être, que des causes simplement occasionnelles des sensations, dont notre ame est affectée, quand ces objets impriment un certain mouvement aux organes de nos sens' (p. 11). Matter is not the efficient, but only the occasional, cause of ideas. Only if God had placed in bodies a perfection equal to that of thoughts and ideas (on a scale of being) could they be the efficient cause of thoughts and ideas; but if they had such a perfection, they would no longer be bodies (p. 12). Similarly, the soul is not the efficient cause of the movement of its body, it cannot move its limbs. Gerdil is following Malebranche here very strictly: I will but do not cause my arm to move.[3] When we say that I move my arm, or that the motion of bodies causes ideas, we need to distinguish what happens in my body from what happens in my soul: 'dans l'ame il n'y a qu'une volonté, ou un désir que son corps soit remué; & ce désir est suivi d'un mouvement dans le corps, ensuite des loix d'union de l'ame & du corps' (p. 47; see also pp. 129–31).

In his various discussions of Locke, Gerdil shows a careful reading of the *Essay* and of the exchange with Stillingfleet (as summarized in the *Nouvelles de la république des lettres*, 1699). He is aware that while Locke belongs to that group of writers who were indifferent to the immateriality of the soul, he was not one of those who sought to prove that all is material. Gerdil summarizes Locke on thinking matter as follows:

M. Locke n'a jamais prétendu prouver que tout ce qui éxiste, jusqu'à Dieu même, soit materiel & étendu; beaucoup moins a-t-il pensé d'en faire un article de Foi. Il prétend seulement, 1. Qu'on ne peut démontrer par la raison, que la matiere ne soit pas capable de recevoir la faculté de penser. 2. Que l'usage qu'ont fait les Anciens du mot *Esprit* & *Ame*, nous autorise à envisager le principe de la pensée, comme une substance qui n'est pas dépouillée de toute materialité. 3. Que la Révelation nous enseigne que l'Ame est immortelle, mais non pas qu'elle soit immaterielle. 4. Que les Peres de l'Église n'ont jamais entrepris de démontrer que la matiere fût absolument incapable de penser. (pp. 189–90)

Other writers, partisans of Locke (pp. 31, 182), went further but Locke's fame and the spread of his suggestion about thinking matter made it necessary to refute even his cautious assertions.

---

[3] For a discussion of this doctrine in Malebranche, see my *Thinking Matter* (Minneapolis, Minn.: University of Minnesota Press; Oxford: Basil Blackwell, 1984), ch. VII.

JEAN ASTRUC

While Gerdil names only one of those he labels a partisan of Locke (Cuenz, discussed below), the second critic, the medical doctor Jean Astruc,[4] is more definite in associating Locke with those he calls 'prétendus esprits-forts', a label in frequent use to group those who attacked religion and who supported materialism. These free thinkers, Astruc claimed, base their materialism on or take support from Locke's suggestion about matter thinking, his causal theory of perception, and his scepticism about the nature of substance. Astruc was, of course, very familiar with physiological explanations of the workings of the body, and also with the close parallels and concomitances between physiology and mental or affective states. It was such physiological correlations, especially when they were very specific, which worried some traditionalists both in Britain and France, for those correlations could easily displace the role of mind or soul in action. But Astruc had a firm theoretical escape from such displacement in his acceptance of occasionalism, with its denial of any interaction between body and soul. The main result of the union of body and soul is the reciprocal correspondence between impressions of the body and affections of the soul. When Locke speaks of matter or body producing pleasure or pain, Astruc says this is just false. Such and such movements of body are followed by such and such sensations or perceptions: that is all we can say we know (p. 92). Similarly for action: such and such volitions of the soul are followed by certain motions of the body. No body is able to act on an immaterial substance (p. 3). Committed to the substance-mode ontology, he is just as firmly committed to *two* substances. The modes of each of these substances differ in kind, as do the substances themselves. The modes *are* states or actions of the substance: just as the heat of the hand and the hot hand are the same, so 'telles et telles *sensations* de l'ame, sont l'ame-meme *sentant* telles et telles choses' (p. 7). Similarly, volitions of the soul *are* the soul willing.

He spins out the usual attempt at a *reductio* of the claim about thought being a property of matter: if it were, it would be long or

---

[4] See his *Dissertation sur l'immatérialité et l'immortalité de l'âme* and *Dissertation sur la liberté* (1755). These two books were published together with continuous pagination. Astruc (1684–1766) was an important medical writer who published many books and tracts on medicine, religion, and natural history. See Janet Doe's article, 'Jean Astruc (1684–1766): A Biographical and Bibliographical Study', *Journal of the History of Medicine and Allied Sciences*, 15 (Apr. 1960), 184–97.

short, it could be divided, etc. He agrees with Locke that we do not know the nature of either material or immaterial substances, but knowing each through its modes is sufficient to convince us of the impossibility of those modes belonging to only one substance. He takes the *reductio* to be a demonstration of this impossibility. Astruc admits that there are many profound thoughts in Locke's *Essay* and in his *Reasonableness of Christianity*, but Locke has a tendency to deal with some topics too quickly and not carefully enough. He discusses the *Essay*, 4. 3. 6, passage on thinking matter, pointing out that, despite what the free thinkers claim, Locke does not say that matter *is* able to think, only that it is impossible to discover from our ideas whether God might not give it the power of thought. He says that the 'prétendus esprits-forts' also argue that God is material, as he charges Spinoza did. He too recognizes that Locke does not go this far, but he nevertheless associates him with several of the clandestine materialist tracts, those by Mirabaud and Fontenelle.

   The work credited to Jean-Baptiste de Mirabaud was published in 1751 under the title, *Le Monde, son origine et son antiquité*. Astruc describes its contents, including the second part on the soul and its immortality. He tells us that this book was suppressed but only after some copies were dispersed. He did not know the author (the work was published anonymously) but he confidently ascribed it to 'quelqu'un de nos prétendus esprits-forts' (p. 39). Locke is not mentioned by Mirabaud, but the arguments supporting the possibility of matter thinking are of the same nature as those outlined by Locke and found in the British debate. The appeal to our lack of knowledge of the nature of matter is one that Astruc responds to, insisting that we know enough to know that matter is extended and has parts and that thought can have neither of those properties (p. 49). Most of his work contains discussions of the views of the ancients on these topics, but the tone of his historical account tends to support the notion that matter could have thought as one of its properties.[5]

<hr/>

[5] The attribution of *Le Monde, son origine et son antiquité* is somewhat in doubt. J. Schøsler in his *Bibliographie des éditions et des traductions d'ouvrages philosophiques français . . . 1680–1800* (Odense: Odense University Press, 1986) credits only the second part of this collection, entitled 'De l'âme et de son immortalité', to Mirabaud. Cf. 'Érudition et philosophie: Mirabaud et l'antiquité', by P. Rétat, in O. Bloch (ed.), *Le Matérialisme du XVIIIe siècle* (Paris: J. Vrin, 1982). Rétat argues that Mirabaud is a good example of the way in which 'le matérialisme au début du XVIIIe siècle a cherché dans l'Antiquité ses modèles philosophiques et a utilisé l'arme de l'érudition' (p. 91). Cudworth in Britain illustrates the same tradition of looking to

The other work which Astruc spends some time attacking was the collection of tracts, all again ascribed by Astruc to 'nos prétendus esprits-forts', under the title *Nouvelles Libertés de penser* (1743). The collection contains a number of tracts dealing with the soul and one on Pascal and Locke on a future life. The third tract in that collection, to which Astruc directs most of his attention, is 'Traité de la liberté'. C. Romeo tells us that this tract, which he thinks was written and circulated in manuscript before 1700, was written by Fontenelle. It was reprinted many times in the eighteenth century, usually in the collection named by Astruc but also along with another important clandestine tract, *Examen de la religion* (1745).[6] This tract on liberty contains nothing directly related to Locke, but Locke's critics heard echoes in it of the system of physical influence which they did find in Locke. That an essay on Locke and Pascal appeared in the same collection reinforced the critic's view that Locke's doctrines lent support to the French free thinkers. Astruc's *Dissertation sur la liberté* (1755), where his attack on Fontenelle's tract appears, is a major attempt to answer writers like Anthony Collins in England and Fontenelle in France. What must have bothered Astruc in particular, with his own proclivity towards physiology, was Fontenelle's use of brain traces and dispositions. In his tract, Fontenelle argued that (1) the mind (*âme*) thinks when the brain is disposed in a certain way, i.e. when certain motions in the brain correspond to certain thoughts, and (2) all objects on which

ancient authors, but he does not endorse the materialism of those writers. Mirabaud was admired by Baron d'Holbach, who used his name (after Mirabaud's death) for his *Système de la nature*. As Pierre Naville remarks: 'Ainsi, l'œuvre clandestine de Mirabaud appartient de toute évidence au mouvement pré-encyclopédiste et maté- rialiste. Mirabaud ne fut pas seulement le prête-nom de d'Holbach pour son œuvre capitale. Il fut l'un de ses pères nourriciers, comme plusieurs autres dont la trace est plus difficile à relever.' (See Naville's informative discussion in his *D'Holbach et la philosophie scientifique au XVIIIe siècle* (rev. edn., Paris: Gallimard, 1967)).

[6] See the article in Bloch, *Le Matérialisme*, by C. Romeo, 'Matérialisme et déter- minisme dans le Traité de la liberté de Fontenelle'. In another tract on the nature of the soul in the collection, *Nouvelles Libertés de penser*, the question is raised: is the faculty of intelligence repugnant to extension? Since a common principle is not to multiply beings beyond necessity, 'if we conceive that the operations attributed to the mind [*esprit*] are able to be the work of matter acting in unknown ways, why imagine a useless being', such as an immaterial substance (pp. 159–60)? The author says that we can easily see that the properties of matter do not exclude intelligence. More positively, the author argues that, for me to know something, there must be something in common between me and the object. How else can an object make an impression on me? If an intellectual substance were united to a material one, intelligence would be destroyed (pp. 164–5). 'It is thus necessary to attribute to matter the operations which we commonly attribute to a spiritual substance' (p. 165).

one thinks leave material dispositions or traces in the brain (p. 119). There is some extended discussion of the ability we have of directing the animal spirits in the brain, but the stress is more upon the necessity of traces for action and thought. The incipient determinism in this tract is what Astruc attacks, since an undue stress upon the role of motions and dispositions in the brain seemed to make man's actions the consequence of those motions. This result was just another feature of materialism.

ANTOINE-MARTIN ROCHE

Roche's detailed discussion and critique of Locke runs through both volumes of his two-volume study, covering almost every aspect of the *Essay*.[7] His two volumes merit a close study. Most of his criticisms of Locke's doctrines are made from a traditional religious position. He manages to find fault with most of what Locke says, from the rejection of innate ideas, to the concept of person, to the account of our ideas of God and infinity. Ambitious and more specific on who were partisans and disciples of Locke, the objective of this study is to make known the nature and excellence of the soul, to establish its pure spirituality against the materialists, and to explain its union with the body. The false system is said to be the common one, a system which attributes to the impressions of sense 'la gloire d'être la source primitive de tout ce qu'il y a de connoissances dans l'homme' (i, p. xi). The soul for Roche is a reflection of God. Of those recent writers who pretend to explain its workings, most end by destroying it: 'Les uns tendent au matérialisme; les autres meme conduisent directement au Spinozisme' (i. 9).

This interesting separation between Spinozism and materialism is formulated as describing two classes of materialists: (1) those who

---

[7] Antoine-Martin Roche, *Traité de la nature de l'âme, et de l'origine de ses connoissances, contre le système de Mr. Locke et de ses partisans* (1759). In the same year, another writer with a similar name uses a similar way of referring to Locke's suggestion about matter thinking. See Charles-François Tiphaigne de la Roche, 'Essai sur la nature de l'âme, ou Examen de cette célèbre proposition de M. Locke: Dieu peut donner, s'il veut, à certains amas de matière, disposés comme il le juge à propos, la faculté d'appercevoir et de penser'. This is part of a 2-vol. work, *Bigarrures philosophiques* (1759). This author spends much of his time dealing with the absurdity of atoms of matter thinking and also with the Locke–Stillingfleet exchange on the topic of thinking matter. His 'Essai' is continued in the second volume. See below, pp. 148–51, for a discussion of this book. For a list of Tiphaigne's other writings, see A. Cioranescu, *Bibliographie de la littérature française du dix-huitième siècle*, iii (Paris: Éditions du CNRS, 1969).

make the soul coextended with all the body and (2) those who claim
that the soul is material. Of the first class, he says it is absurd since it
entails that the soul can be cut and divided, as the body can be.
Roche initially dispenses with the second class of materialists, by
remarking that they devalue the soul (i. 13). He then runs through
the usual defence of two substances. The smallest part of matter,
even the aether of the new philosophers, is extended. To be material
is to be extended. To be a soul is to think. A thought cannot be cut
into parts. Thus thought cannot reside in any matter.

Roche also points out that some materialists say the cause of
sensation resides in nerves and brain; the material soul, they say, is
located in the brain. He refers to several different accounts of the
physiology of the body, both the animal spirit and the vibratory
physiology (i. 34–7). He refers to Thomas Willis and 'several
Gassendists' (i. 71), to Descartes, to a *Lettre à un matérialiste*,[8] and
to Fontenelle (i. 76). Later in this volume, Le Camus's *Médecine de
l'esprit* (1753) becomes the main target of Roche's attack on the
system of physical influences. He tries to show the inadequacies of
physiological explanations of mental phenomena, despite the sometimes *very* specific correlations used by Le Camus. Roche draws
three conclusions from his discussion of the physiology of the body.
(1) It is 'impossible that the sensations, actions of man, and the
movements of the machine of the body have a material soul as their
cause' (i. 78–9). (2) The 'sentiment intérieur' shows that there is in us
a principle of thought, and 'une lumiére eclatante' shows that that
principle cannot be extended. It is simple, one, and immaterial
(i. 80). (3) The cause of bodily movements is not the soul even for
voluntary motions; they are all, as with Malebranche, the result of 'un
Agent fort supérieur à l'Ame', i.e. God (i. 81). The soul wills that
some part of the body move but it does not make it move (i. 82). Our
soul is only an occasional cause.

Roche has detailed discussions of the *Essay* 4. 3. 6 passage on
thinking matter, as well as of the exchange with Stillingfleet. He
speaks of Locke's 'strange doubt' about not knowing enough about
the nature of matter to warrant saying thought as one of its
properties is inconceivable. Roche is equally detailed on some
'modern' writers who have defended this doubt of Locke 'touchant la

---

[8] I have not yet been able to determine just what book Roche has in mind with this
reference. It may be Lelarge de Lignac's *Elémens de métaphysique . . . ou Lettres à un
matérialiste sur la nature de l'âme* (1753).

possibilité de l'Ame matérielle' (i. 101). His references to and citations from these modern defenders of Locke are frustrating, for he hardly ever gives an author's name. In some cases, even the title is so abbreviated that it is difficult to identify. Once most of these works have been identified we have an interesting list of people he characterizes as partisans, disciples, apologists, or reformers of Locke. One of these writers (unnamed and no publication title given) argued that, since new properties of matter have been discovered (e.g. gravitation), there may be still others such as thought that will turn out to belong to matter (i. 101–2). Roche is unimpressed with that argument. Of greater threat is the work of Le Camus who claims 'expliquer d'une maniere méchanique toutes les opérations de l'esprit' (i. 103). Roche notes that this author 'se déclare pour la spiritualité absolue de l'Ame', but Roche doubts his sincerity since his language reads like pure materialism (i. 104).[9]

AUTHORS CITED BY ROCHE

1. *Le Camus*

Le Camus denies that he is a materialist, a denial perhaps necessitated by his speaking, in his preface, of the soul as 'une simple machine qui ne va que par ressorts ou du moins une simple modification de la matière si elle n'est matière elle-même'. While he does seek in physiology the cures of mental ilness ('déraciner les défauts qu'on pense appartenir à l'ame, de la même maniere que les Médecins guérissent une fluxion de poitrine'), he rejects the notion that the finite soul is just a modification of God, as he interpreted Spinoza as doing. Equally, he rejects the notion of Hobbes and Epicurus that the soul is a modification of the body. The soul is not itself body, it is a substance which is reasonable, spiritual, and immortal (*Médecine de l'esprit*, p. ix). The active powers of the soul are the understanding and the will. Le Camus cites Locke as 'ce chef des Philosophes' on questions of human knowledge. Le Camus's account of sensation and perception is very Lockian, thereby making it easy to associate Locke with these physiological accounts. The senses furnish the

---

[9] The full title of Le Camus's book is *Médecine de l'esprit, où l'on cherche, 1. le méchanisme du corps qui influe sur les fonctions de l'ame, 2. les causes physiques qui rendent ce méchanisme ou défectueux ou plus parfait, 3. les moyens qui peuvent l'entretenir dans son état libre et le rectifier lorsqu'il est géné* (2nd edn., 1769; the 1st edn., which I have not seen, was published in 1753).

mind with clear, simple ideas, such as colour, sound, etc. These are called 'apprehensions, perceptions'. Reflection is '*cette facilité que nous avons d'appliquer de nous-mêmes notre attention tous à tous à divers objets*'. These produce different kinds of ideas. Attention is defined as '*la conscience que nous avons de notre manière d'etre actuelle*' (p. 7). All ideas depend upon the senses. Before knowing we must feel, before feeling we must be sensible. Thus, his first section is on sensibility: it is the aptitude of receiving impressions from objects (p. 8). He then gives an account of the fibres and tissues of nerves, their fluids, etc. He speaks of a 'force tonique' of those fibres. The muscles too have a particular force which takes three forms: mechanical, voluntary, and mixed (p. 10). The first of these muscular forces is independent of the soul (e.g. the functioning of the heart); the second depends on the will (e.g. our moving arms and limbs); and the third is action in accord with the general laws of mechanics. These latter can be augmented or diminished by the will, as in breathing. Reflective sensation is characterized as '*l'attention que l'ame porte à ses idées en les comparant entre elles*' (p. 18).

Le Camus gives a large role to another faculty, the imagination: it is '*une force de reproduire ces perceptions pendant l'observation des objets*' (p. 33). The imagination produces ideas or representations of objects. But like the three critics I am discussing, Le Camus declares himself to follow occasionalism. God only is the efficient cause of ideas, he alone is capable of producing motion. God excites ideas in our souls only as a result of the disposition of our bodies. The imagination comes in two forms: one that is independent of our will, the other which is under the control of the will. Even the latter must, presumably, be interpreted as correlation, not as causal control.

2. *Argens*

Another writer Roche identifies as a disciple of Locke is the Marquis d'Argens, the author of *La Philosophie du bon-sens* (1737).[10] In his 'Discours préliminaire', Argens characterized Locke's work as 'vrai dans la plus grande partie de ses principes, juste dans ses

---

[10] This work is divided into 7 parts which are called 'Réflexions'. My references are to the 1768 edn. in 3 vols. The full title is *La Philosophie du bon-sens, ou Réflexions philosophiques sur l'incertitude des connoissances humaines*. This edn. is enlarged and corrected, but it has no substantive changes in doctrines. Argens served in the court of Frederick II (the Great) of Prussia and was the author of two very popular works, *The Chinese Spy* and *The Jewish Spy*.

conséquences, précis dans ses démonstrations'.[11] Argens remarks
that, if he had to choose, he would gladly rank himself under Locke's
guidance, but as the custom in the Republic of Letters is to cite a
variety of authors, he will follow that method. There are frequent
citations from and uses made of Descartes, Malebranche, the Port
Royal logic, and especially Gassendi.

In asserting that, at birth, the soul is a blank tablet, he cites
Gassendi's use of the dictum 'nothing in the intellect that is not first
in the senses'. He then proceeds to explain that external, sensible
objects strike our senses and produce ideas. How they produce ideas
he leaves unexplained. Sensation is one source of the mind's ideas.
The other source is reflection. His summary of the two sources of
ideas is virtually copied from Locke:

> toutes nos idées prennent leur source de la *sensation*, & de la *réflexion*. Par
> la *sensation*, les objets extérieurs fournissent à l'esprit les idées des qualités
> sensibles, telles que sont celles qui nous viennent par le goût, l'attouchement,
> l'ouïe, l'odorat & la vue. Les sens produisent les notions ou les idées des
> odeurs différentes, celles des diverses couleurs, celles des sons, celles de la
> clarté & des ténebres, &c. Par la *réflexion*, l'esprit fournit à l'entendement les
> idées de ses propres opérations; c'est-à-dire, que par les idées qui ont passé
> par nos sens, & qui se sont imprimées dans notre entendement, il s'en forme
> diverses autres par l'assemblage que nous en faisons d'une maniere très-
> variée, comme, lorsque de l'idée d'une Montagne & de celle de l'or, nous en
> concevons une troisieme idée, qui nous représente une montagne d'or.[12]

In rejecting the Cartesians who talk of non-sensory, innate ideas,
Argens cites Locke on the idea of God; he reiterates the doctrine of
sensation and reflection as the only sources of ideas.[13] The discussion of that topic later in this work uses Locke to a great extent. The
section headings there show the close following of Locke: 'Que nous
n'avons point d'idées innées', 'Qu'il n'est aucune regle de Morale qui
soit innée', 'Que nous n'avons point d'idées innées de Dieu'.[14]

Argens also has a section on the connection between words and
ideas (Reflection II, § VII). He uses passages from the Port Royal
logic and Locke's *Essay*. He also follows Locke in the latter's stress
on the limitations of our knowledge. He even sounds like Locke on
the notion of what a non-experiential knowledge of matter would be,
were we able to acquire such knowledge: we would easily be able to
know the operations of matter without experience. He draws an

---

[11] Argens, *La Philosophie*, i. 22.   [12] Ibid. i. 182–3.
[13] Ibid. i. 190–1.   [14] Ibid. ii. 150–61.

analogy between such internal knowledge of the workings of matter and the clock-maker's knowledge of the mechanism of clocks.[15]

Si nos sens pouvoient être assez aigus pour appercevoir les parties actives de la matière nous verrions travailler les parties de l'eau-forte sur celles de l'argent: & cette méchanique nous seroit aussi facile à découvrir, qu'il l'est à l'horloger de savoir comment & par quel ressort se fait le mouvement d'une pendule.[16]

But such knowledge is beyond our faculties. Another area of ignorance is in how thought is able to produce motion in a body, or how body can produce thought: 'Nous ne pouvons pénétrer comment l'esprit agit sur la matière, & la matière sur l'esprit'.

When Argens turns his attention to the nature of the soul, this last example of our ignorance enables him to follow Locke in the suggestion about thinking matter. In section X of Reflection IV, he says that all ancient philosophers have been as little certain about the nature of the soul as are the philosophers of today. He even asserts that it is impossible for us to penetrate into the nature of that being in us which thinks and which we call ourself. That being is 'united to a certain collection of animal spirits which are in a constant flux'.[17] We shall never be able to understand how the soul thinks. Nor shall we be able to know whether the soul is material or immaterial. Faith has to take us to whichever conclusion we draw, but it is clear that Argens sides with saying it is material. He is not quite as outspoken on this conclusion as others were, but most of his discussion seems designed to support it.

In the section on the possible materiality of the soul (Reflection IV, § XI), he quotes from the 4. 3. 6 passage of Locke's *Essay* on the possibility of God adding to matter the power of thought.[18] He says that 'several great men have believed the soul was material, and even several Fathers of the Church'. He lists some early modern writers who held this belief: Averroës, Andreas Caesolpinus (1519–1603), Girolamo Cardano (1501–76), Cesare Cremonini (1552–1613), or Pietro Pompanazzi (1462–1524), and also Hobbes (ii. 200). In a note, he remarks that he has not included in this list Spinoza or Vanini because they were atheists. Some of those on his list have been suspected of atheism, but none have professed openly that they were (ii. 201). In section XIII of this Reflection, he argues that there

---

[15] Ibid. i. 212.   [16] Ibid. i. 212–13.
[17] Ibid. ii. 185.   [18] Ibid. ii. 198–9.

is no proof against the materiality of the soul. In these two sections, and in section XV, he gives reasons against the Cartesians, especially Malebranche, for holding the contrary opinion, that the soul is immaterial.

Thus, Argens gives extensive discussion to the two features of Locke's thought that were viewed by Roche and others as tending towards materialism—the sensory basis of all ideas, and the possibility of a material soul.

3. *Condillac*

Condillac firmly rejected Locke's suggestion of the possibility of certain kinds of matter having the property of thought. In order to reject this suggestion, we do not need to know the essence and nature of matter: 'It is sufficient to remark, that the subject of thought must be *one*. But a system or mass of matter is not *one*; it is a multitude.'[19] Condillac follows the occasionalists in affirming the body to be 'only the occasional cause of what it seems to produce' in the soul. The senses are also only the occasional source of knowledge: 'The soul is therefore able absolutely to acquire knowledge, without the help of the senses' (I. i. i. 8). Condillac even asserts that souls are capable of having and did at one time have ideas prior to the use of bodily senses. That prior time was before the Fall. After the disobedience in the Garden, God deprived the soul of this ability, making it dependent on the senses of the body. Condillac still qualifies that dependence with the clause, 'as if they were the physical cause of what they only occasion'. The occasionalist language is not always used. Sometimes he speaks of external objects *affecting* or acting on us (I. i. i. 4), but he usually speaks of qualities in bodies 'which occasion the impressions they make on our senses' (I. i. ii. 12), or of 'the objects which occasion the sensations of taste, of sound, of smell, of colour, and light' (§ 17). Elsewhere, he seems to distinguish the 'concussion of the fibres of the brain', which he characterizes as 'the physical cause of the perceptions of the mind', from the impressions made on the senses, or 'the agitation of the senses' which cause the perceptions in the mind (I. ii. ii. 24; see also § 1 and § 3). The note in paragraph 24 ends by using occasionalist language: 'Thus, whether we

---

[19] *Essai sur l'origine des connoissances* (2 vols., 1746), I. i. i. 7. I have used Georges Le Roy's 1947 edn. of the *Œuvres philosophiques* (Paris: Presses universitaires de France). Condillac also rejected the talk of the soul being 'only that aspect of body that is more delicate, more subtle, and more capable of motion' (I. i. i. 6).

suppose the perceptions are occasioned by the disturbances of the fibres, or by the circulation of the animal spirits, or by some other cause; it is all the same for the account I have in mind' (I. II. ii. 24). At the very least, the ideas we call sensations 'are such that, if we had been deprived of our Senses, we should never have been able to acquire them' (I. I. ii. 9).

Following Locke in stressing the dependence of ideas and thoughts on the senses (a relation which Locke makes causal but Condillac makes occasionalist), Condillac also identifies reflection as the second source of ideas. Sensation and reflection furnish 'the materials of all knowledge' (I. I. ii. 4). One difference between Locke and Condillac, a difference which worries Roche, is that Condillac identifies the origins of the *operations* of the mind as also being simple sense perceptions. After the Fall, at birth, the soul is without ideas *and* faculties.

Roche groups Condillac with those French authors who are the new disciples of Locke, but unlike some other French disciples, this group (Condillac is the one he discusses but Le Camus may belong here also) modifies Locke in three ways. (1) They openly abandon Locke's suggestion, insisting on the spiritual nature of the soul. (2) While these authors hold that external objects do not act immediately on the soul (God does), they adopt ordinary language and speak of objects producing impressions on the soul. (3) They have said that the soul is able, prior to the Fall and after the death of the body, to acquire knowledge without the aid of the senses (*Traité*, i. 455–8). Roche finds this third feature very important. The second feature is good, since it shows that this group rejects *in theory* physical influence. In fact, he writes as if Condillac *has* accepted Locke's principle of the sensory origin of ideas.

The novel twist to the sensory origin given by Condillac—that the *faculties* too take their origin there—makes it difficult for Condillac to characterize the soul in its first existence in any way. The soul becomes, Roche claims, almost featureless (i. 466). It is bad enough for the soul to be without ideas or thoughts at birth; to be without faculties or the operations of faculties at birth makes it inactive. Such a 'naked' soul, stripped of all the characteristics essential to a soul, violates and degrades the concept of soul. Roche sometimes seems to forget that Condillac writes about the present state, after the Fall. The soul by its nature before the Fall was, and will be again, independent of the body and have thoughts all the time (if indeed time applies to eternity). Locke is even better off than Condillac on the nature of the souls of men (at least, there is no inconsistency in his account, as there is with Condillac's) because, with his extended, semi-material soul (Roche frequently takes Locke's suggestion as if it were a firm assertion), it is easier to conceive such a soul being without ideas or thoughts. The denial of the soul's always thinking by Locke does not contradict *his* concept of soul. Like a watch that is not working, but which we know can be made to keep time, a material soul can be activated by sensory impressions (i. 467). 'But this negation of all thought in an immaterial substance [as Condillac does] is . . . an idea which goes against the light of common sense' (i. 467). To claim that the soul is immaterial but that in its first exist-ence it has no thought at all is to say that the soul is spiritual but not spiritual. Roche sometimes speaks of the soul as a faculty independ-ent of the senses, meaning that its nature is to be active, to have a real power to think, a power intrinsic to its nature. This is a power to know and to love, a power which is inseparable from the soul. To deny such an intrinsic power of a soul would be like denying that a circle is round.[20] He recognized that Locke and 'ses Réformateurs' sometimes used the name 'faculty', but they made it a passive faculty. What worried Roche the most were those disciples who went further than just saying the soul before sensation was a *tabula rasa*: 'ils prétendent que *sans l'efficacité des sens, elle seroit toujours comme une bete brute, comme une machine en mouvement*' (i. 476–7). The programme for the acquisition of ideas offered by Locke and Condillac violates Roche's notion of a soul made in the image of God.

Another writer sympathetic to Malebranche and occasionalism three years earlier expressed the same concern about the doctrine of the sensory origin of ideas; but this writer, the Abbé Mey, directs his attention to Locke.[21] Mey recognized that Locke identified two sources of ideas, sensation and reflection, but his interpretation of Locke's reflection is that it does not produce ideas, it only operates on those the mind already has (p. 166). At least, if the senses failed to

---

[20] Roche is insistent on his claim that thinking is nothing other than the faculty or ability to know and to love (especially to know and love God): these notions, he says, are identical (*Traité*, i. 474).

[21] Mey's *Essai de metaphysique* (1756) is a traditional work, but it is informed by careful discussions of the Arnauld–Malebranche exchange over the nature of ideas, and many references to the Port Royal logic and to Locke's *Essay*. His criticisms of Locke are less shrill than those of Roche, but the two agree on most issues.

produce any ideas, reflection would not occur. Sensing, and thus sensory ideas, do come first in Locke's genetic account of infants. At the same time, Mey points out that another basic claim by Locke is that there can be no ideas in the mind without the mind being aware of them. Thus, having ideas is already a reflective process, a self-reflective operation. This reflective activity, being a product of or a response to sensory ideas, is incapable of giving the mind what Mey calls 'spiritual' ideas, ideas of being, existence, substance, God. He does not discuss those passages in the *Essay* that describe how we form ideas of existence, unity, power, or substance. These are the sorts of ideas that for Abbé Mey can only be part of the mind, they cannot be acquired through sensing. If not part of its nature, then they can only be given to us on specific occasions by God. Taking Locke on his own terms, May states sensations are necessary to get the mind started; for Mey, this means that without sensation the mind for Locke would remain in 'une stupidité monstrueuse' (p. 165). Moreover, the doctrine of the sensory origin of ideas pre-supposes a mind or soul ready to receive ideas, but a soul without any distinctive characteristics, without those properties which for Mey and Roche constitute the very essence of a soul. The comparison of the human soul to animals follows easily for Mey, as it did for Roche.

Cette incompréhensible stupidité est naturelle à l'ame, dans le systême de M. Lock; elle forme son état propre, elle est une suite de sa création: ce fera donc la nature de l'ame d'être brute, sans action, sans vie spirituelle; & incapable par elle-même de changer sa funeste destinée, elle y seroit éternellement condamnée, si les sens ne réformoient & ne perfectionnoient en elle l'ouvrage de son Auteur.[22]

These reactions of Mey and Roche to the doctrines of the sensory origin of ideas and to the *tabula rasa* soul indicate the seriousness for traditional metaphysics and theology of this 'perverse' notion of the human soul. Roche goes into considerable detail about Condillac's account of the acquisition of ideas; he also occasionally cites d'Alembert's 'Discours préliminaire' in the *Encyclopédie* (1751–65) as supportive of the sensory-based account of ideas. Other passages attack the notion, which he found in Locke, Clarke, and Newton, of

---

[22] An equally objectionable consequence of Locke's account for Mey is that we only know the soul by its acts, acts which are added to the blank soul. We do not know its essence; hence, we cannot assert that the soul is not extended.

extension applied to space and the soul. He could not understand how a spiritual being could be extended, since extension for him was a univocal term. Appearing throughout his work are references to and attacks on another 'disciple' and defender of Locke, an author whom Roche identifies only as the 'Swiss apologist for Locke'.

CUENZ'S NEW SYSTEM

The Swiss apologist was a man named Cuenz. A journal, the *Nouvelle Bibliothèque, ou Histoire littéraire des principaux écrits qui se publient*, identified him as 'Conseiller d'Etat de la Ville de St. Gal, chargé ci-devant des affaires de cette République à la Cour de France, et Membre de l'Academie des Sciences et Belles-Lettres de Marseille'.[23] As was indicated in Chapter 1, the title of Cuenz's four-volume work was *Essai d'un sisteme nouveau, concernant la nature des etres spirituels, fondé en partie sur les principes du célèbre Mr. Locke, philosophe anglois, dont l'auteur fait l'apologie* (1742). The title-page of this work tells us that it was published by the editors of the *Journal helvétique* at Neuchâtel. Since this journal was a sponsor of Cuenz's ambitious work, it is not surprising to find its 'Projet de souscription' praising his study: matters of great importance are treated there, the most interesting parts of philosophy, at a modest price, etc. Cuenz had corresponded with the Royal Society of London about his work and he prints that correspondence in this study. The Royal Society seemed to encourage him in his project. The editors of the *Journal helvétique* are suitably impressed with the 'Jugemens qu'une des plus Illustres Societés Littéraires de l'Europe' had made of Cuenz's project. They were also impressed with the support of a number of (unnamed) theologians and philosophers

---

[23] Nov. 1742 issue. This journal was published at The Hague from 1738 to 1744. The main editors were Argens, Barbeyrac, Chais, and La Motte. See 'Table chronologique des périodiques de langue française publiés avant la Révolution', by Jean Sgard, in M. Couperus (ed.), *L'Étude des périodiques anciens* (Paris: Nizet, 1972), 189. In the Mar., Apr., and May issues for 1742, Isaac Watts's *Improvement of the Mind* is extensively discussed and abstracted. Locke is often cited in these articles, although not in connection with materialism. The 1749 issue of the *Journal helvétique* has an 18-page *Précis* of another book by the same author which is preceded by a letter signed, 'Cuenz'. I am indebted to Ann Thomson for calling this *Précis* to my attention. Jean-Daniel Candaux has informed me that Cuenz's first name was Caspar and that he was born in 1720. See Hans Jacob Leu (ed.), *Helvetisches allgemeines eydgenössisches oder schweitzerisches Lexicon* (1747–65), entry under 'Künz'.

from different countries.[24] All of this is typical publishers' 'hype' (together with Swiss pride), but the four volumes, the support by these various groups, and the publicity given by the journal certainly gave the work considerable prominence. With Locke's name on the title page, once again Locke and materialism were associated together. The 'principes de Mr. Locke' included the possibility of matter thinking. Cuenz devoted volume ii to a defence of Locke against the charge of materialism.

In presenting Locke's account of the origin of ideas, the limitations of knowledge, and the relation between soul and body, Roche employs Cuenz as an expositor of Locke's doctrines. There are some citations from Locke's *Essay*, but, more often than not, quotations from Cuenz are presented by Roche as if they catch Locke's meaning. Roche says that Locke's system is the most in fashion, pre-established harmony now has few followers (*Traité*, i. 340–1). Roche takes the basic principle of Locke's system to be that, before impressions from sensible objects, the soul has no ideas of anything, not even of itself (i. 350). For Roche, this means that souls are created in an animal state or worse, for 'a soul without ideas, without volitions, does not differ from a brute'. Roche is astounded to find Locke even comparing the fœtus to a vegetable (i. 355; the reference is to *Essay*, 2. 1. 21)! Locke degrades the infant soul (i. 360). A person for Roche has a rational nature, subsists independently, and is not an accessory to anything else.[25] On this definition, animals are not persons but infants are (i. 360, 362).

The most alarming feature of Locke's account for Roche is the interaction he allows between body and soul. He recognizes that

---

[24] Wade identifies these theologians as Jean-Frédéric Osterwald and Werenfels, from letters in the Bibliothèque nationale (see n. 27 below).

[25] For an acceptable definition of 'personne', Roche quotes from a work whose title he abbreviates as *Ess. de. Mor. Symb.*: 'Par le terme de *personne* on entend une nature raisonnable, qui subsiste à part, qui n'est point dominée, & qui ne fait point partie accessoire d'un autre être' (*Traité*, i. 360). Roche cites ii. 160 of this work as the location for this definition. In *Traité*, ii. 515, Roche gives the title as *Ess. de Morale, Symbole: Du péché originel*. So far, I have been unable to identify this title. The most obvious place to look is Pierre Nicole's *Essais de morale*. These were very popular traditional essays, frequently reprinted into the 18th century. A 25-vol. collection of his writings published in 1740 included his *Instructions théologiques et morales* which devotes two volumes to 'Le Symbole'. However, a careful search of the text has failed to turn up either citation from Roche. The definition of 'personne' is tantalizing, especially having in mind Locke's special analysis of the concept of person. The term had of course been used in connection with the Trinity (there is a long discussion of the three persons of the Trinity in Nicole), but applied to humans it was rare.

Locke is not a materialist, but a number of his principles lead to and support materialism. Locke's account of the origin of sense ideas, and his analysis of action, commit him to influence of mind on body in the case of action, physical influence of objects on the mind in sense perception. Body is the immediate and efficient cause of thought for Locke (i. 377–8, 395–6). Materialism easily follows. The world according to Locke is a reverse world:

1. Instead of conceiving of matter as passive, the English philosopher makes it fully active, even making thought its creation. 2. We believe that the soul is essentially active and that it has thought from the first moment of its creation; but this famous author tells us that from the beginning of its being, the soul is like a mass of matter without life or feeling. 3. Modern philosophers think they have demonstrated that bodies are of a quite different nature from the soul and that it is impossible for bodies to act on the soul. But this great man says that bodies act on the soul, giving the soul even the first germ of a spiritual being, that matter is a creating cause and that without the efficacy of its actions, the soul would be nothing. (i. 398–9)

There are, Roche remarks, some differences between Locke and Cuenz, but these are more a matter of degree than anything substantive: Locke only tends towards materialism, Cuenz constructs a system which says everything—ideas, souls, even God—is material.

The *Nouvelle Bibliothèque* review of Cuenz's four volumes in November 1742 called attention, as Cuenz had in his 'Discours préliminaire', to the fact that part of the stimulus for his study was several articles in Prévost's *Le Pour et contre*, which charged Locke with materialism and linked his name with British deists and others who were considered to be materialists (e.g. Tindal, Wollaston, Collins, Toland).[26] The reviewer in the *Nouvelle Bibliothèque* agrees that the charge against Locke is unjust; Locke was convinced that the soul was immaterial and he clearly did not believe God was material. In finding support in Locke for his own claims about the inconceivability of a being that is entirely non-extended, the reviewer says Cuenz is also unjust to Locke. The reviewer is not impressed with Cuenz's work as a whole: it is repetitious, it lacks systematic order and method, and it seems to be written for Cuenz's friends.

Part of the disorganization this reviewer noted was due to the reference-book nature of much of the four volumes. Cuenz tried to

---

[26] The articles appear in 3, art. 38 (1734), 186; 4, art. 55 (1734), and 7, art. 105 (1735). Cuenz reprints most of them in his 2nd vol.

gather together much of the material relevant to the thinking-matter issue, as it centred around Locke. For example, he reprints a good portion of the *Le Pour et contre* articles, and then discusses their charge. He also reprints the Locke–Stillingfleet exchange, from Coste's version in the note to this French translation of the *Essay* on the 4. 3. 6 passage. He even reprints all but the last dozen small paragraphs of the 'Lettre sur Locke', under the heading 'Lettre d'un anonime sur Mr. Locke' (vol. i, art. VII, pp. 145–55).

All the references to Locke in that 'Lettre' are included in Cuenz's reprint except the list with Locke's name placed in the group with Montaigne, Bayle, Spinoza, Hobbes, Shaftesbury, Collins, and Toland. Perhaps Cuenz wanted to protect Locke from such association in the minds of his readers. In his discussion of this 'Lettre' he says that he knows that many people will think it a crime to print that letter: 'Ils diront que c'est scandaliser tout le Monde, & presenter du Poison aux Ames foibles, à celles qui sont susceptibles de seduction &c.' ('Reflexions de l'auteur à l'ocasion de la lettre precedente', vol. i, art. VIII, p. 156). He does not think there is any such danger in printing this piece, especially since the antidote to its 'poison' can be found in Cuenz's four volumes. Whether Cuenz's system is much different from Locke's suggestion as it is presented in the 'Lettre sur Locke' is dubious, but Cuenz clearly thought there was a significant difference. What is interesting about his reprinting of the clandestine 'Lettre' is that in his 'Reflexions' he gives two quotations from Voltaire's Letter XIII, remarking that he does not know if both letters are from the same hand. Voltaire's Letter XIII goes further towards materialism, Cuenz believes, than does the 'Lettre sur Locke'. The passages he cites from Letter XIII are (1) Voltaire's assertion that the soul is a clock whose operating power the clockmaker has hidden from us, and (2) Voltaire's strong disclaimer that Locke was an evil or irreligious man.

Cuenz also cites many of the tracts and pamphlets in the British debate. One of the more important items in that debate which Cuenz attacked as Humphrey Ditton's *A Discourse concerning the Resurrection of Jesus Christ* (1712). Ditton's appendix on matter and motion was, as Cuenz remarked in a letter of 9 April 1738, a strong attack against Locke's suggestion. Other books from the British debate cited or used by Cuenz include Colliber's *Free Thoughts concerning Souls* (1734), probably from a review in the *Bibliothèque britannique*, Anthony Collins's exchange with Clarke, Toland's

Letters to Serena (1704), the *Philosophie du bon-sens* of Argens, and Boullier's work on the souls of beasts. Cuenz was equally well read in the various journals: e.g. *Journal des sçavans, Nouvelles de la république de lettres, Histoire des ouvrages des savans, Bibliothèque britannique, Bibliothèque raisonnée, Le Pour et contre*. Obviously aware of the British and French literature on the issues surrounding the thinking-matter question, he cites the three systems, those of occasional causes, of pre-established harmony, and of physical influence. Rejecting the first two, Cuenz defends a version of the third. He rejects the label of 'esprit-fort' for himself, along with 'atheist' and 'libertine'. Nor does he consider himself a materialist, which he defines as one who holds that 'matter is the only principle of all that exists in the universe; it denies the existence of a creator God, of revelation, final causes, and a future life', all of which Cuenz claims to accept ('Discours préliminaire', i, p. lxv).[27]

Defending as he does (along with many English writers) the extension of the soul does not make Cuenz a materialist. The extension of space and souls was, of course, not the same as the extension of body. No one succeeded in giving any very clear analysis of this sort of extension, but it was, within Britain at least, a common notion. With strong echoes from Locke's comment to Stillingfleet, Cuenz explains that he believes God created bodies and matter before adding motion to them (i, art. III, p. 14). With respect to man, God clearly gave 'cette Machine humaine' the predisposition of life, thought, and feeling. Man is defined as 'un Tissue indéfinissable d'étendue et de puissance, un Composé de parties internes & externes; . . . il n'est qu'un Etre purement physique' (i, art. III, pp. 18–19). Man as an organized machine has the ability to think. He also has the ability to acquire a 'personality' which makes him responsible for his actions (i, art. III, p. 19). Not quite understanding Locke's distinction between man and person, Cuenz remarks that

---

[27] Ira O. Wade has called attention to some letters of Cuenz which explain that his interests moved from Descartes and Gassendi to Bayle (the article 'Rorarius' in Pierre Bayle's *Dictionnaire historique et critique*, 1697), then to Malebranche and Leibniz (the editor of the *Journal helvétique*, Bourget, whom Cuenz knew, was a Leibnizian). As well, Cuenz indicates that he was strongly attracted to Locke's *Essay*, which he read in French. See Wade's 'Notes on the Making of a *Philosophe*: Cuenz and Bouhier', in Charles G. S. Williams (ed.), *Literature and History in the Age of Ideas* (Columbus, Ohio: Ohio State University Press, 1975). Wade identifies the collection of letters in which Cuenz's are found as Fonds français MSS 24409–21, in the Bibliothèque nationale. For this reference, I am indebted to Ann Thomson, as I am for other helpful references and comments.

man is not responsible for his actions in so far as he is an animal, but only in so far as he becomes a person. Cuenz's odd notion of the soul as an internal organized *spiritual* body to which life and thought have been added was his way of trying to distinguish two sorts of extended beings. His reason for insisting that a non-extended or purely spiritual being is incapable of functioning to produce persons is that 'real Extension, the Matter or the Machine of Man is at least the *instrumental cause*, and the necessary condition of thought . . . and all that depends on it'. He draws the usual distinction between matter 'en tant que Matière' and a being endowed with extension and power. Only the latter is capable of the power of thought. Cuenz also employs Locke's distinction between mobility (the motion of bodies) and motivity (the motion of souls).

It was his notion of *spiritual* bodies that puzzled some of Cuenz's readers. He returns frequently to his theme of thought being added to the machine which is man. He insists that 'in the totality of created matter, there is a part destined and reserved to form the invisible, impalpable, and incorruptible bodies, in which consists the supreme and more noble part of' individuals (i, art. X, p. 209; cf. i. 199). Little help is offered to his readers to clarify this notion of an invisible body; the corpuscular theory of matter employed a similar concept, but clearly reserved for bare, passive particles. Sometimes Cuenz's argument against purely spiritual beings is that, were there any, they would be only a mathematical point (ii, art. IX, pp. 125–6, 168) or a metaphysical point (ii, art. IX, pp. 174, 177). When he talks this way, he is obviously far from Locke's suggestion, but what he seems to be attempting is to find some way of making sense of the suggestion that *some* kind of matter might think.[28] He rejects the notion of thought

---

[28] The notion of a vehicle for the soul, incorporeal or of some subtle matter, was used earlier in the century by William Wollaston, *The Religion of Nature Delineated* (1725). A 2-part review of Wollaston appeared in the *Bibliothèque angloise* (vols. 12, 13), where some attention is given to this notion in his work, and to his extended discussion of thinking matter. The notion of a vehicle for the soul helped Wollaston explain mind–body interaction while firmly rejecting the grosser accounts of thinking matter. See e.g. p. 197 in Wollaston, *Religion*: 'Therefore there must be *some matter* within us, which being moved or pressed upon, the soul apprehends it *immediately*. And therefore, again, there must be *some matter* to which it is *immediately* and *intimately united*, and *related* in such a manner, as it is *not related* to any other. Let us now suppose this said *matter* to be some refined and spirituous *vehicle*, which the soul doth immediately inform; with which it sympathizes; by which it acts, and is acted upon; and to which it is *vitally* and *inseparably* united: and that this animated vehicle has its abode in the *brain*, among the heads and beginnings of the nerves.' (The review quotes a similar passage from p. 193.) Wollaston cites the stoic Hierocles as also

being a property of any bit of matter, reserving that property for complex and special sorts of matter. Hence his distinction between the *human* body and what he calls the *spiritual* body, i.e. the soul (ii, art. IX, pp. 137–9). The clock which chimes and indicates the hour is not brute matter but 'une portion de Matière arrangée d'une certaine façon' (ii, art. IX, p. 139). Similarly, the human machine has been made by the divine craftsman to think, feel, move, and have other powers (ii, art. IX, pp. 142–3).

These last remarks are made when he presents and discusses the Locke–Stillingfleet exchange on thinking matter. Cuenz also cites a popular work by Gravesande, his *Introduction à la philosophie* (1737).[29] He borrows an argument used by Gravesande for a somewhat different conclusion. Gravesande had discussed the identity of substances and the identity of machines, insisting that the identity of those substances that have a faculty of thought requires a personality or person. A person is 'an intelligent substance' with memory, i.e. with 'le sentiment intérieur de son existence actuelle, se trouve jointe la mémoire de son existence passée'.[30] Gravesande probably wrote with Locke's concept of person in mind even though he places too much stress upon memory. He goes on to discuss the various views about the soul's union with the body, saying that he agrees with those who say we do not know substances, only their properties or attributes. He also agrees with those, such as Locke, who say that the soul does not always think. The example he then uses, and the one Cuenz borrows, is offered to support the conclusion that the attributes we know (e.g. thought) may not be the essence of their substance. 'I see an object which is red, but I am not able to discover any other property. Does it follow that red constitutes that object's essence?' (*Introduction*, p. 33). Similarly for thought and the soul.

holding to this notion of a vehicle for the soul. In 1745, Berkeley used a similar notion in *Siris*; see below, pp. 152–3.

[29] The Latin original of this work was published in 1736: *Introductio ad philosophiam: Metaphysicam et logicam continens*. A 2nd edn. appeared in 1737 with additions. J. & A. Verbeek published the French translation in 1737, but the translator seems to be unknown. Gravesande did approve the translation. There were later edns. of the Latin in 1756 and 1765. I have used the edn. in vol. ii of *Œuvres philosophiques et mathématiques de Mr. G. J. 'sGravesande* (2 vols., Amsterdam: M. M. Rey, 1774).

[30] Gravesande, *Introduction*, p. 19. Cf. Cuenz, *Essai*, iii, art. II, p. 69: 'Je sai bien que l'Homme est un Etre moral; mais ce qu'il y a de moral en lui n'est rélatif qu' à sa *Personalité*, qui est une idée morale, et non pas à son Existence phisique.' The echoes of Locke's account of person are evident here.

Cuenz takes this example to support the conclusion that substances such as matter may have properties other than those we perceive.

Cuenz's presentation of the Locke–Stillingfleet exchange runs for close to 200 pages. It contains many 'Remarks' by Cuenz on the different points made by Locke against Stillingfleet. Those remarks are typically somewhat rambling, touching on a variety of related topics, but they also remind the reader that the debate over thinking matter includes questions such as how the soul and body are related, how the soul can move the body, and the nature of extension. Cuenz's discussion of the action of soul on body ('how do I move my arm?') is especially useful for showing the centrality of the mind–body relation in the French literature around Locke's thinking-matter suggestion. Cuenz again borrows from Gravesande who began his discussion of the same topic by remarking that some philosophers have been led astray by the close union of soul and body: they have said that the soul is corporeal (*Introduction*, p. 30). These philosophers have also said that our thoughts are nothing other than 'the agitation of certain particles of matter'. Other philosophers, Gravesande observes, say that bodies could not acquire the property of thought just by the motion of material parts, but God gives that faculty to certain bodies. From this notion, these writers say we cannot decide whether our soul is corporeal or not (pp. 30–1). Gravesande is of the opinion that the faculty of thought could not be the property of an extended being; but, after running through some of the details of the Malebranchian and Leibnizian systems, he says that we cannot rule out influence of soul on body and of body on soul. If there is such an influence, Gravesande believes it is not of the same sort as the action of one body on another (p. 39). Even bodies may be able to act by means other than motion.

Cuenz wants to have influence, not concomitance, but he cannot understand how that is possible unless volitions are physical acts. Gravesande had said that Leibniz's pre-established harmony theory made the soul an 'automate spirituel', a description used by Leibniz himself. Cuenz remarks that the system of occasionalism which says God is the cause of our movements makes the soul passive and turns it into a pure machine. He also comments that the defenders of the systems of occasionalism and pre-established harmony support their positions by saying that if the soul did move the body and its limbs, they would be committed to saying, as the defenders of physical influence claim, that new forces would be added to the universe, thereby running counter to the principle that there is always the same amount of force in the universe (*Essai*, ii. 288). Since Cuenz's system makes the soul part of the world, this objection does not hold against him. What he fails to explain is how there can be two kinds of extended beings both of which conform to the principle of the conservation of force.[31]

CONCLUSION

The 'Avertissement' to Roche's two-volume study describes the author as a saintly recluse, spending his days in a Parisian attic meditating and reading, leaving his attic flat only on Sundays and holidays to assist at divine services. This recluse ate very little, was often so near starvation that friends had to remind him to eat. He had a sincere desire to be unknown and forgotten by men. This pious man, we are told, became increasingly concerned about the growth of impiety and irreligion. One particular event startled him, 'le scandale de la fameuse Thèse' (i, p. v). This is a reference to an event at the Faculty of Theology in Paris, where the doctoral thesis of the Abbé de Prades was censured. The scandal was that a thesis of this nature could be written and even accepted by the Faculty, especially when subsequent to its acceptance the discovery was made that it contained a number of heretical principles. One of those principles, the one that Roche saw as the basis for de Prades's errors, was the Lockian stress upon the sensory origin of ideas. Here is how the writer of the 'Avertissement' describes the effects of this scandal on Roche:

Ce triste objet [of impiety and irreligion] l'occupoit déjà extrêmement lorsque le scandale de la fameuse Thèse éclata; son cœur en fut pénétré. Entre

---

[31] A work which has a balanced discussion of Cuenz, along with other writers on the nature of the soul, is *Recueil de pensées diverses sur l'immatérialité de l'âme, son immortalité, sa liberté, sa distinction d'avec le corps, ou Réfutation du matérialisme; avec une réponse aux objections de Mr. Cuentz et de Lucrèce le philosophe* (1756), by Benoît Sinsart. Locke is a central figure in Sinsart's discussion of materialism, a discussion which is fairly traditional, repeating most of the standard objections against materialism. 'Materialism' is characterized as saying that 'our soul is only matter disposed in a certain way' (p. 7). Sinsart's antipathy to materialism has a strong moral flavour: if it were true, morality would disappear, the consequences would be 'revolting' (p. 181). There are, however, some good arguments in Sinsart's account, especially relating to our ability to move our body. The book summarizes many of the authors who were associated under the label 'materialist' or 'free thinker'. His critique of Cuenz and Cuenz's defence of Locke added to the visibility of Locke's suggestion in France.

les diverses réflexions qu'il fit sur cet étrange événement, une pensée surtout le frappa; c'est la liaison du reste de la Thèse avec ce principe qui en est comme le premier anneau, 'que toutes nos connoissances dérivent des sensations, comme les branches naissent du tronc': . . . Il découvrit tout d'abord la fausseté & le danger de ce principe; mais pour en mieux pénétrer les conséquences, il se détermina à lire les Écrits de M. Locke, Philosophe Anglois, & de ses principaux Disciples. (i, pp. v–vi)

Roche died on 22 January 1755, but not before he had completed his study of the dangerous writings of Locke and those associated with de Prades's thesis.

Locke's doctrines became associated with a number of writers who were viewed as dangers to religion. That association arose, as we have seen, from a variety of sources: from the prominence Voltaire gave to Locke's suggestion about thinking matter; from the appearance of that suggestion in some of the clandestine literature; and, for Roche at least, from the scandal at the Faculty of Theology in Paris. The principle of the sensory basis of ideas (Locke's and Condillac's stress on reflection as another source tended to be overlooked), with its concomitant rejection of innate ideas, was a strong indictment against Locke for many orthodox thinkers. That doctrine about the origin of ideas from the physical stimulus of external objects via physical sense organs identified Locke with the defenders of the system of physical influence.

4
Physical Influence

THE 'system of physical influence' was a label used by Leibniz to refer to the scholastic doctrine of sensible species that come from objects to sense organs and brain, where they are converted into intelligible species. The conversion was considered to be a causal product of the external, sensible species, along with some action by the mind. This system is also ascribed to Aristotle by some writers.[1] As we saw in Chapter 1, this label was frequently associated with materialism, the assumption being that body cannot really affect mind; thus, in order for physical objects to influence the mind, the latter must be physical too. Locke's suggestion about the possibility of thought being a property of the brain combined with his use of a causal theory of perception to reinforce the interpretation of his system as materialist, at least as materialist-inclined. In the eighteenth-century discussions in France, Locke is always linked with the system of physical influence.

It might be thought that there are two sides to the system of physical influence, one side dealing with the fact that I can move my limbs and my body—an influence of mind on body—the other side being the causal theory of perception—an influence of body on mind. Most eighteenth-century discussions in France focus almost exclusively on this second aspect; it was that relation of body on mind that was strictly *physical* influence. Those who opposed physical influence often accepted the mind's ability to move the body or to interfere with the body's physiology. Descartes had identified a number of bodily operations which could be solely a function of the mechanism of the body, but he also stressed the ability the mind or soul has to affect physiology (e.g. in *Les Passions*

---

[1] See *Journal littéraire d'Allemagne, de Suisse et du nord*, 1/1 (1741), where a discussion of an attack on Wolff traces the history of this system. The label, the writer of this review explains, refers to 'l'*influence* des Esprits Animaux qui, selon que l'Ame les determine, lui présente les Idées, & les lui peint, pour ainsi dire, comme sur une Table' (p. 24). The reference to animal spirits is hardly Aristotelian, but it is interesting to see this ascription being made on the basis of what we would now call a causal theory of perception.

de l'âme, 1649). He speaks of the soul 'exercising its function' in a certain area of the brain. The two rival systems of occasionalism and pre-established harmony rejected both sides of the influence relation, insisting that the parallelism between bodily and mental events is either accomplished by God on each occasion (Malebranche) or it is a result of the internal nature of body and mind (Leibniz). No charges of libertinism or of materialism ever arose out of the claim that mind can influence body in some respects. Disagreements on this side of the relation were viewed as metaphysical, lacking in any threat to morality or religion. Mind or soul was, after all, considered to be higher in the scale of being, so no contradiction arises from the claim that it may affect body, a substance lower in the scale. Influence in the other direction was worse since it involved a lesser reality affecting a higher reality. The objections to physical influence on mind or soul by objects was not just a result of metaphysical differences: the objections were laden with emotions.

Just how emotions become entangled in philosophical and theological doctrines is not always easy to determine. A claim that ideas or thoughts are caused by physical motions in nerves and brain, themselves caused by physical stimuli in the environment, has a number of difficulties to overcome and explain. But we would not normally expect to find this claim arousing charges of immorality, libertinage, and materialism. We are properly surprised to discover that this claim was seized upon by the saintly recluse Antoine-Martin Roche as the cause (the 'poison', it was also said by others) of the Abbé de Prades's heretical doctrines. Not every writer who accepted the causal theory of perception was censured or linked with materialism. Locke was the main target.

One clue to the excessive worries about this doctrine may be found in Roche's identifying Le Camus as a disciple of Locke. What Le Camus represented for Roche and others was a too heavy reliance on the physiology of the body in explanations of perception, thinking, and even feeling. The causal theory rests upon bodily physiology: the interaction of body and mind becomes more complex, it becomes more difficult to separate the two. It might in the end account for all thought processes. A man run by detailed, complex physiology begins to resemble Vaucanson's machines.

I think something of this sort of move from causal theory to fears of *l'homme machine* was at work in the minds of many of the French writers who listed Locke and his French disciples as materialists. It will help to understand this move, this cluster of concerns, if we examine de Prades's defence of his thesis. It will also help if we analyse an important discussion of sensation written by David R. Boullier. Finally, a look at some medical treatises which reported on specific correlations between thinking and brain states will suggest some of the grounds for the attention given to the causal theory and to the system of physical influence.

THE ABBÉ DE PRADES'S THESIS

On 18 November 1751, Jean-Martin de Prades, priest of the diocese of Montauban, and Bachelor of Theology in the Faculty of Paris, defended his 'majeure ordinaire' thesis at the Sorbonne. His thesis opened by saying that the first ideas that we acquire come to us from the senses. All other ideas are derived from these sense-based ones. From them we form the ideas of our own existence, of other objects, and of other minds. Worst of all, even our idea of God is constructed from finite properties experienced in ourselves. His general claim entailed of course that there are no innate ideas, a Cartesian doctrine which, in his defence, de Prades charged his critics with turning into a dogma. He went on to say that we should undertake a careful examination in order to discover the nature of the thinking principle in us, suggesting to his orthodox examiners that he was unclear or uncertain about its nature. He did say that 'l'esprit' is active and different in kind from body. He was also careful to avoid saying external objects cause ideas: there is no relation ('rapport'), he said, between sensation and the objects which occasion our ideas. But the combination of denying innate ideas by asserting that ideas come through sensation, and his suggestion that our knowledge of the thinking principle is limited, was sufficient for the Faculty of Theology to charge de Prades with favouring materialism.[2]

Roche concludes his discussion of Condillac by saying that the latter does not draw any evil consequences from his use of a sensory origin of ideas, nor does he say that the ideas of God and natural law are produced by man (*Traité de la nature de l'âme* (1759), i. 504).

[2] For de Prades's published response to the condemnation of his thesis, see his *Apologie de Monsieur l'abbé de Prades* (1752), pt. II. His justification of the first proposition runs to 23 pages. Each of the propositions ('theses' as they were called) comprising his work is printed in Latin and French, followed by his explication. Pt. III of the *Apologie* was written by Diderot. I discuss it in ch. 8.

This newest disciple of Locke, de Prades, is less timid and has more 'partisan zèle' for Locke.[3] De Prades recognized, Roche admits, that the soul is spiritual; he even says Locke went too far in raising the possibility that (this is Roche's gloss of de Prades) the soul might be 'un amas de matiere' (i. 505). But in accepting 'la nouvelle hypothèse' of sense-based ideas, de Prades includes the ideas of God and natural law. For Roche, this inclusion reveals the evil nature of de Prades's use of that Lockian principle. On the idea of God, de Prades has followed Locke's lead in deriving it by extending and enlarging the relevant qualities discovered in our experience. We then apply these qualities to God, to a perfect Being. De Prades was not as detailed as Locke in this account of the origin of the idea of God, but both writers make that idea the work of the human mind. Roche cites passages from de Prades's *Apologie* (see *Traité*, ii. 506–10); he must also have known Locke's *Essay*, 2. 23. 33, account:

For if we examine the *Idea* we have of the incomprehensible supreme Being, we shall find, that we come by it the same way; and that the complex *Ideas* we have both of God, and separate Spirits, are made up of the simple *Ideas* we receive from *Reflection*; e.g. having from what we experiment in our selves, got the *Ideas* of Existence and Duration; of Knowledge and Power; of Pleasure and Happiness; and of several other Qualities and Powers, which it is better to have, than to be without; when we would frame an *Idea* of the most suitable we can to the supreme Being, we enlarge every one of these with our *Idea* of Infinity; and so putting them together, make our complex *Idea of God*.

Matter is not the source of this idea, although some of the qualities and powers can be traced back to our responses to sense impressions. It is what the mind does with the various sensory and reflective ideas that Locke stresses. The complexity and subtlety of Locke's account is missing in de Prades, but what bothered Roche was the fact that this important idea was said by both writers to be made by man, not given to us by God himself.

Roche spends a number of pages arguing against the possibility of our being able to form the idea of God from properties we experience in ourselves. He takes each specific attribute of God (immensity, wisdom, immutability) and tries to show how that property has

---

[3] Roche repeats the charge against de Prades of being the *new* disciple of and of having partisan zeal for Locke, at i. 516 and 518. Later, Locke is described as de Prades's 'illustrious Master' (i. 536). Roche ends his analysis of de Prades by reaffirming that the latter 'embrasse expressément le système de Mr. Locke' (i. 538).

no adequate base in our experience. Part of de Prades's error lies, Roche suggests, in his following Locke's account of the idea of infinity (i. 518). Roche's general principle is that 'It is an obvious error to pretend that the perfect and infinite can become knowledge for us via the imperfect and finite' (i. 522). Roche devotes two more chapters arguing against de Prades's claim to derive natural law from experience. There are numerous references to and discussions of de Prades throughout both volumes of Roche's *Traité*.

When de Prades refers to the origin of our idea of external objects, Roche finds him wavering between using occasionalist and physicalist language, but Roche is convinced that de Prades's considered view is that matter is the *immediate* and physical cause of such ideas. De Prades's justification to his censors at the Faculty of Theology of his first thesis about ideas is a clever and forceful argument, in the course of which he invokes Locke. He begins by remarking that the Faculty has often allowed, or even asserted, that not all ideas are innate. He cites Locke at this point for support, not the wisest move since Locke rejected *all* innate ideas. But de Prades argues that he does not have to show that some ideas do come from the senses, only that this claim does not favour materialism, that it is not incompatible with the spirituality of the soul. 'All the world agrees that all ideas are not innate.' Even those who reject the system of Locke agree that some are acquired via the senses. So, he asks, how does that view support materialism? Is it more supportive of materialism to say *all* ideas, rather than *some*, come from the senses? His most important point is that all suspicion of materialism should have been dispelled by his remark that there is no connection between sensation and the objects which occasion it. For, so he argues, that disconnection still allows for the spirituality of sensations.[4]

De Prades then remarks that the theologians had charged that his system simply drew out the consequences of Locke's insistence that all ideas come from the senses. In the official report on the condemnation of de Prades's thesis, it is revealed that one of the members of the Faculty of Theology, M. Froger, traced the 'poison' in them to the *Lettres philosophiques* of Voltaire, probably a refer-

---

[4] Writing in the *Journal de Trévoux* on the relation between mind and body, Father Tournemine is more precise than de Prades. He says that, on the Cartesian and Leibnizian systems, there is a 'rapport' but no 'liaison réelle' between them. (See 7 (1703), 869.) While Tournemine writes about soul–body relations, de Prades was concerned with the relation between external objects and ideas. But de Prades's point to his censors was meant to deny a 'liaison réelle'.

ence to the letter on Locke. Another member brought to the debate a copy of Locke's *Essay*, in order to show that de Prades's sensualist doctrine (i.e. proposition I) was taken from there.[5] A M. Varré singled out the first proposition, as did the Curé de Saint Benoit, but the curé admitted that it had been defended by others at the Sorbonne.[6] The writer of the 'Avertissement' to Roche's study, as we saw, characterized the events around de Prades as a scandal. It became a *cause célèbre* because the Faculty of Theology fully attended, debated, and approved the dissertation when it was presented. It was only some time later that someone started reading it and became alarmed.

The account in the *Nouvelles ecclésiastiques* reports the charge that de Prades's thesis 'was the result of a conspiracy formed by "pretendus esprits-forts", in order to slip their monstrous errors even into the Faculty of Theology'. The account goes on to express amazement at the fact that this thesis was actually approved. The Faculty should have known better. The account continues by saying that there were a few on the committee who did not find anything reprehensible in de Prades's propositions, but most saw its many faults. In all, after much debate, ten of de Prades's propositions were condemned, including the one on the origin of ideas.

The faults of those ten propositions were described by various epithets: blasphemous, heretical, favouring materialism, contrary to

[5] See John S. Spink, 'Un abbé philosophe: L'Affaire de J.-M. de Prades', *Dix-huitième siècle*, 3 (1971), 160. Professor Spink also tells us that Locke's name appears again in a work by the bishop of Auxerre, Caylus, in 1752: *Instruction pastorale de Monseigneur l'évêque d'Auxerre, sur la vérité et la sainteté de la religion, méconnue et attaquée en plusieurs chefs par la thèse soutenue en Sorbonne le 18 novembre 1751* (1752), 90. On de Prades's use of Locke's doctrine about a sensory origin for ideas, Caylus pointed out that Locke also had doubts about the immateriality of the soul, such doubts making Locke's doctrines doubly dangerous. When Diderot attacked Caylus's pamphlet, he argued that Locke's doctrine about ideas, which was essentially Aristotelian, had not been declared heretical (Spink, 'Un abbé philosophe', pp. 173–8. Cf. Diderot's *Œuvres complètes*, ii. 628–9). For a discussion of Diderot's response, see below, ch. 8.
[6] See the Jansenist, *Nouvelles ecclésiastiques, ou Mémoires pour servir à la constitution Unigenitus*, 8, entries for 27 Feb. 1752 and 12 and 19 Mar. 1752. The account given by de Prades is faithful to the one here. Roche scoffs at de Prades's claim that the sensory origin of ideas was generally accepted, even by a large number of theologians, taking the fact that de Prades's thesis was condemned as evidence against it. Roche does admit that among the Faculty at the Sorbonne, there are now a few who do accept the sensory origin of ideas. He comments that this was not true 30 years ago (*Traité*, ii. 329–31). Roche also has an extended section defending innate ideas.

authority.[7] In the debate before the formal vote of censure, several members singled out the first proposition as especially evil. The judges linked this Lockian principle about the origin of ideas with materialism and the thinking-matter suggestion: we cannot be assured that God 'ne peut pas donner à une certaine portion de matière la faculté de penser'. De Prades agrees that this suggestion of thought being a property of matter is false; it comes about when Locke speculates on the extent, not the *origin*, of knowledge. The claim that all ideas come from the senses does not lead to that conclusion. Condillac, de Prades points out, accepted this claim but draws a quite different conclusion from Locke. De Prades remarks also that Condillac's use of the sensory-based account of ideas has not brought censure on *his* head. De Prades invoked the *Journal de Trévoux*, saying that Condillac's reasonings 'have not alarmed the "Journalistes de Trévoux"'. Moreover, de Prades notes that another thesis, defended at the Sorbonne before his, on 30 October 1751, had subscribed to this principle. That thesis was not censured.[8]

[7] Lawrence Brockliss points out that not only was de Prades expelled from the Faculty, but the person in charge of the defence of the thesis (the *soutenance*), Luke-Joseph Hooke, was removed from his position at the Sorbonne: 'as president [of the defence] Hooke should have read the thesis through first and pointed out to the graduand unorthodox statements' (*French Higher Education in the Seventeenth and Eighteenth Centuries: A Cultural Study* (Oxford: Oxford University Press, 1986), 246, 247n.). For a complete account of the whole affair, see J. S. Spink, 'Un abbé philosophe'. See also A. M. Wilson, *Diderot* (New York: Oxford University Press, 1972), 154–8. It was a very complex affair, with opposition to de Prades reinforced when it was discovered that he had contributed articles to the *Encyclopédie*. Spink points out also that some of de Prades's thesis was taken from d'Alembert's 'Discours préliminaire' to the *Encyclopédie*. Apparently, he also borrowed material from some of Hooke's writings, which did not help Hooke when the censure was made. The complexity of 'l'affaire de Prades' is indicated by the fact that 12 sessions were devoted to debating what action to take and 146 opinions were filed: 'Après avoir consacré onze séances aux opinions des docteurs, on recueillit enfin les voix, le vendredi 21 janvier. Sur les 146 opinants, 105 étaient pour la condamnation *in globo*. Sur la question de savoir s'il fallait entendre le prévenu, 45 se déclarèrent pour et 83 contre' (Spink, 'Un abbé philosophe', p. 161). See also *Dictionnaire anti-philosophique* (2nd edn., 1769), attributed to Louis Mayeul Chaudon, for a brief account of de Prades and the errors of his thesis, entry 'Prades'.

[8] De Prades's claim that acceptance of the sensory origin of ideas was widespread is supported by the review of two books in this journal. These reviews make no criticism of these books, although both books accept physical influence. See the issue for Oct. 1710 on Maubec's *Principes phisiques de la raison et des passions des hommes* (1709) and the issue of Jan. 1715 on Rassiels du Vigier's *Traité de l'esprit de l'homme, où l'on verra la preuve de son existence, l'origine de ses idées pendant son union avec le corps* (1714). Brockliss cites two Paris professors who denied innate ideas, even of God: Robert Basselin, *Dissertation sur l'origine des idées* (1709), and

While that 30 October thesis was not condemned, it was attacked in a pamphlet, *Remarques sur une thèse soutenue en Sorbonne le samedi 30 octobre 1751* (1751). That thesis was the work of the Abbé de Loménie de Brienne, later cardinal, and Minister of Finance, 1787–8, under Louis XVI. J. M. Spink tells us that the author of that pamphlet attack was the Abbé Mey. The *Nouvelles ecclésiastiques* also cites Loménie's thesis, confirming that it too had defended the claim that all ideas come via the senses (19 Mar. 1752). Loménie was also mentioned in the official Condemnation of de Prades. The Abbé Mey's *Remarques* is cited in this March article; it is said to be 29 pages long and to have been written against Loménie's use of the proposition about sense-based ideas. The author of this pamphlet, we are told, said that Loménie drew out the consequences that Locke had begun. This report is confirmed by the Abbé Mey himself in another more ambitious work, *Essai de métaphysique, ou Principes sur la nature et les opérations de l'esprit* (1756). Referring to his *Remarques* as 'une brochure fugitive', without acknowledging his authorship, he comments that the whole first book of Locke's *Essay* is concerned to establish the Aristotelian maxim that there is nothing in the intellect which is not first in the senses (p. 168). We saw in Chapter 3 that Mey shares Roche's worries about the *tabula rasa* soul. In a few paragraphs discussing this pamphlet, de Prades defends Locke from the criticism of Mey in his *Remarques*. De Prades also reports that Loménie said that infants are born without any ideas; that ideas presuppose a soul; and that there are no ideas that are essential to a soul.[9]

The stress that de Prades placed on the occasionalist relation between objects and sensation indicates his awareness of the danger of subscribing to the system of physical influences. Most of the

Guillaume Dagoumer, *Philosophia ad usum scholae accommodata* (3 vols., 1702–3). On the erosion of the doctrine of ideas, Brockliss writes: 'By the mid-eighteenth century the scepticism of Basselin and Dagoumer was no longer exceptional. In 1750 when the *abbé* de Prades was accused by the faculty of theology of defending empiricism, he defended himself by claiming that this was the view of two-thirds of the university's professors of philosophy. Perhaps de Prades was exaggerating, but there can be little doubt that in the second half of the century Cartesian *innéisme* was rapidly falling from favour' (*French Higher Education*, pp. 215–16).

[9] Another pamphlet 'composée au mois de mai et distribuée au mois de septembre' argued that the doctrine of the natural goodness of man is, 'avec le sensualisme de Locke, la source de tout le mal dont la thèse de Prades n'est qu'un symptôme' (see Spink, 'Un abbé philosophe', p. 171). This pamphlet was written by a man named Pierre-Sébastien Gourlin, *Observations importantes au sujet de la thèse de M. l'abbé de Prades* (1752).

strength of Locke's claim about sensation as one of two sources for all ideas lay in the *causal* connection between the physical processes from objects to nerves and brain. While Locke did not give much analysis of the relation between physiology and awareness, he did not deny a connection, as did Malebranche and his followers. Locke's critics in France read him as holding to a causal connection from object to brain to idea. De Prades apparently tried to borrow from Locke (and perhaps from Condillac) while insisting on occasionalism, at least in his *Apologie*. His censors were perhaps more worried by the rejection of innate ideas (especially of God and moral laws) than they were by any implied causal connection; but they also believed that sense-based knowledge could not provide certainty in such important matters as the nature of the soul, of that which thinks. Nevertheless, it is clear that the fear was present, that God's activity and intervention in our knowledge and action were threatened by too much dependence upon physical and physiological causation.

BOULLIER'S DIGRESSION ON SENSATION

In chapter VI of his *Essai philosophique sur l'âme des bêtes*, Boullier summarizes his account of animal souls. Animals have, he says,

a sensitive principle, by which I understand an immaterial being, a thinking substance; in a word, a spirit [*esprit*] which only has confused perceptions. The activity of that spirit is modified and regulated by those perceptions; it has diverse confused desires which correspond to the variety of its sensations.... [T]he spirit is of such a nature that it feels only by means of the organized body to which it is united.[10]

The union of that spirit with matter is so essential to it, the body is so necessary for the spirit to perceive and act, that separation from the material body leaves that spirit useless (ii. 74). In order to help us understand this account of the souls of beasts, Boullier wants us to follow him on 'quelques réflexions que je vais faire sur la nature de nos Sensations'. He does not find that philosophers in the previous century have given any satisfactory analysis of sensations.

Boullier reminds us that those philosophers (he must have Cartesians in mind) have pointed out our tendency to ascribe to objects

[10] David R. Boullier, *Essai philosophique sur l'âme des bêtes: où l'on trouve diverses réflexions sur la nature de la liberté, sur celle de nos sensations, sur l'union de l'âme et du corps, sur l'immortalité de l'âme* (2nd edn., 2 vols., 1737), ii. 73–4. The 1st edn. with a variant subtitle was published in 1728.

the sensations we experience: colours we see when we look at objects, sounds when we hear bells ringing, etc. (ii. 76). Sensations are perceptions which are only found in minds (*esprits*), in a substance which is aware of itself and which is able to act. The body is not aware of itself, it exists without knowing that it exists, it is not the subject of perceptions since perceptions are modes of mind. These same philosophers go further in distinguishing *sensations* from *ideas* (he clearly has Malebranche in mind with this distinction), as well as distinguishing sensations from passions and acts of will (ii. 77). Ideas are perceptions which represent clearly to the soul objects which are distinct from it. The soul is passive in receiving sensations. Boullier summarizes this account as follows:

Les Sensations sont certaines modifications de pensée, ce sont certaines perceptions que l'Ame reçoit, ou que Dieu lui imprime à la présence des objets corporels, & à l'occasion des diverses impressions que les Corps qui environnent le nôtre font sur les organes. Ces perceptions se manifestent elles-mêmes, se distinguent par elles-mêmes, les unes des autres, & quiconque les éprouve, les connoît par cela meme assez clairement. (ii. 79)

He finds this account too brief and filled with difficulties. Some important questions in need of answers are: (1) why does the soul ascribe its sensations to external objects, (2) why are these perceptions so lively but also so confused, (3) why are they always accompanied by ideas, and (4) why are the sensations which are excited, the corporeal object, and the ideas it presents so closely related, even mixed together? He seeks to answer this sort of question, starting by contrasting sensations with ideas. Some of the differences relate to the control we have over our ideas: we can vary them, concentrate upon particular ones. Ideas represent objects clearly, while sensations arise when we just open our eyes or listen. Sensations are also caused by motions and correspond to those motions. Sometimes he speaks of an 'analogy' between sensations and their motion-causes. He also suggests that, contrary to Locke, simple sensations are not really simple (ii. 85). He uses Newton's analysis of light through a prism as an example of a seemingly simple property which turns out to be complex, composed of different properties. A sound too can be composed of several different tones of which we are unaware. Analysis reveals the complexity of the constituents of light and sound. In a similar way, all sensations are really a composite of many little motions, motions that are rapid, successive, and insensible.

These motions are communicated to nerves and brain. The soul is *united to* a particular area of the brain, it is *present to* the sensorium (ii. 90). A sensation is composed of or is a product of several other sensations, and they in turn have as their objects the little motions. Sensations in this account may seem to be physiological, otherwise the analogy with light and sound would fail. Light and the colours it is composed of, a sound and the tones composing it, do not involve mixed categories. If sensations are in the same way composed of little motions, the sensations would also have to be motions. Boullier does not want to turn sensations into physiological motions. The relation between sensations and the little insensible motions is causal, despite his sometimes imprecise account of that relation. 'Product of' rather than 'composed of' is the description he intended.

Sensory perceptions are the means the soul has of perceiving external objects (ii. 91), but Boullier says that such perceptions represent the *motions*, not the external *objects*. For example, 'une Sensation de son, c'est un amas de petites idées successives qui représentent les vibrations du tympan & celles du nerf acoustique produites par un air ébranlé' (ii. 92). He speaks later of the soul being involuntarily attentive or aware of these motions (ii. 100). Later still, he repeats his talk of an *analogy* between our sensations and the motions which cause them, affirming that those motions are not just the *occasion*, but are also the *objects*, of our confused perceptions (ii. 107). Sensations are 'only the confused perceptions of different motions', or 'nothing other than representative ideas of little motions of bodies' (ii. 108–9). Two uses of the term 'sensation' occur in this account: one as a complex of little motions, the other as confused perceptions, or representative ideas, of those motions. I think it is the latter use that Boullier intends.

These little motions are not objects of awareness, they are insensible. We take external bodies to be both the cause and the objects of our perceptions. Boullier agrees with the occasionalists and those who defend pre-established harmony that matter is not able to act really and physically on the soul: God alone can do so (ii. 112, 114). Boullier's *representative relation* is not a causal one, ideas represent but are not caused by matter in motion. The representative relation holds between ideas and motions in nerves and brain, not between ideas and external objects. Using Malebranche's distinction between ideas and sensations, he says:

By sensation, I perceive confusedly a multitude and a series of little motions that I am not able to discern; the sensation reveals to me a clear idea of a circle. . . . In the idea of a circle, I distinguish the circle from the perception of the circle, I easily distinguish myself perceiving the circle by a certain mode of thought, from the circle perceived . . . (ii. 116)

The idea of a circle or of any object is not the circle or object itself, since the idea is a mode of mind. We are unable to discern the rapid successive little motions and therefore we confuse those motions with our perceptions. Instead of saying, 'red is in me and is a mode or way of perceiving a circle', we say, 'red is a mode of being of the perceived circle' (ii. 117). Physical objects do not have such properties.

Throughout this 'Digression on Sensation', Boullier is careful to limit the causal relation to the stimuli from the environment and the motions that those stimuli (themselves motions) give rise to in nerves and brain. The cognitive relation (i.e. the representative relation) holds between nerve- and brain-motions *and* our ideas. If there is an external world (and he remarks that the soul is of such a nature that it is able to have ideas of bodies even if there were no external world), the soul knows that world by means of its sensations. Our sensations 'unite' us with that world. These sensations are not motions but representative ideas (ii. 127). They represent the world not precisely as it is in itself, but as it is in relation to a portion of that material world, our brain. External objects make physical impressions on the brain, the soul then acquires ideas which represent those physical impressions. The soul is said to be 'attentive' to what happens in the brain, but Boullier does not mean the soul watches the motions and impressions in the brain. 'Being attentive' means something like 'is aware of by means of representative ideas'. In this way, 'the soul is united to the material world', cognitively united, just to the extent that the soul has relations to 'that organized portion of the material world', the brain, and to the extent that the material world 'acts on the brain' (ii. 129).

Later in the *Essai*, Boullier gives detailed analyses of the three systems of the relation between mind and body. Chapter XVIII discusses the system of physical influence. In the midst of that analysis, he adds a few more details to the account of sensation and representative ideas. He repeats his account of the brain and impressions. The body is said to be an organized mechanism which receives in its brain (in the sensorium) the different impressions of sensible objects and unites them in 'a very small space' (ii. 388). What happens in the brain is, for an attentive soul, a kind of mirror of the material world. It is not believable that 'our soul independently of any organ would be able to have an immediate sensation of the universe, that it would be able to see light and colour in the vibrations of rays, or hear the sounds by an immediate perception of vibrating air, or perceive all bodies generally, in applying itself directly to them, as it does to its own body'. That his reading of what we might label 'direct realism' is a literal one is reinforced by what he goes on to say: that were direct perception possible, the soul would have to 'spread itself immediately on objects without confusing itself with them and losing itself in their extension'. Direct perception of objects would, in other words, bypass the brain and the body's organs. Instead, the sensorium unites the different impressions and represents in miniature the physical object in the relations it has with the perceiver (ii. 390). The sensorium enables us to perceive 'the image of the Universe which is too large to be seen directly in itself'.

Boullier remarks that everyone agrees that 'our sensible perceptions are limited and that the soul sees material objects only in the relations that they have with our body'. The sensorium is the soul's organ, as the senses are the body's: it represents the universe, bringing the world into 'a tiny point of the brain in the way in which certain optical lenses collect and bring together in a very small circle a great quantity of objects' (ii. 391). The soul is united to the body, it is incapable of having the visible world for its sensorium, i.e. of applying itself to the world. Instead, it applies itself to that small portion of matter which receives impressions from different objects. The impressions our body receives from objects are transmitted to the brain where they become 'un tableau vivant' or mirror of the world. Elsewhere he describes certain impressions as 'signs and fixed characters of our thought, a species of internal writing' (ii. 128).

In this last passage, he was describing the role of the imagination, but the language of signs and internal writing, in the context of his account of motion and representative ideas, could be seen as an echo of Descartes's talk of motion signs to which the mind responds by forming ideas.[11] Curiously, when given the opportunity to talk of signs, Boullier backs off. He adds a brief supplement at the end of

[11] For an account of this aspect of Descartes's analysis see my *Perceptual Acquaintance from Descartes to Reid* (Minneapolis, Minn.: University of Minnesota Press; Oxford: Basil Blackwell, 1984), 22–31.

volume ii in which he quotes from someone who had written to him about his account of sensation. The writer, whom he does not identify, offered two remarks, the second asking whether we should not consider the stimulus of sense organs in relation to the sensations which correspond to that stimulus in the same way that we consider *signs* in relation to the ideas which those signs reveal. The sign relation is arbitrary and conventional, even though we tend to view the relation as natural. If we ask why the structure of our various sense organs is so varied (as between sight, smell, hearing, etc.), the writer of this enquiry suggests it might be because they serve to diversify the signs. Just as words can have different meanings, so the eyes, for example, can respond to different sign-stimuli. It would have been easy for Boullier to accept this suggestion, making the representative relation a sign relation, or, more in keeping with this writer's suggestion (and with Descartes's suggestion as well), making the motions in nerves and brain signs for the mind. But Boullier declines to accept this suggestion. The pain I feel when something pricks my finger is not, he says, perceived by me as a sign. That stimulus serves God as a *signal* for exciting a painful sensation in me (ii. 431–2).

In his account of the mechanism of the body receiving physical impressions from objects which impact on an area of the brain, Boullier was not describing the *physiology* of nerves and brain. He was trying to characterize the *psychology* of sense perception. He assumes that there is a world of physical objects to which our bodies belong. He asserts that our psychological access to that world is mediated by our body's reaction to the physical motions of those objects affecting our various sense organs. He assumes also that the soul has access to that portion of the brain called 'the sensorium' where all physical impressions terminate and are united as in a lens. But what the soul is aware of with its access to the sensorium is not the *physical* impressions. Its access to those impressions results in a cognitive awareness or interpretation: it sees red, hears sounds, feels roughness. The soul confuses these impressions with properties of the object rather than taking them as they are, as modes of the mind's reactions to physical stimulae. The soul also, in good Malebranchian fashion, has an idea of the nature of objects as extended. Unable to separate primary from secondary qualities, the soul ascribes both to the object: it is not only extended and hard, it is red and sweet. Boullier does not give us an analysis of the origin of particular *ideas*, but what is especially important for us to note is the clear causal link between sensation and extended objects. It may be that his distinction between sensations and ideas saved him from the errors of the Abbé de Prades: for *sensations*, not *ideas*, are products of physical influence.

It was just this distinction that Boullier used in his *Court examen de la thèse de Mr. l'abbé de Prades, et observations sur son Apologie* (1753). Linking Locke's name with de Prades's principle of the sensory origin of ideas, Boullier argues that all ideas are innate, in the sense that none can be caused by external objects.[12] Ideas are aroused by means of, by the intervention of, or on the occasion of sensations. Describing in this work the way in which an involuntary impression is received when I see and touch a sensible object, he says that impression makes me judge that there is in objects that which corresponds to the idea, 'because that object must be the cause' of the impression, but he quickly adds: 'at least the object is the sufficient reason for the specific impression that I receive' (p. 8). There is no mention in this work of the system of physical influences.[13] True philosophy, he now says, will credit the correspondence between ideas and certain physical events to the action of God (as Malebranche did) or to a pre-established harmony (as Leibniz did). Sensations for Boullier are not physical brain impressions; they are conscious contents of perception. He defines 'sensation' as 'a perception which is only found in a spirit, i.e., in a substance which is aware of itself', or as a mode of thought (*Essai*, ii. 76, 79). When he writes about sensations in his 'Digression', he does not use the language of physiology for sensations, only for their causes. He cites as sensations the perception of white, round, hard, heavy, resistant. Whether he changed his views on physical influence between 1737 and 1753, or whether he always held to the Cartesian distinction between sensations as linked with the body and ideas as belonging to

[12] Noting the confidence with which de Prades defends this principle, Boullier remarks: 'A ce ton de confiance, on reconnoit le progrès qu'a fait en France depuis peu d'années le Systeme de Locke, & l'on ne sauroit assez admirer l'ascendant qu'une opinion en vogue prend sur les esprits. Il sera bientot aussi ridicule à Paris de croire les Idées innées, qu'il l'eût été il y a trente ans de ne pas croire.' (In the 'Avertissement au lecteur'.) He characterizes de Prades as imprudent and insulting to those who censured him. Boullier confirms that de Prades's thesis made a noise and created a scandal. He finds the thesis false and hateful, the *Apologie* is abhorrent.

[13] Curiously, in this work, the third system is Berkeley's denial, as Boullier interpreted him, of an external world: 'les corps n'ont point d'existence absolue hors de notre esprit' (*Court examen*, p. 35).

the intellect, cannot be determined from his texts. But if sensations are psychological states, physical influence operates at least on that level. The rational, not the sensitive, soul is immune from external physical influences.

THE PHYSIOLOGY OF L'ESPRIT

Boullier's general position is close to that of Malebranche, but (as we shall discover when we examine his discussion of the three systems in the next chapter) he has some sympathy with physical influence. Indeed, his account of sensation and its causes brings him very close to a causal theory of sensation. The causal role of motions in nerves and brain in generating sensations (felt pains and pleasures, seen colours, heard sounds) almost forced him into identifying sensations with the little motions which went into their origin. But sensations are not merged into the physiology: they provide a bridge or link between the ideas of objects given to us by God and the external world which those ideas represent. Confused sensations turn into representative ideas. It is this close link between sensations and ideas that, I think, distinguishes Boullier's account from that of Malebranche. Malebranche developed a detailed theory of the physiology of vision, but the results of the workings of that optical physiology were sights which arise when we look at objects. Seeing for Malebranche was a function of the intellect, not of physiology.[14] Boullier seems to me to be trying to bring these two features in Malebranche's account close together. He does so in large part by suggesting that there is a cognitive relation between the mind and external objects, replacing the causal relation with a representative one. That cognitive relation modifies occasionalism in the direction of physical influence.

Boullier was an outspoken defender of the traditional doctrine of two substances. He was also one of the strongest critics of Voltaire's Letter XIII on Locke. He obviously did not find (at least in 1737) the system of physical influence inconsistent with his traditional view, nor as support for materialism. Why was de Prades's use of the principle of the sensory origin of all ideas seen as favouring materialism, when Boullier's use of that principle (and, as de Prades claimed, that of many others as well) was not criticized? The reason may

---

[14] For Malebranche's distinction between 'looking' and 'seeing', see ch. II in my *Perceptual Acquaintance*.

never be fully uncovered, but part of the explanation lies in the developing detailed physiology produced by the work of medical doctors. It was becoming more difficult to deny an important and pervasive role to physiology in awareness, especially in perceptual awareness. It was both the changed nature of physiological theory, particularly in Europe (the acceptance of inherent forces and powers in muscle tissue), and the specific correlations between physical and mental states that caused some writers to fear that Locke's suggestion of the possibility of thought being another property of the brain was reinforced by these developments in physiology. Any hint that ideas or sensations were caused by external objects and the body's internal physical mechanism was seen as dangerous by many traditionalists.

There was a widespread recognition of the physiology of the body, both in perception and in action.[15] We find references to and discussions of the mechanism of the body in Britain as well as in France. It may be that greater attention was given in France to the details of physiology and to the correlations between physical and mental processes.[16] La Mettrie, with his medical background, devoted much attention to physiology: the association of materialism with a stress on the physiological correlates of thought was reinforced by his writings.[17] There are other even more detailed accounts of specific correlations found in a number of medical books and some articles in French journals.

La Peyronie, Maubec, Luzac

In a short article in the *Journal de Trévoux* for April 1709 (art. 45, pp. 599–621), there is an abstract of a 'mémoire' La Peyronie had presented to the Société royale des sciences de Montpellier. La Peyronie was later cited by Roche as a follower of Locke. That 'mémoire' contained observations on patients with head injuries which affected in different ways their mental capacities and perform-

[15] For the details of the different types of physiological theories employed in the 18th century, see my *Thinking Matter* (Minneapolis, Minn.: University of Minnesota Press; Oxford: Basil Blackwell, 1984), ch. VII.

[16] Robert Whytt in Scotland and David Hartley in England of course made extensive use of physiology in their medical writings.

[17] For a useful discussion of this aspect of La Mettrie, see Ann Thomson's *Materialism and Society in the Mid-Eighteenth Century: La Mettrie's 'Discours préliminaire'* (Geneva: Droz, 1981), chs. II and III. See also Kathleen Wellman, 'Medicine as a Key to Defining Enlightenment Issues: The Case of Julien Offray de la Mettrie', *Studies in Eighteenth-Century Culture*, 17 (1987), 75–89.

ances. La Peyronie was convinced by his case-studies that he might be able to discover 'le lieu du cerveau où l'Ame exerce immédiatement ses fonctions'. A longer article by La Peyronie in the *Mémoires de l'Académie royale des sciences* (Paris) for 1741 (pp. 199–218) presented many case-studies of brain-damaged patients from which he drew conclusions about where the soul did and did not exercise its functions. He explains his goal as follows: 'L'Ame est unie au corps; par les loix de cette union l'ame agit sur le corps, & le corps agit sur l'ame. Quel est le point du corps où s'exécute immédiatement ce commerce réciproque?' (p. 199). That 'commerce' works both ways, from body to soul and soul to body. He uses different terms for designating the place in the brain where this reciprocal exchange and influence occurs: the point, the place, the foyer, or the instrument. Even if we cannot discover the nature of the soul, or the laws of its union with the body, we can, he thinks, discover by anatomical and physiological observations that point, location, or instrument. His method was that of exclusion.

Supposons que toutes les parties du cerveau ayent été détruites, & qu'il n'en soit resté qu'une seule: si après la destruction de ces parties la raison subsiste, si les facultés de l'ame ne sont nullement altérées, il est évident que le siége de l'ame n'étoit point dans ces parties détruites, & il faut nécessairement le placer dans la partie qui reste. (p. 201)

A review of the 1741 *Mémoires de l'Académie royale* article in the *Bibliothèque raisonnée* (35 (1745), 191–3) characterized this method as 'une espèce de démonstration indirecte'. The reviewer also points out that La Peyronie performed many operations on brain-damaged patients, often succeeding in restoring normal functions. La Peyronie's own article is filled with detailed notes and accounts of brain-damaged patients who lived with injuries, and of autopsies he performed after death. Some patients were soldiers wounded in battle.[18] The 1709 article in the *Journal de Trévoux* had

---

[18] His full name was François Gigot de la Peyronie. He was for a time Surgeon-Major in the army. As late as 1744 (three years before his death) he was operating in military hospitals, as mentioned in *Mémoires de l'Academie royale de chirurgie*, ii (new edn., 1769). Vol. i (published in 1761) describes La Peyronie as: 'Ecuyer, Conseiller, Premier Chirurgien du Roi, & Médecin Consultant de Sa Majesté, Chef de la Chirurgie du Royaume, Membre des Académies Royales des Sciences de Paris & de Montpellier'. There is also in the preface to vol. i a long essay on experimental method, presumably by La Peyronie. La Peyronie's work and theory of brain–mind relation are given an extended discussion in the *Encyclopédie* entry 'Ame', in a section added by Diderot on the relation between mind and body and the location of

called attention to the experimental work done by La Peyronie, pointing out the advantages of his work for philosophers and doctors. Philosophers will be pleased if they can know what part of the brain has to be stimulated in order for the soul to have such and such sensations. Doctors will be in a position to cure or at least relieve some patients if they know what part of the brain is affected when the patient exhibits certain defects in specific faculties or mental operations.

It is certain, he thinks, that the soul does not reside 'dans toute l'étendue de la substance du cerveau prise collectivement', a reference to a traditional claim made from before Descartes to the early eighteenth century.[19] The series of cases where injuries to specific areas of the brain affected specific mental functions and left others intact led La Peyronie to the conclusion that it is the 'corps calleux' which is the place where the soul exercises its function (pp. 212, 213, 217). While he once or twice speaks of the soul *occupying* 'le siege', the more usual locution is 'where the soul exercises its function'.[20] He did not think of the soul sitting in the *corpus callosum*. His assumption was that if we are able to act on our body, and if the physiology of the body is to affect our mental states (whether from physical processes within the body or as the conduit for physical causes from external bodies), there must be a feature of the brain through which and by means of which those interactions occur. He

'ame'. The main entry was written by the Abbé Claude Yvon who was widely rumoured to have written part of or influenced de Prades's thesis (see *Mémoires secrets pour servir à l'histoire de la république des lettres en France*, 1 (1777), 4 Feb.1762; known as *Mémoires de Bachaumont*).

[19] *Mémoires de l'Académie royale* (1741), 204. The dictum was usually formulated as follows: the soul is 'toute entière dans tout le Corps, & en meme temps toute entière dans chaque partie du Corps'. This quotation is taken from the French translation of the title of a book by L. Winslow on the soul and its 'location' in the brain. See the *Journal des sçavans*, 14 July 1706. This notion is also found in earlier authors, e.g. Plotinus. See Eyjolfur K. Emilsson's *Plotinus on Sense-Perception: A Philosophical Study* (Cambridge: Cambridge University Press, 1988), 35, 61, 106.

[20] It is often overlooked that Descartes uses this functional formulation, rather than the more literal-sounding 'le lieu'. See his *Traité de l'homme* (1664) and the *Passions de l'âme*. The reviewer of the Winslow book cited in the preceding note remarks that the Cartesians do not say that the soul is *locally present* in the brain, but that with a certain part of the brain it has an immediate and reciprocal correspondence of thought and motion. See also Malebranche, *De la recherche de la vérité*, I. x. iii (*Œuvres complètes* (Paris: J. Vrin, 1958–70), i. 125), where he explains his meaning for the term 'resides', in the expression, 'the soul resides in that part of the brain where all the fibres of the sense organs end': 'Quand je dis qu'elle y réside, je veux seulement dire qu'elle y sent tous les changemens, qui s'y passent par rapport aux objets qui les ont causez, ou qui ont accoûtumé de les causer'.

accepted the system of physical influences. What is probably more important than the identification of this part of the brain is the case-studies he gave of specific correlations between brain and mental states.

Such correlations are also discussed by another Montpellier doctor, Maubec, in *Principes phisiques*. He gives specific physiologies for sensation, passions, judgement, imagination, even speech. His general thesis is that knowledge and awareness are the *natural* consequences of the impressions on nerves and the working of physiology. He starts his account with an extended defence of the claim defended later by de Prades that, as the motto on the title-page says: 'Nihil est in intellectu quod prius non fuerit in sensu'. What he calls 'the principles of knowledge' are said to be purely mechanical, i.e. knowledge and awareness are the result of the disturbances of nerves and the fibres of the brain (p. 18). The nerves are filled with animal spirits which, when disturbed, 'excite in us feelings of pleasure and pain and all the ideas which impress themselves in our mind [*esprit*] in the presence of objects; because it has pleased the author of nature to link perception and feelings with the disturbance of fibres' (pp. 36–7).

Maubec explicitly denied that matter is capable of thought, even though he places so much stress on specific physiological processes for each type of mental operation. It is the mind, he says, not the body, that thinks (p. 19). In 1749, another writer, a professor of philosophy at the University of Leiden, Élie Luzac, defended this same claim against materialists, while accepting the close and specific links between physiology and mental states.[21] He presents case after case where bodily ills have affected mental conditions, such as loss of memory, hallucinations, misperceptions. He also cites such correlations in many normal instances. From all such examples, we cannot conclude, he insists, that the soul is only a mechanism of the body (*L'Homme plus que machine*, pp. 46–7). What these examples show is that the body is the 'instrument' of the soul, in the same way as the musician's violin or cello is his means for making music. Just as the musician is not the same as his instrument, so the soul is not the body. Luzac adds to soul and body a principle of life, a vague, undefined concept: it seems to be a non-mechanical, bio-logical force (p. 53). He also leaves unexplained the relation

---

[21] See his *L'Homme plus que machine: Ouvrage qui sert à refuter les principaux argumens sur lesquelles on fonde la matérialisme* (1748; 2nd edn., 1755).

between this principle and the soul. What his book shows is the impossibility by this time of ignoring or denying the specific correlations between bodily and mental states, but he maintains an uncritical adherence to the immaterialist's two substances and to their inactive matter. Even biological matter has to be activated by a 'principle of life'.[22]

Le Camus, Astruc, Collet

One of the more systematic discussions of the relation between physiology and mental states was Antoine Le Camus's *Médecine de l'esprit* (1753; 2nd edn., 1769). Le Camus's account of sensation and perception is very Lockian. He reproduces Locke's three classifications of ideas: those that are acquired from one or several senses, those that come from reflection, and those that arise from both (p. 35). The terminology of simple and complex ideas is also found (pp. 35–9), Locke's rejection of innate ideas is cited (p. 41); and he says that the soul perceives in all its reasoning 'only the agreement and disagreement of ideas' (p. 47). Combined with this account (which rests on the claim that all ideas depend upon the senses) is a detailed physiology, similar in structure and function to those found in writers such as La Peyronie, Maubec, and Luzac. He refers to a M. Collet who defended a thesis at the Medical School of Paris in 1763, arguing that 'il y a dans le cerveau une fibre destinée pour chaque idée' (p. 43).[23]

Collet's thesis was dedicated to Astruc ('sol meus', he wrote), a fact which gains in significance if we recall the entry 'Brain' in Chambers's *Cyclopaedia*:

[22] His refutation of materialism takes the usual form of asserting matter to be inactive and mind to be active. As many in the British debate did, so Luzac argued that, if any bit of matter thinks, all matter must think (*L'Homme plus que machine*, pp. 21–2); for God to give matter the power of thought would be a contradiction (p. 28); and more specifically, 'si toutes les idées n'etoient que les effets d'un mouvement, communiqué aux nerfs, la pensée ne pouroit jamais etre active & seroit au contraire toujours passive' (pp. 61–2). He identified as Locke's the argument which says that since we do not know the nature of the substance which sustains thought, it may in fact be material (pp. 29–30).

[23] François-Joseph Collet, *Quaestio medica quodlibetariis disputationibus . . . An sua sit in cerebro cuique ideae fibra?* (Held at the Faculty of Medicine, Paris, 27 Jan. 1763). I am indebted to Burton Van Name Edwards for his translation of Collet's *Quaestio*, and to the librarian of the Faculty of Medicine in Paris for sending me a photographic copy of this pamphlet.

From the Texture, Disposition, and Tone of the Fibres of the *Brain*, Philosophers ordinarily account for the Phaenomena of *Sensation* and *Imagination*; which see. Dr. Astruc goes further, and from the Analogy between the Fibres of the *Brain*, and those of Musical Instruments, solves the Phaenomena of Judgment and Reasoning, and the Defects and Perfections of both. He lays it down as an Axiom, that every simple idea is produc'd by the Oscillation of one determinate Fibre; and every compound Idea from contemporary Vibrations of several Fibres: That the greater or less degree of Evidence follows the greater or less Force wherewith the Fibre oscillates. He hence proceeds to shew, that the Affirmation or Negation of any Proposition, consists in the equal or unequal Number of Vibrations, which the Moving Fibres, representing the two Parts of the Proposition, *viz.* the Subject, make in the same Time.

Chambers continues his summary of Astruc's specific correlation of fibres and judgement by taking as an example the ideas of a subject and its attributes or properties. When the fibre which gives the idea of a subject has an equal number of vibrations as the fibre that produces the idea of the attribute, 'we are determin'd to the Affirmation of the Proposition'. If those vibrations are unequal, the judgement will be negative: 'The Evidence and Certainty of a Judgment, Affirmative or Negative, he deduces from the greater or less Consonance or Dissonance of the Fibres of the Subject and Attribute'. According to Chambers's account of Astruc, particular physical explanations in terms of the state and condition of specific nervous fibres were given for phrensy, mania, lethargy, and melancholy.

Collet's *Quaestio medica* is written against the background of Astruc's account. He begins by remarking that no one (aside from Astruc and a few metaphysicians) has been able to explain the mechanism for the production of ideas. Collet is a bit excessive here, or perhaps he was unacquainted with the work of La Peyronie, Luzac, and others at Montpellier. David Hartley's *Observations on Man* (1749) and Joseph Priestley's support for Hartley in England made much of vibratory physiology underlying thought and awareness. When Collet says that the 'knot of the question' about the origin of ideas 'resides in the brain', he is following more writers than Astruc. Collet combines the animal spirit with the vibratory physiology. It was the flow of animal spirits through the 'innumerable, flexible, elastic nerve fibres' which communicated ideas to the mind. Collet assures his audience that God wished man's knowledge 'to depend upon the fibres of the brain'. For this purpose, God 'located in the brain just as many fibres as ideas could be excited in the mind'. Each fibre is assigned its use and function, one fibre for each idea. The union between mind and body is such that 'the mind can perceive an idea arising from the vibration of a fibre'.

Collet follows the tradition of defining sensory ideas as 'the representatives in the mind of some object'; the action by which the representation is made is called perception or sensation. All the action of sensation 'takes place in the striate substance of the brain'. More importantly, he argues that every individual fibre of the brain 'is dedicated to' a particular idea. He also says that the mind *resides* in that area, adding a hesitant remark: 'if any place is to be assigned to it'. The sense organs each have a special series of nerve fibres; for example, in the case of the eyes, different fibres are dedicated to different colours. In the ear, sharp sounds are received in the mind via short fibres, heavy sounds by longer fibres.

Collet repeats Astruc's account of judgement linked with specific fibres, suggesting that the fibres of the brain fall into two main classes:

one of which comprehends all the fibres of subjects, the other all the fibres of attributes; each fibre from the class of subjects will represent all subjects of the same kind; likewise each fibre from the class of attributes will represent all attributes of the same kind. Thus, for example, for all men there will be one fibre in the brain for all stones, etc. Likewise, for all whitenesses one fibre, for all blacknesses one fibre, etc. And from the simultaneous vibration of the fibres of subject and attribute the idea of genus and differences arises, and thence is generated in the mind the knowledge of each thing.

Also following Astruc, Collet cites the correlation of mania, fevers, lethargy, paralysis, apoplexy with 'absurd and inappropriate ideas'. He offers a familiar explanation of the way in which animal spirits in such a body can 'indiscriminately strike the higher fibres of the striate substance', thereby causing certain unusual ideas to be given to the mind.

In his brief comments on Collet's claim that 'each idea has its own fibre in the brain', Le Camus recognized that such a specific correlation between fibres and perceptions or ideas ran the danger of seeming to turn man into an automaton, such as Regiomontanus's or Vaucanson's machines, but he responded by saying that just as the parts of the clock have different properties from the whole, so 'la tete n'a pas idées par elle-même mais par l'arrangement des organes de sens qui y sont attachés et qui reçoive du cerveau, les filets nerveux, cause de leur action tonique, il en résulte un sentiment, une existence ou plutôt une vie que nous appellons *idée*' (*Médecine*, p. 101). He insists that the soul is not lodged in the brain, nor anywhere else in the body. Bodies are extended substances, the soul is a spirit and hence unextended. His occasionalism then emerges: extended things cannot act on unextended ones. There are correspondences between soul and body, never causal relations. God is the mediator between the two substances. These occasionalist remarks make one wonder how Le Camus expected his 'medicine of the mind' to be effective.

CONCLUSION

If Le Camus (and Luzac) could so easily accept both a detailed physiological–mental correlation and occasionalism, why was Roche (and others as well) so convinced that Le Camus accepted the system of physical influences? No one, I suspect, was very clear about when correlation turned into causation. The three systems were seen as alternatives. The similarities between occasionalism and pre-established harmony are evident: both exclude causation from object to perceiver, when that causation is from physical motions to conscious awareness. Certainly, in Malebranche's formulation, occasionalism seems to allow physical to physical causation, even though such causation does not initiate motion, it only transmits it. The question of just how ideas and thoughts are related to their physiological antecedents was one never clearly explained or answered. Nevertheless, writers in Britain as well as in France often expressed concern that, as the mechanism of the body became understood as being more and more complex, as the correlations became more numerous and more specific, either the causation would engulf thought, or thought would be seen as a property of the brain. Locke's association with French materialism stemmed from several doctrines of his *Essay*, not the least of which was what was taken to be his causal theory of perception, the system of physical influences on the mind.

5

David R. Boullier

I n the construction of the story of Locke's doctrines on matter and ideas in eighteenth-century France, Boullier's name has surfaced on two occasions. His critique of Voltaire's Letter XIII on Locke, with its focus on thinking matter, was discussed in Chapter 2. The detailed analysis of sensation which we have just examined in Chapter 4 occurs amidst a comprehensive discussion on the nature of animal souls, with many side comments on human souls and their relations to bodies, to their own bodies and to environmental bodies. He also included in his *Essai philosophique sur l'âme des bêtes* (1728) a presentation of the three systems on the relation between mind and body. Boullier was a defender of traditional doctrines, especially concerning knowledge and perception, the soul, and matter. He was a significant writer on these topics, as well as a useful source for calm and reasoned commentary on the state of philosophy in his day. His writings include some important discussions on miracles, on liberty, and on inertia. Perhaps the most significant of his writings was, as I hope to show in this chapter, the treatise on moral certitude, added to the second edition of his *Essai* in response to a review of the first edition in the *Journal littéraire*.

In a 'Lettre sur l'esprit philosophique de notre siècle',[1] he laments the present age, saying that the previous century was better. He cites Locke as the defender of the claim that the nature of substances is unknown (p. 11). This notion about the limitation of our knowledge was adopted by many, Boullier says, because of the great name of Locke. His worry was that it leads quickly to scepticism. Boullier recognizes that our knowledge *is* limited, but not to the extent of our not knowing whether a man and a tree are just modes of one substance: a typical reading of Spinoza's metaphysics and the feared terminus of scepticism and Locke's suggestion (pp. 14–15). The new metaphysicians say that (1) our ideas have their origin only in the senses, and (2) if bodies did not make impressions on our mind, we would not be able to think or even to know our own mind. In

---

[1] In his *Pièces philosophiques et littéraires* (1759).

Germany, they deny that there are any extended bodies; they say that extension is only a phenomenon, that the world is full of invisible realities, e.g. forces, monads, entelechies (p. 21). For Boullier, there are three ills of modernity: materialism, fatalism, and Pyrrhonism. Free thinkers admit the existence of matter only, they make man into a machine or thinking automaton (p. 22). This latter notion is just an extension of the 'roman de *Descartes* sur les animaux'.

In another work, *Apologie de la métaphysique* (1753), the first part of which appeared in November 1751 as an article in the *Journal des sçavans*, Boullier attacked d'Alembert's 'Discours préliminaire' in the *Encyclopédie* (1751–65) for its defence of the false system of Locke (the rejection of innate ideas and the suggestion about thinking matter). Any suggestion that matter might have properties unknown to us, or that it is active with forces of attraction and repulsion (or thought and volition) is rejected by Boullier in this work and in the 'Lettre' cited above. He says rather strangely that Locke created metaphysics, just as Newton created physics. Since Boullier himself defines metaphysics as the science of ideas (*Apologie*, p. 15), it may be the way of ideas that he considers to be Locke's metaphysics. D'Alembert had said that Locke's metaphysics was 'the experimental physics of the soul', so 'metaphysics' may encompass the account of cognitive faculties and their operations on ideas. It is clear from the *Apologie* that Boullier identified Locke as one of those whose doctrines helped the 'rapid progress of Pyrrhonism and materialism in our century', two doctrines which go together because, 'quand on doute si la Matière n'est pas capable de pensée', we easily end with these two excesses (p. 16).

In another work, *Discours philosophiques: Le Premier sur les causes finales, le second sur l'inertie de la matière, et le troisieme sur la liberté des actions humaines* (1759), Boullier insisted that good philosophy depends on 'the essential distinction between two substances, mind and matter' (p. x). He argues for the traditional view of passive and inert matter. The difference between mind and matter lies there: 'l'esprit renferme en soi un principe d'action & de mouvement; tandis que la matiere est purement passive & démuée d'activité' (p. 22). He refers to an article in the *Journal britannique* (July–Aug. 1754) which reported on a dispute between John Stewart and Henry Home (Lord Kames) on the properties of matter. Boullier's sympathies side with Stewart, who stoutly defended against Kames the passivity of matter. The journal was reviewing the collection *Essays and Observations, Physical and Literary, Read before a Society in Edinburgh* (1754; later called the Philosophical Society of Edinburgh), especially the first two essays by Kames and Stewart, dealing with the laws of motion. Kames refers to Locke's conjecture that 'matter may be endowed with a power of thinking'.[2] The reviewer said that all we can observe, and hence all that we can claim to know, are occasional causes; we cannot discover efficient causes of events.[3]

AUTOMATES CARTÉSIENS

On the traditional view which Boullier shares, matter is incapable of self-motion, it lacks any inherent principles for initiating activity; but when he discusses *organized* matter such as animal and human bodies, Boullier agrees with the Cartesians that many of the actions of those bodies are functions only of the physiological mechanism. This notion of a body run by physiology is not incompatible with those same bodies having attached to them a soul, a principle of activity responsible for specific actions which physiology alone cannot cause. Boullier differs from Cartesians in claiming that animals also have a principle of action (a soul) attached to their bodies. He finds absurd the hypothesis that animals are machines, but he is also aware that libertines favour that hypothesis, wishing to say brutes are not only similar to humans, but their equals.[4] Thus, for Boullier, there is a moral urgency in exposing the absurdity and falsity of that claim, as well as a metaphysical concern to present what he takes to be the correct account of souls, both human and animal.

In the 'Discours préliminaire' of his *Essai*, he speaks of the system of automata, especially of *automates cartésiens* and Locke's suggestion in *Essay*, 4. 3. 6 and 4. 3. 27. He is cautious in his claim for his own system, asserting probability only, but a probability set alongside an absurdity is meant to convince. Boullier has considerable skill in presenting the views of others, even when he thinks they are false or absurd, without allowing his own beliefs to distort that presentation. His account of the Cartesian claim about animals is a good example of this talent. However, he is not reluctant to let the

[2] *Essays and Observations*, p. 5.
[3] *Journal britannique*, vol. 9.
[4] *Essai philosophique sur l'âme des bêtes* (2nd edn., 1737), Preface to the 1st edn., reprinted in 2nd edn., i. xxix.

reader know his own convictions. At the beginning of his presentation of the Cartesian view of animals as automata, Boullier asserts emphatically that feelings can only exist in a mind (*esprit*), never in matter. 'There is a contradiction, a metaphysical contradiction, that matter feels or is capable of feeling, as there is a contradiction in saying it can think.'[5] He says that no one any longer contests the notion that the human body is a machine. Whether a production of man or of nature, a machine is defined as follows: 'J'appelle Machine, un tout formé de l'assemblage régulier de diverses parties tellement disposées, enchaînées & proportionnées l'une à l'autre, qu'il en résulte un mouvement uniforme & régulier, par rapport à ce tout' (i. 17). The human body differs from machines made by man only in the delicacy, the number, and arrangement of the mechanism, and by the composition and infinite variety of its motions: 'It is a machine infinitely more complex and better constructed than all the others; which ought not surprise us since it is made by the Creator of the Universe' (i. 17).

The brain is the centre for all nerves, the reservoir of animal spirits (i. 19). Boullier does talk of reciprocal actions of soul and body in man, but he may only be speaking for the Cartesians. He goes on to explain that saying the soul is *united* to the sensorium (and thereby to all objects) means that 'God gives to the soul a sensation or confused perception' when objects affect the sensorium, reserving that relation for occasionalism, although he has the sensorium *exciting* certain thoughts in the soul when it has received from objects specific impressions (i. 26). The Cartesians (and I think Boullier also) distinguish those motions which depend only on the body from those that depend on the union of soul and body (i. 28). The former are certain bodily habits which come from the repetition of certain actions which leave permanent traces in the brain. Musicians or dancers execute many motions in a very precise manner 'without giving the least attention to them', a single act of the will to play or dance is all that is needed (i. 34). An orator often gives speeches by heart, without having to monitor each phrase and sentence. It is certain, Boullier says, that a man

does a great number of mechanical actions, ... without perceiving that he does so and without having to will them; actions that one can only attribute to

---

[5] *Essai* (1737), i. 17. In this 2nd edn., vol. i contains the treatise on moral certitude, pp. 1–280. The *Essai* then begins with new pagination, pp. 1–154 in that volume, and continues in vol. ii, pp. 1–432.

the impression of objects, and to a primitive disposition of the machine, where the influence of the soul has no part. (i. 33)

The human body could survive without being united to an intelligent principle; but if all actions of man were a result of bodily physiology, the soul would follow blindly the needs of the body, free actions would disappear. Supposing, for example, that an impression of a certain image on the retina, and a specific disturbance of the optic nerve, followed by the flow of animal spirits in specific muscles were the sole causes of fleeing some danger, then the soul would no longer be master of the actions of its body.[6] Considered simply as movements, the external motions of the body are a necessary consequence of internal motions: a play of the machine which does not lead us to any more than a material principle (i. 44). Boullier reminds us that the physiology of the body must function with or without a soul attached. For example, if there is a soul attached to a dog, all the details of the bodily physiology must work before that soul can move the body (i. 45–6). The same by implication is true of humans: they cannot move their body or limbs without the operation of the physiology.

Boullier thinks that the behaviour of animals is more than just motion: there is a sequence, an order, a connection of actions, a uniformity responding in the same way to similar objects and stimuli (i. 46). As we shall see later, it is the series of connected events and actions which Boullier takes as especially important for our morally certain beliefs. The Cartesians say that God could make a machine with these characteristics, establishing a harmony between those motions of the animal, the different bodies that surround it, and the different impressions made on it (i. 49). Pierre Sylvain Régis had mentioned the hydraulic machines that were popular in gardens and grottoes, water-driven statues which performed specific actions when triggered by people stepping on plates planted in the ground

---

[6] 'Il est évident, par exemple, que si de l'impression d'une certaine image sur la Retine, si d'un certain ébranlement du Nerf optique, transmis jusqu'au *Sensorium*, suivoit infailliblement une détermination du cours des esprits animaux dans les muscles des jambes, telle qu'il le faut pour courir, l'Ame ne seroit plus maîtresse des actions du Corps; il ne seroit pas plus en son pouvoir d'empêcher le mouvement résultant de l'impression de l'objet, que d'arrêter l'impression de l'objet même sur ses organes; il ne seroit pas plus possible à un homme de s'empêcher de fuir à la présence d'un objet nuisible, que de ne pas voir cet objet qui s'offre à ses yeux, tandis qu'il aura les yeux ouverts. L'Ame seroit obligée de céder toujours & d'obéïr aveuglément aux besoins du Corps; & dès-là, plus d'actions libres' (*Essai*, i. 38–9).

(i. 53). Boullier also reminds us of the various contrivances made by or credited to artisans, e.g. the flute-player of Vaucanson, the artificial fly, the talking golden head, etc. (i. 55). Suggesting that animals are driven only by the physiological mechanism may be acceptable to some, though for Boullier false, but the danger lies in the extension of this notion to man: 'if God is able to make a Machine which only by the disposition of its internal mechanism executes all the surprising actions that we admire in a dog or in an ape, he would be able to form other Machines which will imitate perfectly all the actions of man' (i. 87). Boullier expresses the fears and concerns of many about this easy move from animal to men machines.

Boullier asserts that the issue is a question of fact: is there or is there not such a principle in beasts as a soul: 'We see the effects, these are the actions of brutes; it is a question of discovering what is the cause of them' (i. 81–2). He insists that the question should be treated in the same way that physicists deal with the search for natural causes or historians go about to assure themselves of certain events. He lays down two rules for moral certitude: (1) God does not deceive and (2) a great number of appearances or effects associated with a cause which explains them proves the existence of that cause (i. 82). With these rules of method, the short refutation of the Cartesians is: 'If beasts are pure machines, God deceives us; that argument is the death blow to the hypothesis of Machines' (i. 83). The longer method used by Boullier to reject the Cartesian view (while at the same time guarding against *l'homme machine*) is to make his case on the more reasonable explanation. Cartesians appeal to an internal principle in the animal machine whose connection with the behaviour of the animal is obscure. Their explanation also goes against common opinion. Boullier's explanation in terms of a soul working with the mechanism of the body appeals to a notion which we can find exemplified whenever we will some action, although he admits that we may not have a clear idea of just how the soul acts.

Vous Cartésien, m'alleguez l'idée vague d'un Méchanisme prétendu possible, mais inconnu & inexplicable pour vous & pour moi; voilà, dites-vous, la source des Phénomènes que nous offrent les Bêtes: Et moi j'ai l'idée claire d'une autre cause, j'ai l'idée d'un principe sensitif; je vois que ce principe a des rapports très-distincts avec tous les Phénomènes en question, & qu'il explique nettement & réunit universellement tous ces Phénomènes. (*Essai*, i. 104, 2nd sequence)

He ends this part of the *Essai* (pt. I, ch. IX) by using the Leibnizian analogy of two clocks, pointing out that once we accept the notion of a soul attached to or linked with the body (whether human or animal), there have been three ways of interpreting that analogy: that the craftsman who made the clocks has to adjust them regularly in order to keep them synchronized; that that craftsman made them so perfectly that the two clocks require no adjustments; or that there is a *real influence* between them. These are, of course, the three systems for explaining the union of soul and body (i. 147).

THE THREE SYSTEMS

Occasionalism

The final chapter of the *Essai* (pt. II, ch. XIX), itself a brief statement of Boullier's belief in the goodness of God and the immortality of the soul, is preceded by four chapters devoted to presenting the three systems on the union of soul (or mind) and body. He says that the system of occasional causes was invented, or perfected, by Malebranche (ii. 330). The system of pre-established harmony has Leibniz for its author. The 'old system of *real influence* of soul on body has been given a new life by today's English philosophers'. Boullier's statement of the third system limits it to the influence of soul on body, which may explain how he could give the analysis of sensation that we examined in the previous chapter (a version of a causal theory of perception) without feeling he was skirting too close to physical influence.

What is interesting about his account of occasionalism are the objections he says have been raised against it, with his comments on those objections. The first objection distinguishes between universal or general causes and particular ones. The occasionalists, so runs this objection, identify the first cause of all but fail to identify the particular causes of each event (ii. 331–2). Boullier characterizes this objection as distasteful (*méprisable*), but whether he is serious is not clear, especially since his comments on the second objection seem to support the first objection, or at least build upon it. The task of philosophy is not, Boullier says in his comment on the first objection, to discover specific causes of events, but rather to follow second causes until we reach the first cause. Moreover, reason informs us by an analysis of the ideas of body and mind that it is impossible for them to act on each other (ii. 333). Allowing that bodies may have a *natural* connection (*rapport*) with other bodies, and that souls have a similar natural connection with other souls, Boullier appears to reserve a place for science: the discovery of causal connections within the realm of matter (and perhaps for the science of man, within the realm of mind). He does not, however, tell us what he thinks science does, how occasionalism finds a place for scientific activity.[7]

A second objection, a more weighty one he says, argues that second causes are, for the occasionalist, both the effects and the rule for divine action: 'the action which produces these effects will also be submitted to them' (ii. 334). In short, 'God will command himself and obey himself in the same instant'. This objection thus stated is rather obscure, but Boullier's explication reveals the point of it. If bodies have no activity themselves, if they cannot act on one another, 'the laws of motion in the System of P. *Malebranche* seem to be only a comedy', since those laws purport to describe the effects of the motion of one body on another. But, so this objection reads occasionalism as saying, bodies cannot cause changes in the motion of other bodies.

Boullier's response to this objection argues that so long as the soul has a real power to produce its own acts, the ability to be the efficient cause of its own volitions (as Boullier seems to accept), the claim that the soul is the occasional cause of certain motions of its body is a different claim from the one the objection allows (ii. 334). I suppose to say that the soul is the efficient (i.e. the producing) cause of its acts of willing is to say the person is the agent of those acts. These particular acts of willing are distinct from the general will of God. God, Boullier says, makes the changes in matter (in the soul's body) dependent upon the soul's volitions. Just as Leibniz's representative perceptions arise in the soul only when certain physical events occur in the world and inside the body, so Boullier is suggesting that specific physical events occur only when specific actions of the mind take place. The volitions of a created mind (*esprit*) are 'really produced by that mind, without being the immediate effects of the will of God' (ii. 335). Those finite acts of will are, in fact, 'the

---

[7] In discussing the question of why I have sensations of light and colours when certain disturbances occur in my brain, Malebranche says that to answer that question we must 'leave the general truths of metaphysics and enter into the principles of physics'. *Entretiens sur la métaphysique et sur la religion* (1688), IV. viii. 92, in *Œuvres complètes* (Paris: J. Vrin, 1958–70), xii.

mediating cause which is interposed between the divine will and the
motions of bodies; they provide the reason for those motions'. Thus,
in dealing with particular actions, we do not have to go back to the
will of God in order to explain those events. The general will is not
the cause of this specific action, e.g. of my walking now (ii. 336). The
general will has willed once and for all that the motions of my body
follow the desires of my soul; the willing to walk now is a mediating
cause between this general will and the motions of my walking.
Boullier is rather emphatic about this way of interpreting Malebranche. All particular instances of willing and moving are subject to
the general law of the union or correspondence between soul and
body, but in each particular case, 'my soul is the true cause of the
motions of its body' because it is the cause of its own willings. That
the phrase 'the cause of the motions of the body' is using the term
'cause' in a sense different from the phrase 'the cause of my own willings' is, I suspect, recognized by Boullier indirectly when he says that
'cause' in ordinary language signifies 'a reason by which one effect is
distinguished from another effect; it does not signify the *general
efficacy* which influences *all* effects' (ii. 337). To ask for the cause is
to ask for the reason why that motion was made at that time. Causal
efficacy has been turned into rational explication, but that rational
explication is stronger than just epistemic: it is metaphysical or
ontological since, unless I will to walk, my body will not move.
Nevertheless, the *efficacy* of my moving my body has been replaced
by *my willing* to walk.

Just as there are general laws which describe and predict physical events (e.g. the explosion of gunpowder when a lighted torch
is thrown into it), so there are general laws which explain how
the torch gets into the powder: my arm moved in such a way that the
torch landed there (ii. 339). These events are covered by reference
to laws of physics.[8] Boullier wants to say that there are other general
laws instituted by God which function in a similar explanatory way:
when I will to move to my arm and throw the torch, the arm moves

---

[8] This comparison between the relation of human action to general laws and the
relation of physical events to general laws is quite explicit in Boullier. 'Par exemple, si
je demande la cause qui à une telle heure du jour a fait monter le mercure dans le
Baromêtre, vous répondriez peu pertinemment si vous m'alleguiez la pesanteur de
l'air. Vous serez mieux de dire, c'est que tel Vent souffle; ou bien c'est que l'air vient de
se dégager des vapeurs qui le rarefioient. Voilà la cause particuliere & prochaine qui
détermine la générale, savoir la pesanteur de l'air, à produire cet effet précis; voilà la
cause dont je m'enquiers, quand je demande raison de cet effet' (*Essai*, ii. 337 n.).

and the torch ends in the powder. Just as it would be undignified and out of character for God to have to bring it about on each occasion that a torch that landed in powder will ignite the powder, so it would be un-God-like to have to intervene to move my arm every time that I will to move it.[9] Malebranche does write in some passages as if he were taking this particularist and interventionist route;[10] some of his followers (e.g. Andrew Baxter in England) definitely did.

The theological debate over premotion

Boullier is giving a sophisticated reading of Malebranche, one that makes occasionalism more attractive, but it makes use of the concepts of 'veritable efficace' and 'pouvoir réel' for the will of man. On the reading of occasionalism which has God intervening on each occasion, man's freedom of will and his responsibility for good and bad actions may disappear: God may become responsible for individual acts of sin. Boullier is here touching on important theological issues which had been under debate earlier in the century. One of the questions was 'what role, if any, does God's grace play in my actions, in my being attracted to good or evil?' There were two positions taken. The first said that God has arranged it so that the good is always more attractive to us than evil, but allowing somehow for our consenting to either. The consenting was within our power, although it was difficult for those who took this position not to make the action follow almost without question from the attraction which God had given to the good. But how to account for acts of sin? The second position gives God a much more active role: he *superadds* attraction to the good on each occasion and gives us a motive which necessitates good action. That motive was sometimes called the 'prémotion physique'.[11]

Chambers's *Cyclopaedia* defines 'Premotion' as 'the action of God

[9] 'Est-il plus indigne de Dieu de remuer le bras d'un incendiaire au moment qu'il a la volonté de jeter une méche allumée dans un magazin à poudre, de remuer dis-je ce bras en consequence des loix de l'union de l'Ame & du Corps, qu'il ne l'est d'allumer cette poudre & de faire sauter le magazin en vertu des loix générales de la communication des mouvemens? Celui du bras qui lance la méche & celui par lequel la poudre s'allume sont tous deux egalement nécessaires pour l'execution du vouloir de ce malheureux, puisqu'il manquera son effet, soit que le bras reste immobile, soit que la poudre ne s'allume point' (ii. 339).
[10] See *Entretiens*, IV. xi, where he speaks of 'cette volonté constante & efficace du Créateur'. (*Œuvres complètes*, xii. 96.)
[11] The language of 'superadding' was also used by Locke for his suggestion about thinking matter.

co-operating with the creature, and determining how to act', or 'an influence or participation of the virtue of the first cause which makes the second cause actually active'. A better explanation of this theological concept is found in Chambers under the entry for 'Predetermination':

the action of God, whereby he excites a second cause to act; or by which, antecedently to all operations of the creature, or before it could operate in consequence either of the order of nature or reason, he really and effectually moves, and occasions it to produce all its actions: that is, whatever the creature does or acts, is really done and acted by the agency of God on the creature who is all the time passive.

There is a thin line between limiting man's actions to willing and consenting and making him the agent of his actions, albeit with God's help.

Boullier does not want to get too involved in the intricacies of this theological debate, but he cannot avoid some reference to it since he wants to modify occasionalism in the ways we have seen: my willing *is* the cause of my acting. Whether I move my body by 'une efficace naturelle, par un pouvoir physique que le Créateur ait donné' to me, there has to be a way in which I can be morally responsible for my actions. Boullier's solution hinges on his distinction between the general framework of laws governing the union of mind and body and particular instances of human actions. God has seen to it at the creation that the motions of my body will follow necessarily when I will to move, but I have the ability to will that action or not to will it (*Essai*, ii. 340). The universe is orderly, there are general laws that explain the communication of motion and the correspondence between willing and bodily motion. Without the uniform, lawful, and orderly flow of events, we would be unable to act in the world. If occasionalism is taken to the extreme of saying that I am not the cause of my particular actions because God is the only efficient and producing cause, the consequence follows: we as agents of actions would be rendered impotent (ii. 341).

In the first *Eclaircissements* (1678) to his *De la recherche de la vérité* (1674–5), Malebranche addressed the question of how, on his account of the active and particularist involvement of God in my actions, he could absolve God from being the author of sin. It is necessary, he says, to distinguish between what God makes happen in us from what we do ourselves.[12] He insists that 'I have in myself

---

[12] *Œuvres complètes*, iii. 17.

a principle of self-determination' (iii. 18). Matter lacks such a principle of self-determination or self-motion. However, what God does for us according to Malebranche seems to leave little room for self-determination. God inclines us towards good in general by giving us a strong inclination towards good; he also gives us the idea which represents some particular good; and he moves us towards that particular good. The presence of ideas of particular goods is important, since those ideas reinforce the movement we have towards good in general (iii. 20). What is left for us to do is to consent or not to consent to the particular goods. This consenting or not consenting is, Malebranche insists, nothing real or positive. Were these acts of consenting real, new modifications of the soul, they would be changes in the nature of the soul substance. Only God can bring about such changes in the real properties of substances. Consenting or not consenting is something we can do, but it is not a real property of the soul: 'God creates in us the properties of speaking, walking, thinking, willing; he also causes in us our perceptions, sensations and motions: in short, he creates in us all that is real and physical' (iii. 31). God also gives us the motive to act, what Malebranche calls the 'motifs physics', but that motive is carefully distinguished from consenting. I have to have a motive before I can consent.

Is that which I can do limited to consenting or withholding consent? In the last book he wrote, *Réflexions sur la prémotion physique* (1715), a reply to a very controversial book by Boursier, *De l'action de Dieu sur les créatures* (1713),[13] Malebranche insists that he has always maintained that the soul is active, but those actions do not produce any physical motion, any overt behaviour. He even says that he has always said that the soul 'was the unique cause of its acts, of its determinations' (*Œuvres complètes*, xvi. 40), but those acts and those determinations turn out to be only its acts of consenting to moral good or evil. Not only do the soul's actions not eventuate in any physical behaviour, they do not add any new modifications to the body or the soul.[14] God gives us the motive to act, the 'Prémotion ou motifs physics' (xvi. 42). Thus, Malebranche's

[13] *De l'action de Dieu sur les créatures: Traité dans lequel on prouve la prémotion physique par le raisonnement* (2 vols., 1713). This work was published anonymously. Its author was L.-F. Boursier (1679–1749).
[14] 'J'ai toûjours soûtenu que l'ame étoit active: mais que ses actes ne produisoient rien de physic, ou ne mettoient par eux mêmes, par leur efficace propre, aucunes modalitez nouvelles, aucun changement physic, ny dans le corps ny en elle-même.' (*Réflexions sur la prémotion physique, Œuvres complètes*, xvi. 41.)

insistence that the soul does have a power to act is a quite different claim from Boullier's interpretation that, by willing, the soul is the cause of its physical actions. All that the power of the soul amounts to for Malebranche is 'un vrai pouvoir de resister ou de consentir à la motion qui suit naturellement de l'apparence de ce bien' (p. 47); this is not a power to produce new modifications, new realities in either soul or body.

The identification of what was and what was not a modification of the soul was important, since Malebranche agreed with Boursier that all modalities of the soul could only have God as their cause. For Boursier, one main difference between body and soul is that the former can acquire new modifications just by a rearrangement of the parts of matter. The soul has no parts, so the only way it can acquire new modes is through God's creative power. It sounds strange to our ears to hear Boursier describing thoughts, knowledge, and affections as realities, as degrees of being, but that is what they were on his ontology. He means that each new perception, each new thought, every increase in our knowledge or love (knowledge and love of God being the two attributes that Boursier was most interested in) requires God's action.[15] Ideas for Malebranche were also 'êtres-réels', so that is why they require God to give them to us on appropriate occasions; we could not create such realities ourselves.[16]

When Boullier was arguing for a specific difference between animal and human souls (*Essai*, pt. II, ch. IV), he took as one example of that difference the ideas that human souls or minds acquire. One explanation for the acquisition of new ideas, new modalities, was the Leibnizian one: ideas, even reflections and habits, develop out of the nature of the soul. Boullier agrees that ideas do not come from any external source: 'the acquisition of ideas belongs to the natural development of a created soul: they are produced by attention, reflection, and reasoning' (ii. 41 n.). Sensations are acquired differently (as we have seen from his digression on sensation): they arise in the soul immediately on the occasion of the action of external objects on our body. Thus, Boullier disagrees with Malebranche on two points: ideas are a product of mental operations and physical actions result from acts of willing, albeit the 'result from' relation is indirect.

---

[15] Condillac discusses Boursier's book as one of the systems he presents in his *Traité des systêmes* (1749). He says it is unintelligible (p. 210).
[16] *De la recherche de la vérité*, III. ii. iii, *Œuvres complètes*, i. 423.

The parallel between the causes of ideas and the causes of bodily actions in Malebranche's system is illustrated in a striking manner by Robert Basselin's *Dissertation sur l'origine des idées* (1709). Basselin sets out to show that all ideas come from the senses, even the ideas of insensible objects. He explicitly denies that we see all things in God (Malebranche's main doctrine), that we are born with any ideas, and that God forms our ideas or perceptions on the occasion of objects being present to us (p. 5). As Boullier argued later, so Basselin maintains that we form our ideas ourselves. He calls attention to several paragraphs in Malebranche's *Recherche* (III. ii. iii; *Œuvres complètes*, i. 423–4) where Malebranche talks of ideas as real beings and where he argues that finite minds cannot create new beings such as ideas. Basselin formulates Malebranche's claim about ideas by saying that the *understanding* cannot form them. Similarly, the *will* cannot perform any action. Basselin's novel way of showing the parallels between ideas and actions on Malebranche's system is to substitute in the III. ii. iii passage acts of will (e.g. knowing, loving) where Malebranche's text speaks of ideas. For example, where the text reads: 'Personne ne peut douter que les idées ne soient des êtres-réels, puisqu'elles ont les proprietez réelles', Basselin writes: 'Personne ne peut douter que (les actions de la volonté) ne soient des êtres-réels, puisqu'elles ont des proprietez tres-réelles' (p. 10). Or, where Malebranche's text says that men lack the power to create and therefore cannot produce ideas, Basselin substitutes 'cannot produce actions of the will' (p. 11). He carries out the substitution through four paragraphs. The language used is that of the controversy over efficacious grace and the notion used a few years later by Boursier of ideas, perceptions, and affections being realities. The context of Basselin's discussion in his opening pages is this theological issue about God's role in our actions.[17]

Pre-established harmony

Chapters XVI and XVII of Boullier's *Essai* are devoted to a discussion of Leibniz's system. It has, Boullier says, the advantage of novelty, it is the newest theory (ii. 343). He rejects this system mainly because he thinks it leads to idealism and scepticism about bodies and other minds. Leibniz agrees with Malebranche in denying any real influence of the two substances, but, unlike Malebranche,

---

[17] I am indebted to Lawrence Brockliss for calling Basselin's book to my attention.

Leibniz thinks of the body as a machine which, from the moment the Creator forms it, works alone without the craftsman having to direct or repair it. Its actions are co-ordinated with all other bodies in the universe. The soul is 'a principle which moves itself, which develops itself by adding new modifications' out of its own nature (ii. 345). These changes are co-ordinate with changes in its body. Boullier reports the language used by Leibniz of a 'spiritual automaton', insisting that liberty is impossible since 'a preordered mechanism regulates before my birth, the series of future movements of my hand, my tongue, my whole body' (ii. 347–8). Boullier finds this system bizarre and incomprehensible, comparing it to astrology (ii. 351–2). Moreover, on this system, the body is useless to the mind, the mind and body each go their separate ways. Leibniz's soul would be isolated in the universe, it would have no good reason to believe there is any other being in the world (ii. 357–8). Leibniz's system, like Berkeley's, leads into idealism, it reduces us to the 'certitude of our own existence, i.e., of our mind'. The soul is unable to extract from its nature or experience any sufficient reason or proof that there is an external world (ii. 363). It cannot even conclude to the existence of its own body, since all the representative impressions it has come from its own nature.

En niant toute influence réciproque des uns sur les autres, en rejettant toute causalité, soit réelle, soit occasionelle, soit physique soit morale, on m'ôte le moyen de découvrir l'existence des autres Esprits par les phénomènes des Corps, ou de m'assurer de l'existence des Corps, par les changemens qui arrivent dans mon propre Esprit. (ii. 364)

In short, Boullier concludes, on this system 'I am both the spectator and the spectacle'.[18]

Boullier contrasts Leibniz's system with the ordinary belief we have in an external world. If this belief is true, then Leibniz's system is false, and if that system is true, we must reject our ordinary belief (ii. 366). Just as there are no reasons that an individual soul can find within itself to believe in an external world (or even in its own body),

[18] 'Voilà quel est l'Automate spirituel de Mr. *Leibnitz*. Il roule éternellement sur lui-même, *ipse suis pollens opibus*, comme les Dieux d'Epicure, abandonné, dès qu'il sort des mains du Créateur, à l'infaillible direction de sa propre nature, au dessus de l'influence de tout Agent, & dans cet état solitaire, incapable de se convaincre qu'il y ait au monde d'autres Créatures que lui, pas même par révélation; puisqu'une Révélation seroit un miracle, qui viendroit troubler cette merveilleuse harmonie que la sagesse du Créateur rend inviolable' (*Essai*, ii. 382).

so we cannot, on Leibniz's system, infer mental phenomena from watching a body behave (ii. 371–2). Boullier is trying to take the position of a Leibnizian soul and then asking what beliefs in or inferences to an external world could that soul have or, if we assume that we could observe bodies behaving, how could we from those observations conclude that there was a soul or mental operations linked with it? For Boullier firmly believes that the behaviour of some animals does lead us to the belief in some form of mental activity, but he does not think that Leibniz's metaphysic allows either move. The question could be put: 'how does Leibniz's spiritual automaton know or even believe that its ideas do in fact represent a world outside?'

Boullier is also interested in the question of how Leibniz reached his conclusion about mind and body. Did he reach first the notion of a body as an automaton, 'all of whose mechanically prepared movements would work together to express all that happens in a soul', or, as Boullier believes, did Leibniz start with his notion of an 'automate spirituel', all of whose 'ideas, sensations, actions, passions occur in a specific order by the necessity of a primitive law founded on' the nature of the soul (ii. 374)? Boullier is surprised that Leibniz seems to have ignored the fact that his notion is contrary to our feelings which convince us that 'we are free, masters of our will', true agents. He also thinks Leibniz ignored the daily experience we have of all sorts of involuntary impressions affecting us each moment. Once we accept this notion of a spiritual automaton, the corporeal one follows (ii. 375).[19]

In short, Leibniz defends a grand paradox by one even larger. The incomprehensibility of his corporeal automaton is absorbed by an even more incomprehensible notion of isolated soul-substances (ii. 375–6). Pre-established harmony leads into scepticism, fatalism, and 'egoisme' (ii. 389).

Physical influence

Boullier's discussion of the third system is brief and more favourable. He says it is less subtle, less refined, but closer to the views of

---

[19] Nevertheless, Boullier finds the idea of a corporeal automaton equally difficult to accept. He uses an interesting metaphor for understanding that notion: 'une tablature réglée, pour tout ce qui s'est passé dans cette Ame depuis la naissance de Cesar jusqu'à sa mort, vous pouvez supposer dans sa machine, une autre tablature que la Toute Puissance divine y aura mise pour s'accorder juste avec la précedente, & pour en faire résulter toutes les actions de Cesar' (*Essai*, ii. 375).

ordinary people: 'it admits a real efficacy in the soul for moving matter' (ii. 385). Boullier presents this system as the influence of mind over matter. God gave to the soul that power, but limited to its own body. Boullier does not find this notion very clear, but it is certainly more reasonable to locate such a power in an active substance (the soul) than in matter itself. Boullier mentions and rejects in a footnote an objection raised by Boursier in his treatise on premotion: to attribute to the soul a power to move its body requires the extension of that power to all bodies, especially if that power is a natural one. Boullier finds this objection frivolous, there is no reason why the soul could not have such a limited power without its having the power to move other objects. The power we have to move bodies is limited by the general laws of the union of soul and body (ii. 385 n.).

The serious problem facing the system of physical influence is that it does not explain how the soul reacts to the impressions of objects on its body. Physical influence explains actions but not sensations. It is here that Boullier clearly intends his account of sensation to aid the system of physical influence. He says that he cannot decide between occasionalism and physical influence, but his sympathies are clearly for some version of the latter. He is hesitant about saying that we are aware of our ability to move our body, but we have seen that he does make my willing to move the cause of my moving. The account of sensation helps him apply physical influence in the other direction. Sensations occur when the action of the soul is obstructed; sensations arise whether I want to have them or not. Foreign objects modify the soul (ii. 387). If his account of sensation explains how the influence of bodies on the soul (or on awareness) operates, without violating the engrained doctrine about no action between different kinds of substances, then Boullier has a neat analysis of physical influence. Somehow that action of body on soul has to be mediated, it cannot be directed. The mediation occurs by the causal effects of bodies on the sensorium. Direct access to the external world is not possible, but the sensorium 'mirrors' the world, doing so in terms that the mind can understand. Boullier is not very clear about the precise nature of the sensorium mirror or the *tableau vivant*, but he is obviously looking for a way to have a causal theory of perception, physical influence in the direction from body to mind.

My willing is the mediator of my walking, mediating between the General Will of God and particular instances of willing. Particular human *acts of willing* cause the body to move now, and *particular bodily motions* cause sensations in the mind. Both the acts of will and bodily motions have an indirectness. I do not cause my arm to move directly (that is, I do not bypass the physiology) but I do cause my soul to will the movement of that arm. Because of God's general laws, my willing now does cause my arm to move. Similarly, physical objects do not directly cause my sensations: the sensorium is the mediator there. Boullier does not want to settle for occasionalism in this direction, any more than in the other direction. When the brain is affected in a certain way, we see red, feel pain, etc. He wants a close relation between the motion of bodies and the mind's sensory awareness. That is where the mirror and the *tableau vivant* come in: they are available to the mind and they *are* the external world in relation to us.

EXPLANATION AND MORAL CERTITUDE

Of the three ills of modernity identified by Boullier (materialism, fatalism, and Pyrrhonism), it was the first that loomed most importantly in his writings. His attack on Voltaire's Letter XIII was a strong reaction against Locke's suggestion of the possibility of matter having the property of thought. Boullier considered this possibility as tantamount to reducing thought to operations of organized matter, the usual reaction to Locke's suggestion among his British opponents. Few who discussed that suggestion understood that reductionism need not be the result of a property such as thought being attached to (or even being natural to) the mechanism of the brain. The lack of understanding here is similar to the failure to understand Spinoza's metaphysics of one substance with two kinds of properties. Spinoza's substance has the properties of extension and thought. If extension as a property of a substance makes or reveals that substance to be a material one, thought as its property ought to make it immaterial. But none of the critics and quick rejecters of Spinoza appreciated this point: they missed the familiar, comfortable *two* substances where the two properties belonged to different substances. A difference of *kind* between properties required, it was generally believed, a kind-difference of substances. Much of the reaction against Locke's suggestion was, I suspect, coloured by the existing abhorrence of what Hume called the 'monstrous hypothesis of Spinoza'.[20]

[*See p. 128 for n. 20*]

For Boullier, the spectre that hovered over his *Essai* was not Spinoza's one substance but Descartes's animal machine. The results were the same: a mechanical explanation of life, of the actions and behaviour of animals and, eventually, of man; the twin dangers of *automates cartésiens* and *l'homme machine*. Leibniz's character-ization of some monads as *automates spirituels* reinforced Boullier's fears. The consequence of such a view of man was the impossibility of freedom and the elimination of moral responsibility. As he wrote in the 'Avertissement' to the second edition of his *Essai*, responding to criticism of the first edition in the *Journal littéraire*: 'the word "liberty", when speaking of the action of a spiritual automaton, means the same as the word "necessary" when that word is used for the motion of a mill-wheel' (i, p. xviii). Boullier's commentary on the three systems of the relation between mind and body is influenced, and his criticisms of each are guided by his firm conviction that materialism and mechanism are false. He claimed, as we saw, that the question for the Cartesians is one of fact; questions about mind and body should be pursued by the same method as is used in science and history. It is more difficult to see how one would apply the evidential method of science to these issues, but Boullier does present a convincing case for some strong similarities between historical explanations and explanations of behaviur. The *Essai* has a few remarks on method and principles of explanations, but he gives a full and very interesting account, in the treatise added to the second edition, of how we reach conclusions which go beyond and claim to explain observed phenomena.

In that 'Traité de vrais principes qui servent de fondement à la certitude morale', Boullier distinguishes two kinds of demonstra-

---

[20] For a discussion of Hume's satirical account of Spinoza, see my *Thinking Matter* (Minneapolis, Minn.: University of Minnesota Press; Oxford: Basil Blackwell, 1984), ch. III. Locke was associated with Spinoza as early as 1705 by some of his less impressive opponents in Britain. (See my *John Locke and the Way of Ideas* (Oxford: Oxford University Press, 1956), 144–6, 161, 179–80.) That the association was also made by at least one serious and well-informed writer in France is suggested by two letters from Barbeyrac to Pierre Desmaizeaux. In one letter dated 22 Dec. 1706, Barbeyrac expresses surprise that Desmaizeaux says Locke was a Spinozist, since he (Barbeyrac) can find no evidence for this claim in Locke's published works. In a letter of 7 May 1707, Barbeyrac again expresses surprise at the suggestion that Locke believed there was only one substance. (These letters are in the British Library, Add. MSS 4281, fos. 21, 23. I am indebted to Professor James Moore for calling these letters to my attention and for providing me with photographic copies of them.)

tion: geometrical and moral.[21] For the latter, he illustrates the method leading to such demonstrations with some extended and fascinating discussions of historical knowledge. He includes under moral certitude truths which are neither evident to the eye nor necessary to the mind but which are susceptible of proofs which make doubt impossible. To prove that objects exist in the past or beyond present experience, there need to be some phenomena whose occurrences and connections suppose the reality of other objects (i. 5, 1st sequence). For historical events, human testimony is one of the main sources of evidence (ibid. 7–8). But testimony by itself is not sufficient. The circumstances under which it was given as well as the kind of person giving it are important. If possible, a full knowledge of the person giving the testimony is needed: his character, motives, interests, causes able to influence him, accuracy of observation (ibid. 10). A single report is often corroborated by others, but he recognizes that there can be instances where a group gets together to hide the truth. Sometimes this is for good reasons, as when your friends hide from you the death of a close relation; they do this only for a time (ibid. 13–14). For historical claims, such as 'there was a man called Julius Caesar', there are so many events linked with that person, the thoughts and actions of Caesar which have affected other persons and events, that it is impossible to doubt his existence (ibid. 16, 25).

Boullier speaks of the moral order of society, with laws founded on human nature (ibid. 20–1). What he has in mind is the fact that people do tend to react in similar ways under similar conditions. He links the moral order of society to traditions that develop in that society and which are often transmitted via oral history (ibid. 36–8). He recognizes that 'the historian speaks to posterity from the point of view of his time', but reports from different societies can help in uncovering the past (ibid. 81). Boullier has some interesting remarks about the role trade and commerce have played in transmitting and preserving social memories (ibid. 84–5). He believes traditions are specific to areas, times, and particular groups; there are no universal traditions of humanity (ibid. 86), although he has a section in which he suggests that if there are traditions which are universal, they

---

[21] The reviewer in the *Bibliothèque raisonnée* says that the term 'demonstration' is often used in a loose way, but he assures us that the proper meaning relates to the certainty of proofs where the contrary to a proposition implies a contradiction. See *Bibliothèque raisonnée*, 19 (July–Sept. 1737), 11.

would have to date from the first man and from a time when there was only one family (ibid. 87–8). Tradition, monuments, and records can support one another in revealing to us past events and happenings. So tightly connected are these various evidence-bearing items that doubting that there were such people as Plato or St Augustine is virtually impossible. To doubt that such well-reported people existed in the past, in the face of all the documents and reports, would require us to suppose a 'Cabale de Faussaires', a 'Concert de Témoignages', who themselves wrote the books and letters that talk of those persons, who fabricated whole events, etc. (ibid. 91). Boullier sketches in some detail what would have to have happened were claims about such historical figures false. Of course, some of the details that have survived in reports and records may be wrong or distorted, but that there were such persons is beyond doubt. What is especially important for Boullier is the complex cluster of interlocking testimony, oral traditions, books, records on which our moral certainty of such events and figures rests.

When he comes to the certitude of causes in physical science (ch. III), the same stress is found on the connectedness of the phenomena to be explained. Causes are the 'invisible facts to which phenomena give testimony'. A hypothesis is an arrangement of diverse imagined causes from which we try to derive consequences which are the phenomena we began with (ibid. 101). He uses the example of a large machine of whose inner workings we can only glimpse a part. How to explain what the other parts are and how they work, based on the outward appearances? The universe is such a machine of which we only see parts; it is a mechanism of many material agents connected in complex ways (ibid. 102). To offer an explanation of one segment of the universe, we need to know what is most consistent with the 'General System of Nature'. If we were able to know perfectly that general system, we should be able to know the true causes of specific events. Since everything in nature is connected, we should need a complete history of effects, were we to discover causes (ibid. 105). The principles of the universal history of nature would lead us to demonstrations, not just to hypotheses. An immense variety of effects could be deduced from those general principles. Since we do not have such complete and perfect knowledge of nature, the search for causes that explain phenomena is more piecemeal. Boullier compares this search to the cryptographer seeking the key to enable him to decipher a coded message. At some point, the letters fall into order and the cryptographer finds he can make sense of a few sentences, then of whole pages. In a similar way, a scientific explanation of one set of phenomena often fits with and helps explain other phenomena (ibid. 108–9). Such is the nature of the physics of discovery (ibid. 113). Of competing hypotheses, moral certitude goes with those that explain the most phenomena with the simplest principles and the fewest causes (ibid. 117–19).

Chapter V gets to the main reason for this treatise: how we 'demonstrate' the existence of minds (souls) and immaterial agents in animals and man, given that all we witness (except in our own case) is behaviour. The choice for explaining the behaviour of animals and man is between mechanism and immaterialism. Boullier's general claim is that if one of these hypotheses can explain, make sense of, more phenomena, then it should be the one we accept. Are there clear criteria which tell us when these conditions have been met? Boullier thinks that by using ordinary examples he can convince us of the difference between competing hypotheses and which one is consistent with our experience.

He takes an example of entering a room where he watches a ball flying from wall to wall, conforming to the rules of a game, but he sees no players in the room. He would have to conclude that he was watching a game and that there were some players invisible to him. 'To say that there is some hidden mechanism which makes the balls behave as they do, or to say that these effects are the results of some natural law unknown to me, would be extravagant' (ibid. 136–7). No law of mechanism can make sense to me of what I witness, assuming (though he does not say this) that experience has already exposed me to games and to the motions of bodies. He then treats the behaviour of animals in the same way, stressing some of the special features of that behaviour: when they begin and end some bit of behaviour, the speed of their motion, etc. These features vary, thereby reinforcing the belief that the behaviour is not mechanical. Furthermore, the behaviour of animals seems to be interest-related: self-preservation, hunger, fear, etc. (ibid. 138). In the case of what I take to be another man like me, it is the mass of phenomena which convinces me that it is not an automaton. A few human-like motions of arms and legs might pass as the product of some mechanism, but the variety of motions makes that hypothesis more difficult to accept. He gives an example of a 'Cavalier' entering his room and doing all sorts of actions and gestures but not speaking. The complex set of behaviours, stopping and starting, playing the lute, writing, some of those activities clearly related to others, assures him that it is a man, not a machine.[22]

If the sceptic tries to make a case for mechanism explaining these activities, Boulier says that the springs and drives required by such a machine for so many different and related actions would have to be very complex. He also believes that not all of the actions of that being can be explained by the known laws of nature. If that being was a machine, it would have to be a 'miraculeux Automate', requiring a very skilled artisan. But if we suppose this possible for God, we must conclude that God would have constructed such a complex machine in order to deceive us. In making such a machine, God would have had to interrupt the ordinary course of nature (ibid. 143). As we have seen, Boullier bases much of what he says on the firm belief that God is not a deceiver.

He goes on to point out that for other sorts of phenomena (e.g. the growth of plants, the attraction of iron to a magnet), he finds no reason to invoke an immaterial principle, but the behaviour of animals is different.

Mais quand je vois dans un Animal des mouvemens irréguliers, arbitraires, détachez les uns des autres, mais pourtant liez d'une maniére intime avec les sentimens, les besoins, les vues, les intérêts qu'auroit une Ame supposée hôtesse de son Corps; quand je vois qu'une telle Ame, intéressée à produire toutes ces actions, est un centre qui les lie, un Principe qui tout d'un coup me les explique; je conclus que cette Ame en est la vraye cause, & qu'elle existe par conséquent. (ibid. 151)

He even admits that each individual movement of an animal might be produced by a mechanical spring, but to say the complex whole was so caused strains our credulity (ibid. 152). To those who say that a perfect imitation of a man could be given by a cleverly built automaton, Boullier replies that if in fact such an automaton did deceive us, the only conclusion to draw is that its maker designed it to deceive us (ibid. 154–5). If mechanism as the cause of such complex behaviour is ruled out, what is left, Boullier argues, is that that behaviour is at least related to, if not run by, an immaterial principle, a soul. We can conclude that the way these figures behave indicates they have souls. The same conclusion must be drawn for

---

[22] As we saw in ch. 1, Crousaz, Roques, and Bayle used similarly constructed examples to attack Leibniz.

animals, since their behaviour is similar to that of the man who entered his room but did not speak.

Besides the outward similarity of some animal behaviour to ours, another way to reach the conclusion that there is in animals a sensitive principle is to examine the internal structure of their organs (ibid. 165). There are three kinds of organs: those that control the vital processes, those that transmit to the brain different impressions of objects, and those that produce different actions. He then appeals to an argument for final causes: what the organs do is what they were designed to do. He claims that the Cartesians are unable to show how the retinal impression by itself is able to cause the animal to respond as it does; a mechanical explanation will not do (ibid. 168–9). He speaks of the eyes and ears, together with the accompanying nerves, having a *natural* aptitude to cause sensations in the soul (ibid. 170), but he admits that we are ignorant of the precise connection between a motion and a thought, between the organization of the eye or ear and a sight or sound, between the physiology and the sensations. He goes on to say that it is not just the disturbances of the air, the structure of the organ, the nerve action that cause the sensation. We assume as well that the disturbance which the sensorium receives 'a de si justes proportions avec le sentiment de l'Ame dont il est suivi, que sans lui ce sentiment ne naîtroit point dans l'Ame' (ibid. 172–3). God at the Creation instituted this proportion, this natural connection between feelings and specific modifications of the brain.

It is clear from these remarks that Boullier is firmly convinced that there is an external world with which we interact in some form. But before turning to the question of the demonstration of bodies, he distinguishes between the ideal or intellectual world and the real world. Even if there was no real world, only ideas that I have of such a world, we have ample evidence for the existence of an intelligence behind the world of ideas. A book with pictures of a palace and the palace itself both suggest some intelligent designer (ibid. 195). 'Ainsi le Monde réel, ou le simple spectacle d'un tel Monde, supposent avec une égale nécessité, une Cause intelligente hors de moi' (ibid. 195–6). God could make us hear a discourse which no one spoke, he could create all the books in my library, making the authors exist only in my imagination. The question is: has he done so? Boullier's answer is no, because it would be contrary to God's wisdom and goodness to deceive us. But there are more direct means to reach the conclusion that an external world exists. Citing Berkeley as one who has denied such a world (ibid. 208–9), Boullier stresses, as he has in other sections, the complexity of and relations between sensory phenomena. It is this connectedness which convinces us that all is not an illusion. Moreover, Boullier is conscious of his own body, that he can move his arms, walk, etc. External objects are the instruments for creating sensations in our soul or mind (ibid. 212). Without a world of physical objects, we would be at a loss to explain the order and connection of our perceptions, a claim Boullier can make because he rejects occasionalism.

In another section, Boullier compares the *phenomena* we see with a painting. In virtue of certain general laws, the painter is able to use colours and shapes on a canvas to *represent* objects. We do not mistake the shapes for real objects. If the painter intended us to take his painted shapes as the real objects, he would have moved from representation to imposture (ibid. 232). In a similar way, the phenomena that I see and which represent their causes are not the same as their causes. If the intention of God was to make automata that would make us mistake the machine for a man, that again would be deception.

CONCLUSION

The review in the *Bibliothèque raisonnée* of the second edition of Boullier's *Essai* was devoted to presentation and criticism of the treatise on moral certitude.[23] It was not a favourable review. Some good points are made against Boullier, but the anti-Catholic bias of the reviewer may have interfered with his judgement. It irked the reviewer that Boullier, pastor of the Walloon Church in Amsterdam, dedicated this edition to Fontenelle, 'un Philosophe, qui fait profession de la Religion Catholique'. The likely reason for the dedication is that Fontenelle was the Secrétaire perpétuel of the Académie royale des sciences in Paris, a person who might give some visibility to Boullier's book.[24] The reviewer also did not believe Boullier's

---

[23] *Bibliothèque raisonnée*, 19 (July–Sept. 1737), 1–46.
[24] The reviewer suggests that other Huguenots will be surprised by this choice of persons for the dedication. 'Quoi, diront-ils, n'y avoit-il donc dans les Provinces-Unies aucun Réformé, qui fût digne que Mr. Boullier lui dédiât son Livre? Ou s'il n'y en avoit point, les grands Hommes sont-ils si rares ailleurs parmi les Protestants, à Genève, par exemple, en Prusse, ou même dans l'Eglise Anglicane, dont Mr. Boullier

methodological principles would enable him to identify the 'false' traditions accepted by the Church of Rome. Whatever the reason, the *Bibliothèque raisonnée* reviewer did not do justice to the details of Boullier's account of the beliefs we form about past events and other people. The reviewer praises Humphrey Ditton's account of moral certitude (expressing surprise that Boullier did not refer to it), but Ditton hardly ever gets beyond general remarks.[25] The strength of Boullier's treatise lies especially in his careful account of historical research, the relation between present-day records and testimony and the truths we seek to uncover or confirm about the past. His somewhat briefer account of scientific method is less original but consistent with generally accepted views and practices. Where he is most vulnerable is of course in his effort to support his claim for some kind of soul or immaterial principle in animals, but the Cartesian view was seen by many as counter-intuitive. Boullier was very traditional in his acceptance of final causes, in his argument that what a particular sense organ does is what it was designed to do, but that is a product of his general theological beliefs. He is on stronger ground with his many effective examples showing how any inference from the complex and diverse behaviours of bodies like our own in ordinary life situations to a mechanical explanation is incomprehensible. What his treatise on moral certitude does not do is settle the debate between the three systems of mind and body, but it does reveal, as we have seen from our analysis of his *Essai*, that Boullier's sympathies were with interaction both ways, i.e. with physical influence.

lui-même est Prêtre, qu'il ait été obligé de choisir pour Patron de son Ouvrage un Philosophe, qui fait profession de la Religion Catholique?' (Ibid. 6)
[25] Ditton's discussion is in his *A Discourse concerning the Resurrection of Jesus Christ* (1712; 2nd edn., 1714), pt. II.

6
Systems of Philosophy

THE ills of modernity for Boullier were, as we saw, materialism, fatalism, and Pyrrhonism. For many, these 'isms' went together, one reinforcing the other. To identify the limits of human knowledge does not seem to be a step towards either of the other two diseases, since even those who defended religion and morality against these modern evils were the first to point to man's finiteness, in life and in knowledge. What counted against you in their eyes was what you said man cannot know. To say, as Locke and others did, that we cannot know the nature of soul or body, not the essential natures, only their observable or experienced properties, inevitably clashed with orthodox convictions which assured their holders that the soul is immaterial, active, and simple; that matter is material, passive, and divisible into parts: these were the orthodox beliefs which became for them dogmatic claims to knowledge. Similarly, to suggest that the properties of soul might become properties of matter, even by the power of God, was for many an impossibility, an absurdity. The question of possible interaction between a soul and *its* body was not so easily resolved, but, especially at a time in France when occasionalism was once again in the ascendancy, physical influence of body on soul, or intentional action of soul on body, was not the favoured hypothesis or system.

HUME AND THE RENOVATION OF PHILOSOPHY

Besides those specific doctrines linking Locke's name to materialism—the causal theory of perception, the stress on sensory origins of ideas, the suggestion of matter thinking—there was also at work in the larger intellectual context a growing distrust of systems, of abstract systems purporting to render the world intelligible in terms of very general principles and concepts. In 1739–40, David Hume ridiculed standard metaphysical systems: they have led us into paradoxes and dead ends, they use meaningless terms, they are more concerned with rhetoric than with logic or reason. Hume's opening charge in his *Treatise of Human Nature* is well known:

Principles taken upon trust, consequences lamely deduced from them, want of coherence in the parts, and of evidence in the whole, these are every where to be met with in the systems of the most eminent philosophers, and seem to have drawn disgrace upon philosophy itself. (Selby-Bigge edn., p. xiii)

In that introduction to his work on the 'science of man', Hume urged the use of reason, 'the tribunal of reason', as the way to disclose the inconsistencies of old systems, their use of eloquence instead of reason. But reason comes close to being replaced in the *Treatise* by experience and the invisible hand of nature. The old dogmatisms are replaced by a cautious scepticism and careful attention to observation and experience. Hume was not opposed to systems—he characterizes his own work as a system several times (e.g. in the section on scepticism with regard to the senses, pp. 199, 202)—but any system of philosophy, any metaphysical system, must be constructed on the base of observation and experience. Even general principles are allowed by Hume, so long as they emerge from close acquaintance with the phenomena being studied, e.g. the mind or soul, the passions and emotions. Truth, Hume warned (a warning he repeated in his *Philosophical Essays*, 1748), does not come easily in the physical or in the social sciences; it may even be abstruse and require effort to understand once it is discovered.

In his *Traité des systèmes* (1749), Condillac expressed similar attitudes towards previous sytems. Criticizing those systems which claimed to derive truths from such general principles as 'the same thing cannot both be and not be', or 'whatever is included in clear and distinct ideas of objects can be affirmed of those objects', Condillac charged that these principles do not lead to any useful knowledge. He also rejected suppositions or hypotheses which were not firmly grounded in careful attention to phenomena: 'Si les suppositions ne paroissent pas impossibles, et si elles fournissent quelque explication des phénomènes connus, les philosphes ne doutent pas qu'ils n'aient découvert les vrais ressorts de la nature' (*Œuvres philosophiques* (Paris: Presses universitaires de France, 1947), i, ch. I, p. 121). The best 'principles' are 'facts'; hence Condillac's efforts in his *Traité des sensations* (1754) to study each sense modality in order to uncover what each contributes to our knowledge of the world. In the work on systems, he illustrates the difficulties and errors of basing a system on general, abstract principles, or on suppositions, by discussing Malebranche, Leibniz, and Spinoza. Descartes had been added to the list of metaphysicians rejected in his earlier *Essai sur l'origine des connoissances humaines* (1746). In that early work, he remarked in the Introduction that metaphysics has fallen into disrepute because of its abstract nature and its indifference to precision and exact observation. He distinguished two kinds of metaphysics, both of little value. The one is ambitious, claiming to penetrate the mysteries of the universe, the other recognizes the limits of the human mind and contents itself with vague notions and meaningless words. Descartes, Malebranche, and Leibniz have been seduced by their systems, failing to see that these have not revealed the essence or nature of mind, body, or matter. 'We only see what is near to us', Condillac says in summing up the systems he rejects, 'but we believe we see all that exists'.

J. H. S. Formey also expresses views about systems of thought similar to those of Condillac and Hume. In his Introduction to the French translation of Hume's *Philosophical Essays*, Formey criticizes both ancient and modern philosophers.[1] The earliest philosophers tried to 'pierce the veil of nature' and discover the first elements of matter. Formey says that the whole history of ancient philosophy is a mass of errors and absurdities. If we did not understand the extent to which human pride can go, we would be astonished at the audacity of the dogmatism of these early philosophers (*Essais philosophiques*, i, p. iii).[2] Modern philosophers (and here Formey means natural philosophers, scientists) have made great discoveries. Our century, he says, is one favourable to observations and experience (i, p. iv). The researches of these modern philosophers are however still far from 'being able to form a complete system where all the phenomena are interconnected and lead to first causes', but they are now in a position to draw the limits and extent of possible knowledge while still increasing our know-

---

[1] *Essais philosophiques sur l'entendement humain* (2 vols., 1758). The translator of the *Philosophical Essays* was J. B. Mérian. The *Philosophical Essays* were later entitled the *Enquiry concerning Human Understanding*.

[2] Formey's judgement on the history of philosophy is not quite so harsh in his *Histoire abrégée de la philosophie* (1760). He there says that a good history of philosophy is useful for learning what has been said by past philosophers. Nevertheless, to the question he raises in this *Histoire*, 'is the history of philosophy the history of truth?', Formey replies sharply: 'Non assurément: & encore moins celle de la Vertu. Les erreurs & les passions y tiennent la principale place, y jouent le plus grand rôle' (p. 14).

ledge in certain areas (i, pp. iv–v).[3] Nevertheless, modern philosophers (and now he means 'philosophers' in our sense of the word,
modern system-builders) have come to an impasse, they simply
repeat what has been said about God, the world, soul, body, etc. Two
routes have now been followed, neither of which Formey approves.
One route is that of a new dogmatism, where philosophers make new
hypotheses arbitrarily, they favour a flamboyant style of writing and
an imposing tone. The main aim of these new dogmatists is to acquire
a reputation (i, p. vii). The other route is that of Pyrrhonism: the
recognized limits of knowledge lead these philosophers to deny the
very possibility of *any* knowledge; man is only capable of producing
errors and falsity (i, pp. viii–ix). Formey's passionate rejection of
such sceptics is apparent in his comment:

Voilà la carrière dans laquelle sont entrés plusieurs Ecrivains distingués de
nos jours; voilà la gloire à laquelle ils aspirent. Ils entassent Objections sur
Objections contre les Vérités les plus généralement reconnues; ils sement
partout le doute & l'incertitude, & mourroient contens si comme d'autres
Samsons ils pouvoient s'ensévelir, eux & leurs Concitoyens, sous les ruïnes
de cet Univers. Ordre, beauté, régularité, enchaînement, proportions, fins,
plan, sagesse; sont autant d'idées pour lesquelles ils ont une aversion
décidée, & dont ils voudroient effacer jusqu'à la moindre trace. (i, pp. ix–x)

Formey consoles himself with the thought that the excesses and
absurdities of these writers, and of the free thinkers who take
comfort from scepticism, are so obvious that their books are no
longer dangerous (i, p. xii). He predicts the imminent return of good
sense and the demise of these extravagant dogmatists and sceptics.

How much confidence Formey really had in this optimism is not
clear; the confident tone of these remarks is a prelude to his justify-
ing publishing a French translation of Hume's *Philosophical Essays*:
'Ces considérations ont surmonté la repugnance qu'on avoit d'abord
eue à faire paroître en François les *Essais philosophiques* de M.
Hume' (i, p. xiii). The general Pyrrhonism that pervades Hume's
work, even the attacks on the fundamental truths of religion, will,
Formey forecasts, probably detract from rather than spread the
influence and knowledge of those *Essais* (i, p. xiv). Besides, this
book has been read already by many people, even by Frenchmen, in
the original English, so the translation will add little to what is

[3] In his *Histoire*, Formey defined philosophy as 'l'assemblage, la totalité des
bonnes explications, & des raisons satisfaisantes, par lesquelles on a joint à la notion
des faits, celle de leur possibilité dûement constatée' (p. 10).

already known about the evil doctrines of Hume, or what has been said about Hume in French-language journals.[4] Just in case his optimistic prediction proves ill-founded, just in case his conviction that Hume's philosophy no longer requires serious refutation is too optimistic, Formey uses the rest of his long Introduction to present the reader with Leland's criticisms of Hume's account of causation, probability, and his rejection of miracles.[5]

There is, of course, a world of difference between Hume's *Treatise* and his *Philosophical Essays*, not in the central doctrines on the origin and connection of ideas, or even in the accounts of causation and necessity, but in the confident tone of the writing, the scope of his analyses, and the bold programme for the science of man in the *Treatise*. The *Essays* give more attention to the various forms of scepticism and to the sceptical nature of his own account. When the *Essays* are placed, as they were in this French translation, together with Hume's writing on natural religion, the essay on miracles, and the short essay on the Epicureans, it is easier to understand Formey's reactions. Had the *Treatise* been given wider circulation in France, had Hume's readers paid more attention to other aspects of his total system in that work, a more sympathetic reaction might have surfaced. One feature in particular that might have mitigated the 'repugnance' felt by Formey towards Hume's doctrines is the satire on Spinoza in the section on the immateriality of the soul (I. IV. V). That section should have pleased Spinoza-haters in the eighteenth century, of whom there were many.

The *Treatise* did receive two long reviews in the *Bibliothèque raisonnée* in April–June of 1740 (24: 324–55), which dealt with Books I and II, and in April–June of 1741 (26: 411–27), which discussed Book III. These two reviews gave a fairly full coverage of the main doctrines in that work, but the section satirizing Spinoza is only mentioned (and Spinoza's name is not cited). Hume had said (with tongue in cheek) that he was going to show how the doctrine of the immateriality, simplicity, and indivisibility of a thinking substance is a true atheism. While I am sure Hume took great delight in such a statement, the review in the *Bibliothèque raisonnée* fails to

---

[4] Formey refers to a review of the *Essays* in a publication he cites as *Mélanges littéraires* (1756). He also mentions the German translation by Sulzer (*Essais philosophiques*, i, p. xvii).

[5] See John Leland, *A View of the Principal Deistical Writers that Have Appeared in England in the Last and Present Century* (2nd edn., 1755), ii, Letters I–IV.

mention that this claim, which the reviewer terms a 'singular paradox', occurs at the beginning of Hume's satire on Spinoza.[6]

One other feature unique to the *Treatise* which might have softened some of the critical reaction is the contrast between the youthful confidence of the main body of that work and the despair (feigned or real) expressed in the conclusion to Book I. Hume had tried to resolve the conflicting accounts offered by several philosophical systems on our knowledge of body, the nature of matter, and, most important of all for Hume, the analysis of personal identity. Causation and the formation of belief were exhaustively treated earlier, the first of these breaking sharply from traditional accounts. Having rejected all previous accounts on these various topics, revealing inconsistencies in them, Hume found that he was unable to construct replacement accounts for these concepts which would be accepted by the tribunal of reason. His system, he now realized, ends by replacing reason with the imagination (that magical faculty of the soul, as he termed it), and by custom, habit, and the association of ideas. Hume did believe he had discovered genuine

---

[6] For a discussion of this satire, see my *Thinking Matter* (Minneappolis, Minn.: University of Minnesota Press; Oxford: Basil Blackwell, 1984), ch. III. In this satire, Hume said that he was going to show that immaterialism is an atheism. Was this notion borrowed by Jacques-André Naigeon in his *Encyclopédie* entry 'Unitaires', where he lists as one of the claims of this sect: 'Que l'immatérialisme est un athéisme indirect'? One interesting peculiarity of the review of the *Treatise* in the 1740 *Bibliothèque raisonnée* is that it is in very large part a translation of Hume's *An Abstract of a Book Lately Published, Entituled, A Treatise of Human Nature* (1740). The similarity between the first dozen or so pages of the review and the *Abstract* are so startling that a copy of the *Abstract* must have been open before the reviewer as he wrote the review. Professor E. C. Mossner conjectured that the reviewer may have been Pierre Desmaizeaux: 'If so, it was also he who wrote the friendly puff in the *Bibliothèque raisonnée*, which, in the event, was to prove the only friendly one ever published' (*The Life of David Hume* (Oxford: Oxford University Press, 1954), 119). In light of the extensive use of the *Abstract* made by the reviewer of the *Treatise*, we might better say that Hume wrote the friendly puff in the *Bibliothèque raisonnée*. (I called attention to this curious feature of that review in 1979: see my 'Hume's *Abstract* in the *Bibliothèque raisonnée*', *Journal of the History of Ideas*, 40 (1979), 157–8. Jørn Schøsler is correct when he points out that the reviewer does add comments of his own, some rather critical, so the review is not only a translation of the *Abstract*. See Schøsler, *La Bibliothèque raisonnée (1728–1753)* (Odense: Odense University Press, 1985), 71–2 n. 14.) Mossner says that Desmaizeaux, who was 'the London correspondent' for the *Bibliothèque raisonnée*, was 'one of the few, except close personal friends' who knew Hume was the author of the *Treatise*. A notice in the *Bibliothèque raisonnée*, under 'News from London', in 1739 had given Hume as the author (14: 216). Did Desmaizeaux, if he was the reviewer, know that the *Abstract* was by Hume? A listing of new books in vol. 14 (Jan.–Mar. 1740), 436, of the *Bibliothèque britannique* credited George Turnbull as its author.

operating principles of human nature, but he was also aware, as he said at the beginning of part IV, section IV, that the faculty of the imagination included bad as well as good principles. It became important for Hume to 'distinguish in the imagination betwixt the principles which are permanent, irresistable, and universal . . . And the principles, which are changeable, weak, and irregular' (p. 225). The same faculty to which Hume appealed had, he was aware, produced the scholastic empty concepts of occult qualities. He re-affirmed this duality of the principles operating in that faculty when he wrote the Conclusion to this book: 'For if we assent to every trivial suggestion of the fancy; beside that these suggestions are often contrary to each other; they lead us into such errors, absurdities, and obscurities, that we must at last become asham'd of our credulity' (p. 267).

Hume had talked confidently about this distinction between the good, meaningful, and useful work of the imagination and the fanci-ful, frivolous products, but he really had provided no clear, rational criterion for identifying either. Thus, his despair and frustration with the realization that Book I of the *Treatise* was a sustained attack on reason (at least the reason used by philosophers) as a guide to truth: the choice left, he ruefully remarks, is 'betwixt a false reason and none at all' (p. 268). Total scepticism threatened to engulf him; he was strongly inclined to abandon all philosophy just when he was ready to begin the main part of the *Treatise*, a detailed description of the passions and how they relate to the self.

The reason I suggest that, had Formey been aware of the senti-ments expressed in Hume's Conclusion, he might have had a more sympathetic view of Hume's system, is, firstly, because this shows that Hume was genuinely trying to fight off the threatened scepticism and anti-rationality his system seemed to court, and secondly, because after all the despair, Hume reaffirmed his faith in philo-sophy and the search for general principles of human nature. True, Hume gave up on the traditional goals of metaphysics—to discover the essential features of nature, nature's secret springs and prin-ciples—but his faith in making progress in the science of man remains intact through his despair, even about his admittedly in-adequate account of the person (p. 273).[7] Hume's science of man,

---

[7] The significance of Hume's disappointment over his account of personal identity (see the Appendix to the *Treatise*, ed. Selby-Bigge, pp. 633–6) can be appreciated by comparing pp. 263–71 in the Conclusion to bk. I with the letter Hume wrote describ-

his account of the passions, is closer to Condillac's notion of a system than it is to those of writers such as Formey, Antoine-Martin Roche, or Gerdil. Hume participated in the renovation of philosophy and the nature of systems of philosophy that Condillac tried to foster by his concentrated attacks on the systems of Descartes, Malebranche, and Leibniz.

SYSTEMS AT WORK

L.-F. Ladvocat

There were any number of systems of philosophy or metaphysics published in the century, before and after Condillac's analysis of the very concept of 'a system'. Some of these are more or less textbooks for the student or interested reader, repeating the old doctrines, using the standard language. Some are worth little attention. An example of this type would be the work of an obscure man, Louis-François Ladvocat. The 'Privilege du Roi' to his *Nouveau Sistême de philosophie, établi sur la nature des choses* (1728) identifies him as 'Doyen des Maîtres ordinaires de notre Chambre des Comptes à Paris'. This work is an odd mixture of Aristotelian and scholastic doctrines, some use of Locke, and even some definitions from Spinoza, although Ladvocat (and those granting the Privilege and the Approbation) does not give any indication that he knows where these definitions came from. For example, the definition of attribute: 'J'entends par attribut, ce que l'entendement conçoit de sujet ou de la substance, comme constitutif de son essence' (i. 73–4). There are other examples of Spinoza's language here and there. Ladvocat also borrows Descartes's talk of formal and objective reality of ideas, without much understanding. What is of more interest is his explicit use of Locke's account of ideas of space and solidity (i. 33, 35, 73, 93, 251–63). Locke is characterized as 'un de nos meilleurs Philosophes, & des plus profonds' (i. 251).

Claude Mey's critique of Locke

A much more impressive but still fairly conservative system is that of Claude Mey, *Essai de métaphysique, ou Principes sur la nature et les opérations de l'esprit* (1756). I have already referred to Mey's role in

---

ing his own nervous disorder. See Letter no. 3 of Mar. or Apr. 1734, in *The Letters of David Hume*, ed. J. Y. T. Greig (Oxford: Oxford University Press, 1932), i.

'l'affaire de Prades' and his criticisms of Condillac. This work devotes an entire chapter to Locke's account of the will (ch. XII, pp. 293–317). Mey also gives a very clear exposition of Descartes's doubt (pp. 13 f.); he spends some time discussing Arnauld on true and false ideas, defending Malebranche against Arnauld (pp. 190– 212); and there are a number of references to Boursier's work on 'prémotion'. He confronts the suggestion that matter might be made to think, but he simply repeats the standard arguments against that possibility, arguments found in much of the British literature: e.g. if any bit of matter thinks, all matter must think; bodies are divisible, thought is not (pp. 37–47). Spinoza's doctrine that mind and body are not two different substances but two different modes of one substance is identified and dismissed as absurd and inconsistent: it makes that one substance both extended and non-extended (pp. 45– 6). Mey reads the system of Locke as holding to two substances but saying that we cannot be sure that the modifications of spiritual substance are 'really spiritual and different from corporeal' ones, because we lack an adequate idea of spiritual substance (p. 45). Locke's system is less absurd than Spinoza's because it does admit two substances; but in leaving open the possibility of thought being a property of corporeal substance, Locke fails to detect the contradiction that would result: a substance could both be extended and think (p. 47). Mey also has some brief comments on what he takes Locke to say, that we do not have an idea of substance (pp. 48–9).

By far the most interesting chapter in Mey's book is the one on the origin of ideas (ch. VII, pp. 159–89). There, he discusses the Port Royal logic, Malebranche, and Locke, as well as the earlier systems, which he characterizes as bizarre and ridiculous, of the Epicureans and the Peripatetics. The 'new philosophers' reject these systems and claim that all our ideas depend on the impressions of sense; the mind has no knowledge which does not come by that route. Mey recognizes that Locke does not base all knowledge and ideas on the senses; reflection is another source. However, as Mey reads Locke's account, the operation of reflection waits upon the senses to produce ideas. Even if reflection goes beyond the senses in giving us ideas of our mental operations, and even if it does produce some ideas of our own existence, it fails to yield any of what Mey terms 'spiritual ideas', nor does it give us any understanding of what we are (p. 167). In the final analysis, the principle of the sensory origin of ideas is simply false for Mey, since extended bodies are incapable of being the cause of ideas in a mind. We saw in Chapter 3 Mey's objections to the *tabula rasa* mind, that notion in effect denies the spiritual nature of the soul and presupposes causal influence of bodies on soul. Were it the case that conscious mental acts could be caused by physical influence, those mental events would not be part of the essence or nature of the soul, since at birth on the *tabula rasa* notion there is a soul without any mental contents or acts (p. 171). Mey inveighs at great length against the system of Locke on this point (pp. 171–4). Not only does Locke's *tabula rasa* soul deprive the soul of all 'les traits de grandeur qu'elles a dans sa nature', it overlooks the truth of original sin. Original sin, Mey assures his readers, is not just a feature passed on from Adam's crime, it is now part of man's nature, it is very real even in infants, and it can only be ameliorated by baptism (pp. 178–9).

Mey's *Essai de métaphysique* is a well-written, clearly argued presentation and criticism of several systems dealing with the nature of human knowledge and the workings of the mind. While he is partial to Malebranche, he gives an unusually penetrating account of Arnauld's system of ideas (pp. 192–212). His criticisms of Locke are perhaps more rooted in his own metaphysical concepts than are his expositions of Descartes and Arnauld. Locke's account of the various features of the understanding had implications for someone such as Mey which clashed with the accepted ontological and theological doctrines about the nature of the soul. Those doctrines are another example of the abstract *systems* attacked by Condillac, but what is significant about Mey is his ability to understand and to present, with minimal influence from his own views, doctrines which in the end he rejects. His is a work well worth study.

Caspar Cuenz's fifty-five articles

In the same year that Condillac's *Traité des systêmes* appeared (1749), a writer much less impressive than Claude Mey, a man we have met before in this story, Caspar Cuenz, published an outline of what he claimed again was a 'nouveau systême', a system which he argues escapes Condillac's censure of abstract systems of thought. In the November 1749 issue of the *Journal helvétique*, Cuenz characterizes Condillac as a 'Grand Partisan de *Locke*, Emulateur de la gloire de cet Illustre Philosophe' (p. 349).[8] Cuenz claims that his new

[8] 'Lettre de l'auteur de précis d'un sistême touchant la formation, la propagation & la nature de l'etre humaine', *Journal helvétique* (Nov. 1749), 349–72.

system contains neither abstract principles nor hypotheses. His outline consists of fifty-five articles, all of which he insists are consistent with what 'revelation teaches about our state in the next world' (p. 350).

Cuenz's fifty-five articles are, as one might expect, a compendium of that system which was embedded in his 1742 rambling four-volume defence of Locke against the charge of materialism. Locke is only mentioned once in this outline (along with Cudworth, Grew, Addison as defenders of the chain of being), but Cuenz refers to his earlier work several times. What is fascinating in his outline, and in the brief commentary that follows the fifty-five articles, is that he saw no incompatibility between his notion of the soul as a machine and traditional Christian doctrine. In the outline, he describes the human being in the womb (the foetus) as 'une petite Machine, invisible & impalpable' (p. 357, art. XXXIX). Adam and Eve, and all humans thereafter, were composed of two organized machines: one is a visible, palpable, and perishable body, the other is a little invisible, impalpable, and indestructible machine 'placed in the Corpus Callosum' (p. 359, art. XLIX). Both these machines are animated by a principle of life, vegetative in the body, sensitive in the little machine in the brain. The personality and moral character of humans are conserved in the insensible and indestructible machine (art. LIII).

Cuenz reaffirms his belief that his new system should put to rest all those interminable disputes between what he calls here 'les trois Sistêmes des Immaterialistes' (i.e. physical influence, occasionalism, and pre-established harmony), all of which assume the immateriality and non-extension of immaterial beings (p. 364). He even believes his new system ought to convince free thinkers and Pyrrhonians of the errors of their thinking. Of even greater interest is Cuenz's appeal to the physiological work of La Peyronie. He draws the very inference from that experimental work that so many feared: that the soul really is located in the brain. He takes La Peyronie's 'siege' literally, but by making the soul an invisible, impalpable machine located in the *corpus callosum*, Cuenz thought he could have materialism and immortality too. He did not, of course, think he was advocating materialism, since one of the two machines composing humans was, on his account, invisible and impalpable! His readers could see nothing but materialism in that odd notion, if they could indeed make any sense of it at all.

Sinsart and Denesle

In referring to those materialists who say man is composed of two machines, Sinsart clearly had Cuenz in mind (*Recueil de pensées diverses sur l'immatérialité de l'âme* (1756), 137). Early in this work, Sinsart refers to Locke's suggestion about matter thinking, adding that 'a hundred voices have been raised assuring us that the soul is only organized matter' (p. 2). His objections to this claim are, for the most part, the usual ones so often employed in the British debate. However, there are several considerations advanced by Sinsart which move beyond those naïve reactions. In one passage, he presents an argument from experience, our experience of being aware of our sensations and feelings, our thoughts and volitions. What we are not aware of are the dispositions or motions of our brain (p. 49). Sinsart thinks this fact about awareness rules out the brain as the cause of thought and feeling, which of course it does not; but he was close to suggesting that there is at least a phenomenal difference between what we are aware of and what the physiologists say occurs in nerves and brain. He recognized the close correlation between brain states and thoughts (pp. 106–9); what he resisted was the attempts to identify the latter with the former. The seeing of light or colour is not motion in the optic nerve. What occurs in sense organs and nerves is only motion; the body does not see nor does the physiology will or decide to walk (p. 117).

There is much discussion of Locke's suggestion in Sinsart's book. He admits that Locke did not accept his own suggestion, did not, that is, believe that God had added thought to organized matter. It has been his followers, more daring than Locke, who have loudly proclaimed that the soul was material (p. 191). For Sinsart, the very suggestion was 'revolting'. Sometimes, he seems to think that suggestion was that any bit of matter, even a rock, could be made to think. At other times he does use the phrase 'organized matter'. He was convinced that there is an essential repugnance (an incompatibility) between thought and matter such that not even God could make matter think (pp. 189–91). Like many opponents of Locke in Britain, Sinsart feared that this suggestion would or even already had led to immorality, supporting the free thinkers and libertines (pp. 369–70).

The two-volume work of Denesle, *Examen du matérialisme, relativement à la métaphysique* (1754), says that 'le système de la matière pensante révolte la raison et choque le sens commun'

(i. 324). Denesle says that young men easily fall prey to materialism. As Sinsart had done, so Denesle distinguishes the motion of our body from the sensations we feel (i. 3–4). The physiological mechanism is only the occasional cause of our experience of seeing. To say that a dead body no longer feels is misleading since it never felt (i. 6). There is much discussion in this book of Leibniz's pre-established harmony system, whose denial of any connection between soul and body seemed to Denesle to make matter too independent of mind, active on its own. Just how his own following of occasionalism avoids this danger is never made clear.[9] What Denesle's study indicates again is the extent to which the British vocabulary around thinking matter had spread. Locke is not mentioned by Denesle but it is difficult not to hear echoes of the British debate in what he says. Spinoza also appears, representing the one-substance evil that must be avoided.

Tiphaigne de la Roche's examination of Locke's suggestion

Another more interesting work confronts Locke directly: Charles-François Tiphaigne de la Roche's 'Essai sur la nature de l'âme, ou Examen de cette célèbre proposition de M. Locke' (1759).[10] As Antoine-Martin Roche had done, so Tiphaigne speaks of Locke and his 'school'. He identifies two different groups: those who say man is a composite of mind and body and those who say man is a pure machine, but 'une machine pensante' (i. 119–20). He refers to the 'doubts of Locke and his school' about the nature of substance. The second view about man says that since God is able to create a mind and then to unite it to a body, he is also able to give to matter arranged as he judges suitable 'la faculté d'appercevoir et de penser' (i. 123). He insists that, although the doubts about man's nature seem reasonable, and the suggestion of these writers seems mild and intriguing, this doubt is in fact dangerous and leads to 'un état violent' (i. 126). The immortality of the soul is of great importance, but if it is material, it cannot be immortal. Tiphaigne is not interested in what God is *able* to do, but only in what he *has* willed (i. 128).

[9] W. H. Barber (*Leibniz in France, from Arnauld to Voltaire* (Oxford: Oxford University Press, 1955), 161, 167) thinks it doubtful that Denesle had ever read Leibniz; he probably picked up his knowledge of Leibniz from Fontenelle's 'Eloge' of Leibniz delivered before the Académie des sciences in 1717. For a review of Denesle's book, see *Journal de Trévoux* (Dec. 1754).

[10] This work is in Tiphaigne's *Bigarrures philosophiques* (2 vols., 1759), in i. 114–244, and ii. 207–94 (consecutive paging).

Chapter IV of this work argues that, if matter thinks, motion necessarily accompanies thought, since motion is the way matter changes and operates. He points out that, for Locke and almost everyone else, thinking is a form of acting; thus, if it is matter which thinks and perceives, that activity must be motion. Tiphaigne does not seem to allow, on Locke's suggestion, two different kinds of action by the brain. 'Supposons un amas de matiere arrangée de la maniere que Dieu le juge à propos pour qu'elle pense; toute l'école de M. Locke nous assure que jamais cet amas n'aura de pensées, si les objets ne viennent à agir sur les organes dont il est pourvu' (i. 132). It is of course one claim to say that, without stimuli on sense organs, perceptions will not occur, but quite another to say the motion of nerves stimulated by the external object *is* thought. Tiphaigne is correct when he says (ch. V) that the motion that must accompany thought, if matter thinks, can only be an internal motion of the nerve fibres. The same would be true for occasionalism and pre-established harmony: there is a correlation between physiological and mental events for all three of the systems of the relation between mind and body. Tiphaigne is not very clear about the difference between thought *being* motion of nerves and thought being *accompanied by* such motion, but he does make an important point about the physiological events being of the same kind, whether it be in optic, auditory, or other nerves. The senses, he says, are instruments which advertise what is going on outside the body (i. 137). The motion which is set up by sight is different from the motion set up by hearing, and the same for other sense modalities. Thus, he argues, these motions must act on different parts of the thinking matter (i.e. the brain), since we often see, hear, and touch at the same time. The question then is: 'how can that matter deal with all the different motions hitting it at the same time?' (i. 140) Even with one sense modality, e.g. sight, the motion related to our seeing a circle is presumably different from the motion related to our seeing a triangle (i. 144). The answer to Tiphaigne's question is just as important for occasionalists as for those who defend physical influence. There is a hint at this point in his text that he may have some understanding of this point, since he employs the language of 'occasion' in his examples. Nevertheless, the question has not been answered.

Tiphaigne de la Roche accepts some sort of corpuscular account of matter, insisting that the elements, the atoms, can neither move nor think (i. 155–6). Chapter VIII draws the general conclusion that

no body, no bit of matter, whether 'brut' or 'organique' is able
to think (i. 166). Nor can two atoms which are unable to think
constitute through their union a whole which can think. This same
argument appears in part II, in volume ii of his *Bigarrures philosophiques*. Chapter II of that part carries the title, 'Examen de
quelques pensées de M. Locke' (ii. 220–64). The Locke–Stillingfleet
exchange over thinking matter is discussed (ii. 226–32), quoting
passages from Locke's reply. He falls back on the familiar argument
that God cannot make matter think because it is not in the nature
of matter to have such a property; God would have to change the
nature of matter. The two substances, mind and matter, are *essentially* different. To suggest, as Locke did in replying to Stillingfleet,
that either substance could have the property of thought because
both are substances waiting for God to give them some properties
would be like saying 'qu'un morceau de glace peut, aussi bien qu'un
fer rouge, avoir la puissance de brûler, parce que l'un & l'autre sont
également corps' (ii. 235). Tiphaigne de la Roche does recognize
here that Locke assumes that body and mind are the same with
respect to being *substances*, that their differences lie in their properties (ii. 240). Thus, Locke is able to assume that solidity is
compatible with the faculty of thought, but that is just what Locke
has to prove (ii. 245).

Just as some writers were disturbed at what they took to be
Condillac's and Locke's account of the soul—that it enters this world
without content or faculties—so Tiphaigne de la Roche, and many in
the British debate over Locke's suggestion, rejected the notion of a
substance without any properties. A *bare* substance, a substance
which has neither extension nor thought in the beginning, was not a
concept that was intelligible. The scenario that Locke presented to
Stillingfleet did use such a notion of a bare substance for one of the
substances, but the second substance was created already having
extension and solidity: motion was added later by God. The other
substance in Locke's scenario was just said to be an immaterial
substance without any qualities, or none that Locke mentions. The
decision for God in this scenario was: to which of these substances
should he add the property of thought? Of course, the two examples
are not parallel, since the one substance created by God already has
two properties, the other one has apparently no qualities at all,
except perhaps the odd quality of being a substance. It is easier to
think of thought being added to a bare substance than it is to think of

it being added to a substance with the properties of extension and solidity. Locke seems to have thought that his Creation scenario presented real options for God. But with one of the two substances already defined in the familiar terms of material substances, most readers saw Locke's options as going against the nature of material substance, were God to add thought to it as another property. Tiphaigne's reactions to Locke's suggestion are thus familiar from the British debate; he makes some of the same criticisms against that suggestion. He also spends time discussing Voltaire, saying that Voltaire developed these notions of Locke (ii. 265 ff.).

Berkeley's system

Bishop Berkeley is not a central figure in our story, although he was well known to the French reading public through journal reviews, articles, notices, and in translation.[11] One of Berkeley's books *is* related to our story because of the extended review and critical comments in an issue of the *Bibliothèque raisonnée*: *Siris*. The review is of the French translation of 1745, *Recherches sur les vertus de l'eau de goudron, où l'on a joint des Réflexions philosophiques sur divers autres sujets importans*.[12] This mysterious, mystical, almost hermetic work of Berkeley was mainly known in Britain for its recommendation of tar-water as a cure for all ills. That aspect of that work was ridiculed and attacked repeatedly in Britain. The reviewer of this French translation fairly summarizes Berkeley's account of the making and use of tar-water, but he goes on to present and reject

[11] e.g. the *Analyst* is listed in *Bibliothèque raisonnée*, 12 (1734), 476, and reviewed in 14 (1735), 400–30; listed and reviewed in *Bibliothèque britannique*, 3 (July–Sept. 1734), 457; the *Querist* is listed and described in *Bibliothèque raisonnée*, 44 (1750), 477; the *Defence of Free-Thinking in Mathematics* is listed in both journals (*Bibliothèque raisonnée*, 14 (1735), 469; *Bibliothèque britannique*, 5 (1735), 412); and his *Discourse Addressed to the Magistrates* is trans. and repr. as 'New Method of Refuting Libertines' in *Bibliothèque britannique*, 11 (1738), 308–47. His *Alciphron*, *Three Dialogues between Hylas and Philonous*, and *Siris* were all translated shortly after the English edns. appeared.

[12] *Bibliothèque raisonnée*, 35 (1745), 36–77. This book was also listed and given a paragraph description in the 'New Literature' section in 33 (July–Sept. 1744), 236–7. Another review appeared in the same year in the *Bibliothèque françoise*, 41: 16–27. The relevance to our study of this translation would be increased if the tantalizing suggestion were true that the translator was David R. Boullier. Geoffrey Keynes reports Jessop's discovering of the catalogue in the Surgeon-General's Library in Washington, DC, attributing the translation to Boullier. I have not found any other support for such an attribution. See Keynes's *Bibliography of George Berkeley, Bishop of Cloyne: His Works and His Critics in the Eighteenth Century* (Oxford: Oxford University Press, 1976), no. 73.

in some detail the metaphysical system, the 'Réflexions philosophiques' contained in that work.

The reviewer notes the many topics discussed by Berkeley, from science to metaphysic, commenting that some of the science is founded on facts, but the metaphysic is pure conjecture. Even with science, Berkeley rejects Newton's space and attractive forces. In Berkeley's system, bodies do not have any force, or any internal principle of motion. 'All natural phenomena which we see are the immediate effect of God's action, according to general laws. It is only minds [esprits] which are the true agents, true principles of action' (*Bibliothèque raisonnée*, 35 (1745), 46). Minds or spirits are the only substances in this system, the corporeal world has no absolute existence: that world is regarded only as a group of appearances which are regulated and ordered by God. The motion of bodies 'is merely an image and shadow of the power that resides in spirits' (p. 47). The reviewer identifies the summary as 'l'idée générale qu'on peut se former de son Systême', a system some of whose features are 'revolting', others of which pose enormous problems. The reviewer even suggests that some aspects of this system may scandalize theologians.

The summary of Berkeley's system up to this point contains nothing radical or unusual except the part about physical events being appearances. There were many theologians and even scientists who accepted the passivity of matter and who identified God as the only active cause. The rejection of material substance, the inclusion in his system of only one kind of substance was worrisome for the reviewer (in the end, he labels Berkeley an 'egoïste'), but what he found most disturbing was Berkeley's strange notion of fire or light as the vehicle for spirit. Berkeley speaks of the fire from the sun, of light, and aether as the active agents in the universe. More precisely, *soul* is the active agent, fire or light is its 'envelope'. What this envelope encloses is the World Soul. The human soul in action is a pale copy of that World Soul, the animal spirits playing the role of the vehicle of our soul.

Besides the implication that God is the cause of evil, since he is the cause of all, the reviewer argues that, even with respect to man, the human soul cannot be the only cause of bodily motion. Experience shows us, he says, that soul does act on body, but it also shows that our body affects our thoughts and feelings (p. 54). There is 'in the machine of the body, an active force, a moving force which is not the immediate effect of an immaterial Being' (p. 54). He cites as examples the bodily functions of digestion, the circulation of the blood, the beating of the heart, etc.

Si l'Ame, aidée du *Véhicule* qu'on lui donne ici pour *Envelope*, est le seul *Agent*, la seule *Cause efficiente* de tout ce qui se passe dans notre Corps, elle est donc aussi la cause de toutes les maladies qui viennent d'un principe interne, & elle devient son propre Boureau en détruisant son Tabernacle. (p. 55)

The reviewer is clearly on the side of physical influence, but it is not just his difference over which of the three systems of mind and body to accept which forms his objection against Berkeley: it is that odd notion of animal spirits for man and fire for God being the vehicle of the soul which the reviewer finds most objectionable. It seems to be the term 'envelope' that bothers him; he takes it more or less literally, as if the soul is enclosed in a sack. Had Berkeley talked more of the animal spirits being the means whereby the soul can act on the body and on external objects by moving its limbs, he might have been seen as following a more or less standard account. The difficulty comes when he tries to unite soul and animal spirits, leading the reviewer to ridicule the notion that the soul moves through the body, as physiologists said the animal spirits do. The reviewer does not at this point call attention to Berkeley's claim that all bodily phenomena are just appearances of the infinite soul, thereby rendering all talk of soul operating on its body out of order. The reviewer fails to see how 'encasing' the soul in animal spirits enables it to act on corporeal phenomena (if, indeed, that action even makes sense on Berkeley's system) any more than acting on its own. What the reviewer misses, I think, is that the 'envelope' or 'vehicle' was Berkeley's way of relating mental and physical, mind and body, or, ultimately, God and the world. Underlying Berkeley's doctrine is the familiar assumption that action of spirit or soul on bodies, and action of God on the world, require proximity of actor and that which is acted on, an assumption found throughout British literature on perception: 'no thing can be or act where it is not'.[13]

The only other way to account for the action of spirit or soul on matter is, the reviewer suggests, to follow Cuenz's assertion that all

[13] This formulation can be found in many books and pamphlets. As an example, see Clarke's formulation in his exchange with Leibniz, *A Collection of Papers, Which Passed between the Late Learned Mr. Leibnitz, and Dr. Clarke* (1717), Clarke's Second Reply, para. 4.

beings are extended, that the notion of an unextended being makes no sense. In a clear and succinct summary of Cuenz's *Essai d'un sisteme nouveau* (1742), the reviewer remarks that Cuenz (he calls him 'Quenz') claims that the notion of an unextended spirit is a fiction or a being of reason. Cuenz's talk of the soul residing in an invisible, impalpable, and indivisible body, and his talk of the power of the soul resulting 'du Souffle Divin', is very similar to Berkeley's account in this book (p. 61). The reviewer thinks Cuenz's system is in some ways better than Berkeley's, but it too has great difficulties (pp. 61–2). The reviewer thinks our knowledge is too limited to enable us to discover how a thinking being acts on bodies, but he can find no reason for saying God needs a vehicle or instrument to enable him to create the world and act on it (p. 62). Since we know so little about the nature of our soul, it is rather silly to give it an envelope in order for it to act.

The reviewer is suspicious of any system which offers to explain all events by one central concept, such as Berkeley's ethereal fire (pp. 63–5). The suggestion that all the elements of bodies came originally from fire goes against the known facts, which show us that one element cannot change into another (pp. 66–9). The work of Boerhaave and other scientists is cited to refute that aspect of Berkeley's account. The reviewer also defends pure space against Berkeley's rejection of it, his defence resting upon the claim that he has an idea of space distinct from bodies that are in space (p. 71). He accepts a notion of space that Berkeley rejects, the notion of space as an area (or even as a substance) into which bodies can be placed. He reads Berkeley's rejection of absolute space as saying that bodies 'have no other place or location than in the soul or mind'. Berkeley makes a cryptic remark about Plotinus, that the soul is not in the world, but the world is in the soul, adding that the soul is in the mind and the body is in the soul.[14] The reviewer takes this to be Berkeley's own view, a view which the reviewer characterizes as 'un jargon inintelligible' (p. 73). Berkeley is accordingly pronounced 'un Egoïste', the name given to certain philosophers who deny the existence of bodies and the reality of such phenomena as attraction and repulsion. The usual claim about Berkeley then follows: 'Suivant cette Hypothèse, il n'y a proprement ni Ciel, ni Terre, aucune Substance corporelle, & le Monde sensible que nous voyons, est

---

[14] For this notion in Plotinus, see Emilsson's study, *Plotinus on Sense-Perception* (Cambridge: Cambridge University Press, 1988).

un Monde imaginaire, il n'y en a point d'autre que l'intellectuel'
(p. 74).

CONCLUSION

In the review of Condillac's *Traité des systêmes* in the *Bibliothèque
raisonnée* (44 (1750), 122–48), the reviewer expresses his belief
that if Condillac is successful in showing the futility and abuses of
abstract systems, he may be able to bring peace to the society of
learned men. The reviewer thinks that all that has resulted from the
quantity of abstract, speculative systems of thought has been hatred,
division, and persecution (p. 123).

Ces beaux Systêmes ont-ils rendu les hommes plus éclairés? Point du tout; ils
n'ont répandu par-tout que ténébres & obscurités. Ont-ils corrigé leurs
mœurs; les ont-ils rendus plus doux, plus humains, plus charitables, plus
bienfaisans? Vous le savez, Lecteur. (p. 123)

The implied answer to all these rhetorical questions is a firm 'no'.
The reviewer agrees with Condillac's stress on the senses as the
origin of knowledge; thus, the further removed abstract principles
are from ordinary experience, the more useless and unreliable they
become. It is easy to be misled by words, to believe some system
produces real knowledge when all it does is play with words, words
which have very little meaning, as Locke has shown (pp. 128–9).
   One of the most striking abuses of abstract systems, the reviewer
agrees with Condillac, is the prejudice of innate ideas (p. 132). The
attack mounted by Condillac against the Cartesian dictum that whatever is included in a clear and distinct idea can be affirmed as true is
outlined in the review. Condillac's attack on the void is also mentioned (pp. 132–3). Any system not based on finding the origin of
ideas and knowledge in the senses is liable to these errors. Ideas are
only sensations, so we can easily discover their content. A system
that relies on innate ideas already starts from vagueness, making it
difficult to reach a clear understanding of those ideas (p. 134).
Condillac even finds Malebranche's account of ideas unclear, comparing him unfavourably with Locke: Locke does not have the defects that Malebranche has, Locke correctly identifies the origin of
knowledge, but he does not provide as many details as we would like.
   The reviewer concedes that there are defects in Malebranche's
system, defects that stem from his theology. 'Il est d'ailleurs bien

difficile, pour ne pas dire impossible, de concilier la Théologie avec la Philosophie' (p. 137 n. *a*). Malebranche accepts all the doctrines of the Church without examination: grace, Trinity, conception, incarnation, etc. In contrast, Locke submits faith to reason; the principles he needs for his religion are few and simple. He makes Christianity a *reasonable* religion. Malebranche determines the nature of the soul through his religious faith, Locke looks to reason and concludes that he does not know the nature of the soul, even saying, 'peut-être n'est-ce que matière' (ibid.). The reviewer does not take sides on this feature of the two philosophers, leaving it to the reader to choose, adding the remark: 'Il en est des opinions comme des ragoûts, elles ne sauroient également plaire à tout le monde.'

The reviewer does take issue with Condillac's claim that Locke had discovered the origin of knowledge, invoking Gravesande's authority in saying that the obscurity around the origin of ideas has not yet been entirely dissipated. To Condillac's remark that details are lacking in Locke's account, the reviewer disagrees, pointing out that Locke himself thought the subject might be covered in a few sheets but found to his dismay that a very long book resulted (p. 138 n. *a*). That Locke benefited from Malebranche's earlier account is true, even though Locke does not acknowledge it, a feature, the reviewer suggests, of 'Haine nationale' (p. 138 n. *b*). An even more negative remark occurs in another note added by the reviewer where he says that, as regards innate ideas, Locke 'n'a rien prouvé, & que toute la question reste encore indécise, du moins à l'égard de l'Homme' (p. 139 n. *a*).

Schøsler sees these comments by the reviewer as indicating a change in the attitude of the journalists of the *Bibliothèque raisonnée* towards Locke. That may be true, although some of the comments in these notes are a bit equivocal. What is useful for us to note is the role given to Locke by Condillac and the reviewer in this wider topic of the nature and value of systems. Condillac saw Locke as attacking many of the standard metaphysical concepts, attempting to base his account of man and his understanding on a careful attention to his own experience. Condillac also cautions, as did Locke, against the use of hypotheses in science; hypotheses not firmly rooted in experience are as bad as the reliance on abstract principles in metaphysics. A descriptive anatomy of the soul, of its actions, abilities, limits, as Hume had also insisted, was replacing the metaphysics of traditional systems. If, on this review of Condillac, the journalists were ambivalent or openly critical of these features in Locke, as Schøsler suggests, they were not as unsympathetic towards Locke's insistence on the limitations of knowledge as most of the other reviews involving Locke were. Malebranche *had* come back into favour, but whether this was because, by 1750, the system of physical influence had run its course, had been replaced by occasionalism, or because of the theological aspects of Malebranche's systematic treatises, cannot be determined. There *may* be a connection between the programme of founding the science of man on experience and observation, and the system of physical influence; our own experience seems to convince us that by taking thought we can move our arms, shoot arrows from bows, greet friends. Experience also seems to make it difficult to deny all influence of physical objects on awareness.

Malebranche, and most orthodox writers, began their accounts with basic principles, e.g. that material and immaterial substances cannot interact, that what we know must be near or present to the mind (this latter principle clearly confirming Condillac's remark about the ambiguity of the words in such systems). Leibniz had his own set of principles (e.g. sufficient reason, indiscernibles, the best), but the dominant factor behind his pre-established harmony theory was the concept of individuals or particulars, the fully formed particular, whether material or immaterial, that unfolds internally, interacting with other particulars only cognitively by correspondence and representation. All such systems, Condillac says, seek to *explain* phenomena, with little concern about deriving principles from experience. As d'Alembert, paraphrasing Condillac (and borrowing from the review), remarks in his *Encyclopédie* (1751–65) entry, 'Système (métaphysique)': 'If the suppositions do not appear to be impossible, and if they furnish some explanation of known phenomena, philosophers think they have discovered the true forces or springs of nature'. D'Alembert explicitly summarizes the main points of Condillac's *Traité*, indicating his agreement with Condillac's rejection of the abstract systems of Descartes, Malebranche, Spinoza, Leibniz, and Boursier. He repeats the four main features of Condillac's account: that abstract systems usually end with empty words, that appeal to innate ideas must be rejected, that hypotheses should be used sparingly and only when they are carefully based on experience and observation, and that the best principles are facts. As Condillac did, so d'Alembert fits Locke easily into the rejection of systems; Locke, they saw, accepted all four of these 'principles' about systems. Locke represented attitudes that were systematically articulated and developed by Condillac, and then became embodied in much of the programme of the *Encyclopédie*, certainly as conceived by d'Alembert and Diderot.[15]

[15] I have no reason to believe d'Alembert was not working directly from Condillac's *Traité*, but his entry follows closely the review in the *Bibliothèque raisonnée*. Of course, book reviews in the journals then were usually excerpts, whether placed in quotation marks or not, from the books being reviewed. The points from Condillac selected by the reviewer and by d'Alembert are almost identical. The language is that of Condillac in both cases. One example from Condillac that appears in the review and in d'Alembert's entry is this curious remark: 'Mais il ressemble, comme le remarque *Locke* en pareil cas, à des hommes qui sans argent & sans connoissance des especes courantes compteroient de grosses sommes avec des jettons, qu'il appelleroient louis, livre, écu. Quelques calculs qu'il fissent, leurs sommes ne seroient jamais que des jettons: quelque raisonnement que fasse un Philosophe, tel que celui dont je parle, ses conclusions ne seront jamais que des mots' (*Traité des systêmes*, p. 36). The version in the review and in d'Alembert's entry of this remark is shortened a bit. (See *Bibliothèque raisonnée*, 44 (1750), 129, and *Encyclopédie*, xvi. 777b–778a.)

7

Journal Presentations

THE Republic of Letters was well served by reviews and discussions in journals of the books and pamphlets that came off the presses in the eighteenth century. Especially useful were those French-language journals which played a role in transmitting the British thinking-matter debate to European readers. Most of these journals were published in Holland, the one exception being the *Journal helvétique* in Switzerland. Jean Le Clerc's three journals covered the period from 1686 to 1727: *Bibliothèque universelle et historique* (1686–93), *Bibliothèque choisie* (1703–18), and *Bibliothèque ancienne et moderne* (1714–30). The *Bibliothèque raisonnée* (1728–53) and the *Bibliothèque britannique* (1733–47) are the most important for our study since their coverage of the books in the British debate is more comprehensive than Le Clerc's. The Swiss *Journal helvétique* is mainly useful for its articles on the three systems of mind and body. A few other journals have been used in the previous chapters where they carried some material relevant to specific issues: e.g. the *Journal des sçavans, Journal of Trévoux, Bibliothèque françoise*.

The *Bibliothèque britannique*'s subtitle indicates its British orientation: 'Histoire des ouvrages des savans de la Grande-Bretagne'. That journal was the successor to the *Bibliothèque angloise* (1717–28), which had the same purpose. The *Bibliothèque britannique* is better for our purposes than the *Bibliothèque angloise*, for, besides covering new books published in England, Scotland, and Ireland, the *Bibliothèque britannique* indicates in its 'Avertissement' that its editors will call attention to and present for its readers 'disputes on matters of religion or philosophy', precisely the areas relevant to the topics of this study. The rationale for concentrating on England was, the 'Avertissement' says, because that country, more than any other, 'is rich in works remarkable for their novelty, their singularity, or the strength of feeling', character-istics which result from the liberty that prevails in that country and the appeals made to the 'tribunal of reason'. Moreover,

les Anglois ont fait dans la plus sublime Metaphysique & dans la plus
profonde Theologie, des progrès qui sont aussi peu connus de la plûpart des
autres Nations de l'Europe, que les découvertes faites dans les Arts & les
Sciences, ici & ailleurs, sont connuës au delà des Pyrenées.

The *Bibliothèque raisonnée*'s scope is much larger: 'des ouvrages
des savans de l'Europe', but its coverage of the British debate over
thinking matter is extensive. Of even greater importance is the way in
which that debate is located in the context of European (mainly,
French) books on the topics of mind and matter, the nature of the
soul, the developing discoveries and theories in physiology, and our
perceptual knowledge of objects. It too gave credit to the attention
given in England to theology and religion:

En *Angleterre*, toutes les Professions se mêlent de Théologie, & sur un
Ouvrage de Belles Lettres, de Medecine, de Politique, de Mathématique, ou
de Philosophie, vous y en verrez vingt autres dont la Religion fera le sujet. (1
(1733), ix–x)

I indicated in my Introduction that Jørn Schøsler has given us a
detailed account of the treatment of Locke in the *Bibliothèque
raisonnée* (in his work of the same title), as found in its various
reviews of books using or attacking Locke's doctrines. In this
chapter, I want to give a similar survey of both the *Bibliothèque
britannique* and the *Bibliothèque raisonnée*. There will inevitably be
some overlap with Schøsler's analysis with respect to the *Bibliothèque raisonnée*, but my survey will have a narrower focus, singling
out for special attention some of the main books in the British debate
over thinking matter. As Schøsler's study makes abundantly clear,
the presence of a variety of Locke's doctrines in the reviews and
comments in the *Bibliothèque raisonnée* is striking throughout the
entire run of that journal. In both journals, there are also a number of
books reviewed which may not directly relate to Locke's suggestion,
but which illustrate, through European books, some of those themes
found in the British debate. Some of this latter sort of books help us
place Locke's doctrines in the ongoing discussions in the larger
Republic of Letters.

I shall organize my discussion of both journals around two main
topics: (1) books dealing with the nature of the soul and its relations
to the body, and (2) various medical books analysing the physiology
of the body, especially as that physiology relates to the correspondence between particular physiological events and mental processes

or states. In each of these groupings, there are some reviews which are of special significance for the topics discussed or for the length of the review.

MIND AND BODY: *BIBLIOTHÈQUE BRITANNIQUE*

In the April–June issue of 1734 (3: 39–75), the second edition of Peter Browne's *The Procedure, Extent and Limits of Human Understanding* (1728) is reviewed along with the second edition of his *Things Divine and Supernatural: Conceived by Analogy with Things Natural and Human* (1733).[1] As there was in Browne's *Procedure*, so in this review there are many references to and discussions of Locke. Molyneux's sending Locke a copy of Toland's *Christianity Not Mysterious* is mentioned on pp. 41–2, Browne's criticism of Locke's broad use of the term 'idea' is discussed on pp. 46–8 (the reviewer says that most logicians agree with Locke's definition as 'that which is present to the mind when it thinks'), and Browne's objections against Locke's ideas of reflection are cited on pp. 50–1. Browne's discussion of Locke's suggestion about thinking matter is mentioned and briefly discussed on pp. 55–6; the reviewer remarks that Browne 'se met dans une grande colére contre Mr. Locke' on this topic. Browne's rejection of Locke's account of abstraction is briefly cited on pp. 58–9.

In the July–September issue for the same year, there is a long 'Eloge de Mr. Samuel Clarke', with rather detailed analyses of Clarke's career and all of his publications (3: 414–51). Clarke's exchange with Anthony Collins over Dodwell's defence of the natural mortality of the soul is discussed on pp. 420–1. Collins had referred to Locke's suggestion, agreeing that our knowledge does not enable us to reject the possibility that the soul may not be immaterial.

Two other authors who were prominent in the British debate, Samuel Colliber and Andrew Baxter, are given long reviews in issues of the *Bibliothèque britannique*. Colliber's *Free Thoughts concerning Souls* (1734) is listed in 2, issue for Jan.–Mar. 1734, with a summary of its contents (pp. 463–4). This work was a set of four interrelated essays on the nature of the human soul, its comparison

[1] The review is carried over to 4 (Oct.–Dec. 1734), 1–19, where the review of the *Analogy* appears.

with the souls of brutes, the supposed pre-existence of souls, and their future state. A fifth essay on creation is added at the end. Colliber also published an earlier book, *An Impartial Enquiry into the Existence and Nature of God* (1718) which contains an appendix on space and duration. *Free Thoughts* is reviewed in two volumes, 4 (1735), 275–98, and 5 (1735), 129–49. Colliber attacks materialism by arguing that no single particle of matter could have the property of thought, nor could any organized combination of material particles (or of animal spirits) give rise to thought. Both of these suggestions had been taken as the consequence of Locke's talk of matter thinking. The reviewer in volume 4 identifies 'nos Matérialistes modernes' with this latter view (p. 279). He notes that Colliber says that experience shows us that the soul is 'affected or wrought upon by the Matter of its Body'.[2] The soul knows matter 'not by penetrating its Substance, . . . but by receiving its Impressions'.[3] Since the soul can be affected by the body and also act on its body, it must have something of the nature of both soul and body: it is, Colliber argues, a 'Being of a Middle Nature between the Nature of its Body and that of the Deity'.[4] The reviewer finds this conclusion 'extraordinary' if not contradictory (p. 282). Colliber quotes Locke's *Essay*, 2. 23. 28, for support.

> Hence may be conjectured, that created Spirits are not totally separate from Matter, because they are both active and passive. Pure Spirit, *viz.* God, is only active; pure Matter is only passive; those Beings that are both active and passive we may judge to partake of both.[5]

Colliber omitted the opening phrase about conjecturing. The reviewer finds it difficult to conceive a simple substance, which the soul is supposed to be, that could share the nature of both material and immaterial properties: 'We have', he says, 'no idea of that kind of substance'.

Colliber also argued that we can have a knowledge of bodies even without our normal sense organs, or when the link with the earthly body is very tenuous. This claim, which he develops in his fourth essay, is based on his notion that the *soul*, not the sense organs, sees and hears. In this life, seeing and hearing are dependent on sensing,

---

[2] Colliber, *Free Thoughts*, p. 29.   [3] Ibid.   [4] Ibid. 22.
[5] The reviewer replaced the English citation from Locke with the French translation in the 1729 edn., the 2nd rev. edn. of Coste's earlier translation of the *Essay*. The quotation can be found on p. 329 of that edn.

but he constructs a model where all the sensory fibres have been severed from their connection in the brain. So long as the 'Spirits in the Brain are still affected or wrought upon in the usual manner, the Soul, whose seat is among those Spirits, might still have the same Sensations' (Colliber, *Free Thoughts*, p. 87). Moreover,

if the grosser Substance even of the Brain itself were dissolv'd, yet if the Spirits, or any other Subtile Particles were still capable of being wrought upon by Objects and of affecting the Soul as usual, the Soul tho' separate from the Body, might, by their means, be capable of its usual Sensations. (ibid.)

The reviewer finds these claims dubious, but he suggests that they confirm his suspicion that Colliber leans towards materialism. There is at least an acceptance by Colliber of physical influence. It is true that, however tenuous the connection is between soul and some material component, Colliber is reluctant to dissolve entirely the connection between the middle being which is the soul and some bit of matter. At the resurrection, all souls will be given another body, perhaps similar to our present one, but even if unlike, it will be material in some way (*Free Thoughts*, pp. 115–17).

Andrew Baxter's *An Enquiry into the Nature of the Human Soul* (1733, 2nd edn. 1737) is listed in the April–June 1737 issue (vol. 9) with the comment, 'C'est un Livre tres bien écrit, & digne de la curiosité des plus profonds Métaphysiciens' (pp. 219–20). A review did not appear until the first issue of 1739 (12: 296–331). Baxter's work was one of the most important defences in Britain against materialist developments. His own metaphysic is openly Malebranchian. As did most traditional writers, he insisted that matter was passive and inert. Only immaterial substances can be active. He ascribed to matter the property of *resistance*, a *vis inertiae*, insisting that this property did not make matter in any way active. The reviewer is rather sceptical of this claim, suggesting that in resisting a force which tries to move or to stop it, matter is exhibiting some kind of activity (pp. 298–9). The reviewer even invokes Toland's *Letters to Serena* (1704), where Toland advanced the notion that all insensible parts of matter are continually in motion (pp. 300–1). The activity of matter is, for Toland opposed to passivity. Usually, activity of matter was seen as favouring materialism, as indeed Toland was seen as doing. A change was gradually taking place such that, by mid-century, Newtonians were talking of attractive and repulsive forces as being part of the nature of matter. But Baxter writes to support the standard notion that only an immaterial being can be the cause of motion. As his reviewer correctly reports, for Baxter attraction, repulsion, elasticity are all only 'effects produced by an immaterial cause' (p. 306).

Baxter's Malebranchianism had tried to give man some active role in human actions, rather than leaving all causation to God. He assigned the internal physiological motions of our body to God as their cause, and he denied that any mechanical or biological cause could be found for those processes. Voluntary action requires physiological and muscular events. Voluntary actions consist, Baxter said, in setting the mechanism of the body at work: 'we are free to excite motion in the hand, or foot, or not to excite it; but we are not free to excite it with, or without the help of mechanism; if it is begun spontaneously [i.e. voluntarily], it is executed or performed mechanically'.[6] What we do is *will* the action; God sets the mechanism in motion. On the occasion of my willing to move my arm, God, an immaterial mover, exerts his power and moves my muscles. The reviewer quotes the following passage from Baxter:

When one discharges an arrow out of a bow, the spontaneous mover (the immaterial part, or soul) *wills and designs* the production of the action: and this entitles it *his action*, in all the moral consequences of it, whatever they are. This mover doth moreover something that sets the mechanism of the body at work; and thus far only it is an agent. (*Enquiry*, i. 176)

The reviewer takes this last sentence to be saying that the soul 'makes a very small impression on some part of the body' (*Bibliothèque britannique*, 12 (1739), 309); he rightly goes on to query how, on Baxter's doctrine, the immaterial soul can exert even a small amount of power on matter. But he misreads Baxter. What I do, all that I can do, is to will and design the action of pulling the bow. If I do not will and design that particular action, the action will not occur, but what I do cannot go beyond the willing and designing. Baxter does not help the reader understand what is being said when he refers to 'the particular mover in the human body' having 'but a small share in producing' the motion of arm, bow, and arrow (*Enquiry*, i. 177), but it is clear that the man who pulls the bow is a mover only in the sense that *his willing* to pull the bow is necessary for the action to occur.

[6] Baxter, *An Enquiry into the Nature of the Human Soul* (3rd edn., 1745), i. 145–8.

He exerts no power on the bow or on his muscles. The reviewer's misreading of Baxter leads him to ascribe to Baxter the doctrine of 'prémotion physique' (*Bibliothèque britannique*, 12 (1739), 311, 313). Any attempt to involve the soul in bringing about the actions we perform, inside the general framework of God as the ultimate cause of those actions, tends towards that particular theological doctrine, as we saw with David R. Boullier in Chapter 5.

Besides willing and designing actions, Baxter's soul has the additional power of perceiving. *Activity* and *perceptivity*, he says, are inseparable from the soul (*Enquiry*, i. 248). He tolds a view very similar to Colliber's, that the soul perceives even when separated from the earthly body, but Baxter does not offer details of how this is accomplished, other than to say it is part of the nature of soul. Neither powers, of activity or perceptivity, can belong to matter. Not even God could add such properties to material substance, as Locke had suggested, a suggestion which the reviewer notes Baxter rejects.

The issue of the *Bibliothèque britannique* for July–September 1739 carried a review of Archibald Campbell's *The Necessity of Revelation* (13: 222–61).[7] Campbell had raised the question of how we can know the soul is immortal and immaterial. His answer was through revelation, but he cited Cicero as an ancient author who had no notion of an immaterial soul. The reviewer at this point refers to Locke's exchange with Stillingfleet on this question (pp. 250–1). Campbell quoted from the 4. 3. 6 passage on thinking matter, insisting that since, as Locke says, our knowledge is so limited that we cannot rule out this possibility, we must rely on revelation. Earlier in Campbell's book, Locke's *Reasonableness* had been cited and discussed.

In a notice of Hume's *Treatise* in the October–December issue for 1739, Locke is mentioned as one of the philosophers the author was responding to (14: 216). In the same volume but the January–March issue for 1740 (14: 432–3) a work of some importance in the British debate is listed among new books: *An Essay towards Demonstrating the Immateriality and Free-Agency of the Soul* ('MDCCLX', misprint for 1740). It is listed with a full descriptive title. This anonymous work was a careful attack on Samuel Strutt and Anthony

---

[7] The full title is: *The Necessity of Revelation, or An Enquiry into the Extent of Human Powers with Respect to Matters of Religion, Especially Those Two Fundamental Articles, the Being of God, and the Immortality of the Soul* (1739). Campbell was the Regius Professor of Divinity and Ecclesiastical History in the University of St Andrews.

Collins, two of the better British writers who were seen as following materialism.

In 1740 (16: 209–10), the *Bibliothèque britannique* lists, with a brief description of its contents, a book by Vincent Perronet, *Some Enquiries, Chiefly Relating to Spiritual Beings* (1740), a work that cites Locke often on a variety of topics, always favourably, and which attacks materialism. Perronet had earlier published two defences of Locke on personal identity, the second of which was listed and described in *Bibliothèque britannique*, 11 (1738), 208. None of these books is very interesting or important, but this notice in the *Bibliothèque britannique* kept Locke's name before the French reading public.

In 1739, the Jesuit G.-H. Bourgeant published a small pamphlet, *Amusement philosophique sur le langage des bestes*.[8] Ostensibly defending the thesis that animals speak and understand each other, Bougeant attacked the Cartesian view that beasts are machines. He admits that one could argue that what we take to be men talking to one another are really only clever machines, but this is not a belief we can sustain, particularly when we are one of those interlocutors. Similarly, the behaviour of animals leads Bougeant to the belief that they too have feelings and knowledge (pp. 5–6). Just how serious Bougeant was is not clear, but, in the course of his pamphlet, he touches on most of the issues in the thinking-matter debate, from the notion of just one substance to the claim for a tight dependence of thought on physiology. The reviewer of an Englishman's attack on Bougeant, John Hildrop's *Free Thoughts upon the Brute Creation*,[9] characterized Bougeant's pamphlet as an amazing 'jeu d'Esprit' (p. 219). The reviewer cites Hildrop's rejection of Locke's suggestion about thinking matter and Hildrop's reference to the exchange on this topic between Locke and Stillingfleet. Hildrop's brief discussion of Locke on thinking matter follows a longer discussion arguing that animals do understand and even reason. He writes against the Cartesian beast machine. Hildrop recognizes that Locke agrees with

---

[8] Bougeant was a prolific writer on theology and the Christian religion. For a complete list of his works, see A. Cioranescu, *Bibliographie de la littérature française du dix-huitième siècle* (Paris: Éditions du CNRS, 1969). The *Amusement philosophique* was reprinted several times in the century. I have used the 79-page edn. of 1757. Cioranescu does not list this edn.

[9] *Bibliothèque britannique*, 21 (July–Sept. 1743), 213–44. The full title of Hildrop's book is: *Free Thoughts upon the Brute Creation, or An Examination of Father Bougeant's Philosophical Amusement, &c., in Two Letters to a Lady* (1742).

him on animals, but he objects to Locke's reluctance, in *Essay*, 2. 11, to allow the reason of brutes to come from the same immaterial principle as in man (i.e. a soul). Since Locke has rejected innate ideas, our ideas must come from the same source, sensation, as do those of brutes (*Free Thoughts*, p. 15). Hildrop finds a connection between Locke's comments on reason in animals and the thinking-matter suggestion:

He [Locke] concedes, indeed, to the main Point, and allows the Rationality of Brutes; but, for fear of allowing them immaterial, and consequently immortal Souls, he frequently insinuates, that Thought, Rationality, or Reflection is not the absolute Privilege of immaterial Beings, but may be communicated by the Power of God to certain Portions of Matter, differently modified. . . . (pp. 15–16)

The discussion of Locke and Stillingfleet occupies five more pages, with Hildrop's comments on the nature of matter.

What the reviewer of Hildrop's book found odd was the seriousness with which Hildrop took Bougeant's suggestion of a language of animals. Hildrop goes into great detail (pp. 20–50) about the possible ways in which animals and even insects communicate, those ways of communication being languages. He uses extensive quotations from Antoine Pluche's *Spectacle de la nature* (1732–50) to indicate the social nature of animals; community and communication naturally go together. The reviewer is amused that a work which in France was seen as playful has been taken by this Englishman as 'un objet à l'Esprit libre & profond' (*Bibliothèque britannique*, 21 (July–Sept. 1743), 214). Nevertheless, Locke has appeared again in the context of discussions in France over the nature of the soul.

MIND AND BODY: *BIBLIOTHÈQUE RAISONNÉE*

The *Bibliothèque raisonnée* did not review Baxter's book, but in its listing of Baxter's *Enquiry* among new books in the Apr.–June 1735 issue, a paragraph description was appended. The focus of that description is Baxter's attack on Locke's suggestion about matter thinking (14: 471). This brief notice is balanced, as Schøsler points out,[10] by a similar notice of another book in the British debate, John

---

[10] Jørn Schøsler, *La Bibliothèque raisonnée (1728–1753)* (Odense: Odense University Press, 1985), 21.

Jackson's *A Dissertation on Matter and Spirit* (1735), which, the notice says, 'refute les raisons que Mr. Baxter a alleguées pour prouver l'immaterialité de l'Ame' (p. 472). Jackson shares many beliefs with Locke about our lack of knowledge of substance. While these two notices are both descriptive of the books, Schøsler believes that 'le journaliste ne cache pas son admiration pour la métaphysique antilockienne de Baxter: "C'est de la plus fine Métaphysique"'.[11]

In his careful analysis of the treatment of Locke by the journalists of the *Bibliothèque raisonnée*, Schøsler divides his survey into three periods. The first period, 1728–40, finds the journal opening with a review of Humphrey Ditton's *A Discourse concerning the Resurrection of Jesus Christ* (1712), and closing with its review of Hume's *Treatise*. Schøsler's survey includes books and notices on any aspect of Locke's thought, not just those doctrines seen as materialist-inclined. Thus, a review for April–June 1729 of several pamphlets dealing with different views on religion by Turrettini and a M. de Bionens (2: 312–41) indicates that this controversy involved, among other works, Locke's *The Reasonableness of Christianity* (p. 334). Similarly, the French translation of a work by Turrettini is reviewed in 1731 (6: 45–71); Locke's *Reasonableness* is cited again (ibid. 56–7, 59). A descriptive notice of Collins's work on liberty and Samuel Strutt's attack, together with a few other pieces on the same topic, comments that Locke's account of liberty was attacked by Strutt (4 (1730), 458).

Attention was also given to Locke's own works. The second French edition of the *Essay* received a review in the Apr.–June issue of 1730 (4: 343–57), the edition in which Coste included the exchange between Locke and Stillingfleet. This edition also contained an eighteen-page 'Eloge de M. Locke' by Coste. Schøsler considers the reviewer's praise of Stillingfleet and his several critical observations on Locke as evidence that he wished to leave the impression that Locke was 'un philosophe dangereux, peu original, têtu et parfois faux'.[12] Schøsler also calls attention to the long review of the anonymous *Two Dissertations concerning Sense and the Imagination* (1728), sometimes credited to a Zachary Mayne, which was a

---

[11] Schøsler, *La Bibliothèque raisonnée (1728–1753)* (Odense: Odense University Press, 1985). Vol. 22 also listed another work of some relevance to the British debate, William Windle's *An Enquiry into the Immateriality of Thinking Substances* (1738).

[12] Schøsler, *La Bibliothèque raisonnée*, p. 16.

sustained attack against Locke's failure to distinguish ideas from notions (2 (1729), 293–311). The author of that work, in a third essay on consciousness, reminds us of Locke's account of personal identity. There are also a few pages in which he argues that perception and consciousness cannot be properties of the body, but in this work there is no overt reference to Locke and thinking matter. From the opening remark by the reviewer, that 'l'Auteur de cet Ouvrage nous paroît meriter un rang distingué parmi les Auteurs Metaphysiques', and a few critical remarks about Locke in the review, Schøsler concludes: 'Il semble donc légitime de soutenir que le B.R. exprime ici—comme dans l'article sur l'ouvrage de Ditton—une méfiance apologétique à l'égard de la métaphysique de Locke'.[13]

The review of Ditton's *A Discourse concerning the Resurrection of Jesus Christ* (1 (1728), 15–29) only devoted a page and a half to the Appendix where Ditton launches a full-scale attack on materialists who say matter can be made to think. This was a very important work in the British debate. While Ditton attacked deists and other unnamed materialists, readers of his Appendix in England, and readers of this French review, would have associated his attack with Locke's suggestion. In a similar way, a brief mention of 'the hypothesis of Mr. Locke' in a review (10 (1733), 92) of J. P. de Crousaz's *Examen du pyrrhonisme* (1733) probably does, as Schøsler suggests, show that Locke's suggestion was well known in France by the years 1728–33.[14]

The second period into which Schøsler divides the *Bibliothèque raisonée* coverage of Locke spans the years 1741–9. In that period, volume 27 was an unusually rich source for Locke doctrines. Two of the items in that volume have already been discussed in earlier chapters: Boullier's attack on Voltaire's Letter XIII (ch. 2) and Formey's *La Belle Wolfienne* (ch. 1). A third item, Voltaire's explication of the Marquise du Châtelet's *Institutions de physique*, 1740 (an account of Leibniz's and Wolff's system), has a few references to Locke on space and essence, but nothing on soul or matter (27 (1741), 433–64).

In volume 29, there is a long review of the fifteenth volume of the works of the Abbé de Saint-Pierre, mainly on natural law (1742: 147–76). Locke's rejection of innate ideas is cited in the review (pp. 159–61, 164). The article is followed by another one on natural law, a review of a book by Casto Innocente Ansaldus, *De principorum*

[13] Ibid. 11.   [14] Ibid. 19.

legis naturalis traditione (1742). This work is primarily concerned with natural law, but the reviewer also calls attention to Ansaldus's defence of the immateriality of the soul and to two other writers (Gravesende and Musschenbroek) who discussed the question of matter thinking (pp. 202–3). The review ends with a reference to Boullier's rejection of Cartesian animal machines. Locke is not mentioned in these contexts, but since he is cited on other questions raised by Ansaldus, readers of the review may have found it easy to associate Locke with these topics too.

Over the next few years, from volume 32 to 44, there are a number of similar reviews of books touching on this topic of the nature of the soul. In some cases, Locke is explicitly mentioned by the reviewer; in others, the association with him is just under the surface. For example, the lead review in Jan.–Mar. 1744 (32: 3–58) is a fifty-six-page discussion of Saint-Hyacinthe's *Recherches philosophiques* (1743). Saint-Hyacinthe took the standard view of matter, that it is composed of insensible particles. Bodies are an organized whole made of these individual particles. Saint-Hyacinthe argued that a whole could not have properties different from those of its parts. The reviewer insists that a whole *can* have new properties not found in the individual atoms. This was an issue in Britain between Anthony Collins and Samuel Clarke, Collins arguing as the reviewer does. The rest of this review is devoted to talking about machines and automata. Locke is not mentioned in any of this discussion but Schøsler is probably correct when he says that readers of the *Bibliothèque raisonnée* would have made the connection.[15] If they read Saint-Hyacinthe's book, those readers would have found a discussion of the 4. 3. 6 passage in Locke's *Essay* on thinking matter (*Recherches philosophiques*, p. 486). While Saint-Hyacinthe talked of the body as a hydraulic machine, whose movements are independent of the soul's will (motions of the body are functions of fluids in the body), he took the Malebranchian route of limiting the soul's action to willing. He did talk of two kinds of extension, one for body, the other for souls. Spiritual extension is

---

[15] Schøsler, *La Bibliothèque raisonnée*, p. 42. The full title of Saint-Hyacinthe's book is *Recherches philosophiques sur la necessité de s'assurer par soi-même de la vérité, sur la certitude de nos connoissances, et sur la nature des êtres.* A book which attacked Locke's account of religious knowledge is listed in this same volume of the *Bibliothèque raisonnée*: John Ellis's *Some Brief Considerations upon Mr. Locke's Hypothesis, That the Knowledge of God Is Attainable by Ideas and Reflexion* (1743) (p. 226).

not incompatible with sensibility and activity (p. 496). As Cuenz did also, Saint-Hyacinthe challenged the notion of a being not extended in some way.[16]

Volume 33 carried the review of Reinbeck's attack on Voltaire's Letter XIII which I discussed in Chapter 2. In volume 34, a review of a book on experimental physics by the Abbé Nollet contained a paragraph description of Cuenz's notion of the soul as an invisible, impalpable, but extended being, undoubtedly reinforcing again the association with Locke, since Cuenz's four-volume work carried Locke's name in the title (34 (Jan.–Mar. 1745), 103–4). In part II (Apr.–June 1745) of this same volume, there is a letter taking the journalist to task for supporting Locke's suggestion about thinking matter (pp. 472–3). The author of this letter admits that the journalist does not say God *has* given thought to matter, only that God *could* do so.

Volume 42 for 1749 has several items of interest. In a review of Élie Luzac's *Essai sur la liberté* (1749), the reviewer tells us that among the superstitious and fanatics, '*Locke* est regardé comme un impie, parce qu'il prétend que Dieu peut bien avoir donné à une certaine portion de matière organisée la faculté de penser & de raisonner' (p. 21). There is much discussion in the same article of La Mettrie and his brand of materialism (pt. I, pp. 20–33). Article III in this volume discusses an *Essai sur l'étude des belles-lettres* by Edmé Mallet (1747). The reviewer gives a long quotation from the book in which Locke is listed with Hobbes and Woolston as modern philosophers, as writers favouring an excessive liberty and who hold dangerous views. These English writers have influenced French writers and have encouraged materialism and incredulity. Under the topic of 'metaphysics', Mallet says that Locke is very dangerous for having dared to say that a portion of organized matter would have been able to receive from God the faculty of thought. The author said Locke was grossly deceived in this possibility, but the reviewer says in Locke's defence: 'Peut-on se tromper quand on doute, & quand on doute si modestement est-on si blâmable?' (42: 44). Another review in this same volume, this time of an anonymous work on the passions (*Essai sur les passions & sur les caractères*, 1748), refers to the three systems of mind–body relation, taking the

---

[16] Cuenz was a friend of Saint-Hyacinthe. See Elisabeth Carayol's *Thémiseul de Saint-Hyacinthe, 1684–1746*, Studies on Voltaire and the Eighteenth Century, vol. 221 (Oxford: Voltaire Foundation, 1984).

side of physical influence, even insisting that the body is the first to act, acting on the soul by giving it its first perceptions. 'Even if there is a soul', the reviewer says, it is inert and without ideas or sensations until the body and its physiology set to work (pp. 142–3). This notion of the blank soul was, as we saw earlier, precisely what Roche found so objectionable in Condillac and the Abbé Mey criticized in Locke.

In the remaining years of the *Bibliothèque raisonnée*, 1750–3 (Schøsler's third period), Locke and his doctrines continue to be mentioned in reviews, but the thinking-matter issue has disappeared. Schøsler thinks the attitude of the journalists towards Locke has changed, has become more critical and negative. Malebranche begins to appear and receive attention. The important attack on Locke by the occasionalist Gerdil does not get mentioned or reviewed. Nor do Astruc's similar attacks. The extended critiques by Antoine-Martin Roche and Tiphaigne de la Roche were not published before this journal ceased appearing. Nevertheless, the exposure to the French-reading public of Locke's doctrines, including the suggestion about thinking matter, in the pages of the *Bibliothèque raisonnée* was constant and extensive from 1729 to 1750.

'RÉFLEXIONS SUR LE PYRRHONISME'

In the final issue of the *Bibliothèque britannique*, article III was an unsigned letter headed 'Réflexions sur le pyrrhonisme, ou Lettre à Mrs. les auteurs de la *Bibliothèque britannique*' (24 (Jan.–Mar. 1747), 281–356). As we shall see, this letter is not really about Pyrrhonism except in the general sense that what the author complains about are the many claims by writers, especially in the *Bibliothèque raisonnée*, that some of the fundamental beliefs about the soul have not been established as truths. The writer of this letter surveys and criticizes a number of the book reviews in the *Bibliothèque raisonnée* that I have just discussed. His general charge against the editors of that journal is that, if not actually in agreement with some of the radical doctrines of the free thinkers, deists, and materialists, they are at least too anxious to present the views of those writers. The term 'raisonnée' is, he says, a proper characteristic of those who write for the *Bibliothèque raisonnée*: in fact, they reason too much, seek to demonstrate what cannot always be demonstrated. Even in mathematics, assumptions are sometimes necessary, not everything can be demonstrated. If we take the model of demonstration into other areas, e.g. into theology, we may quickly be driven to the conclusions of 'les Esprits-forts'. These men are not content with moral demonstration, i.e. probability: 'La simple *Possibilité* qui n'établit rien, qui ne prouve rien, leur fournit toutes leurs Armes offensives & défensives' (p. 285). These free thinkers pretend to defer to certain 'Grands-Hommes', they are happy to rest in the shadow of the 'célébre Locke', repeating after him 'that they do not find any absurdity in the belief that, through his Omnipotence, God has communicated to a certain portion of matter the faculty of thought' (p. 285).

This correspondent agrees that God can make things that are infinitely above our understanding. It does not take a great philosopher such as Locke to convince us of this feature of God's power. But just consider the possibility that Locke and the free thinkers ask us to accept. Especially when we consider the complex machines made by man, why is it so difficult to conceive of God making a machine that infinitely surpasses those constructed by man (p. 286)? Pushing the supposed parallel that some writers drew between human and animal souls, and in particular the parallels often drawn between artificial machines and the feared man-machines, the writer sarcastically remarks that, in the latter, all we can observe or discover are volitions, memories, intentions. Actions follow intentions. With artificial machines, all we observe are figure and motion, not the least sign of spontaneity. Where, he asks, is the comparison, the parallel? He has, of course, gone beyond what can be observed in the case of the willing, acting machine, unless he means to talk from the first-person perspective, which he does not do. Nor did any of those who defended Locke's suggestions want to say man was or might be a machine. They may not always have been clear-headed about what Locke's suggestion implied, but few if any meant to say that, were thought a property of the brain, man would then be a machine, in the sense in which Descartes said animals were machines. It is instructive about the fears that many people had, when confronted with a suggestion such as Locke's, that they so easily jumped to the conclusion that the possibility of God giving to some matter the faculty of thought would mean that man would be a machine, complex but nevertheless a machine, a clockwork man.

This correspondent seizes on that feared result of materialism, sketching in the consequences of that possibility. He asks his readers (and the editors of the *Bibliothèque raisonnée*) to consider two societies. The first is a society of men who have great powers of judgement, depth of insight, and delicate minds: all the traits which characterize 'un Grand-Homme' (p. 287). These men are also visionaries on one point: they believe they have a certain book which tells them of a supreme Being who has revealed himself to men, teaching men that they have a principle internal to them which is distinct from matter (the soul) which will never die, etc. The writer draws out rather vividly the various aspects of such a belief for morality and social stability (pp. 288–90).

He then contrasts this society of men with a group of 'philosophes' who, by reasoning founded on their 'beaux *Peut-être*' have discovered that, 'yes, there is a Being existing by himself, but about whom they know very little and have no interest in knowing'. These 'philosophes' also conclude from their mere 'perhaps' that that Being has placed in a great park, as a way of amusing himself,

toutes sortes d'Animaux, les uns plus grossiers, les autres plus adroits, mais tous également Machines; & dont, après un certain Nombre d'Années, il ne restera plus rien, puisque les Ressorts des uns & des autres seront dissous, & tomberont avec les Rouäges dans la Pourriture, & dans l'Anéantissement, autant que la Solidité des Atômes le peut permettre. (pp. 290–1)

Then these 'philosophes' discover among these machines a particular kind which they call 'man'. These machines surpass the others in complexity, delicacy of structure (p. 291). It is not surprising that these machines come to imagine 'that there is something in them more than figure and motion'. Moreover, these man-machines believe that they would have to be great philosophers in order to persuade themselves of the contrary.

The animal-machines which the society of 'philosophes' call 'man' think, reflect, have specific values, and seek happiness; but those values and that happiness must be found in this world, since, so these philosophers tell us, there is no other world. The sketch this writer gives of these mortal man-machines ends with a Hobbesian war of all against all (pp. 292–3). He goes on to paint the short life of these man-machines as sad and empty, once they become convinced by the philosophers that there is no future life (pp. 294–5). This writer asserts that even if he were one of these Sages, these wise 'philosophes', who had made these discoveries or whose beliefs he had reasons to accept, he would keep it secret because of its deleterious effects on society (p. 296). He wants to know to which of his two societies do the authors who write for the *Bibliothèque raisonnée* see themselves belonging, the society of 'philosophes' or the society of those visionaries who believe in God and in real good and evil and immortality?

In raising this question, this writer recognized that some would say that journalists have an obligation to present different points of view, not to judge which books to review on the basis of some prejudice the journalists have. On the other hand, some people will say (and this writer agrees) that journalists have a duty to ignore some books, those that should never have been published because of the wrong or bad views they contain. What would we say, he asks, if a doctor was to announce a new medicine which cures diseases but then proceeded to administer mortal poison under the pretext that it was agreeable to the taste (p. 298)? It is precisely this double action which the writer thinks the authors of reviews in the *Bibliothèque raisonnée* have often taken.

In the *Bibliothèque raisonnée* review of Saint-Hyacinthe's *Recherches philosophiques* (32 (Jan.–Mar. 1744), 3–58), the reviewer had warm praise for the author, in part because of the traits of objectivity and impartiality displayed. Even in his presentation of Spinoza's philosophy, the reviewer points out how Saint-Hyacinthe avoided the usual labels (atheist, impious, monster) and gave a clear account of Spinoza's system (p. 6).[17] While the writer of the 'Réflexions sur le Pyrrhonisme' does not comment on Saint-Hyacinthe's including Spinoza in his account of systems of philosophy, it is a good illustration of a philosophy that the writer thinks should not be discussed. What the writer does select to censure in the *Bibliothèque raisonnée* review is the naturalistic definition of virtue and happiness. Even though the reviewer takes great pains to criticize this view, the very fact that it is discussed is objectionable to the writer. Moreover, he suspects that the reviewer has some sympathy for that naturalistic and secular account.[18]

---

[17] The reviewer says that Saint-Hyacinthe had read Spinoza's *Œuvres posthumes* three times in his efforts to understand and 'enter into the thought of that famous Jew' (p. 15).

[18] At the end of his critique of this part of Saint-Hyacinthe's account of virtue, the reviewer says: 'Voilà mes engagemens remplis. J'ai fait voir les pernicieuses conséquences des Principes de notre Auteur, & je souhaite que quelque habile homme entreprenne de lui démontrer qu'il est dans l'erreur, & qu'il doit nécessairement s'être égaré dans la *Recherche* qu'il a faite *de la Vérité*' (p. 38).

On the topic of the nature of the soul, the reviewer points out that Saint-Hyacinthe asserts that the soul is an active, spiritual, simple substance entirely different from matter (32: 44). This should please the writer on Pyrrhonism; but, once again, the reviewer has included a discussion of the opposed view, that the soul is material. The reviewer calls attention to the argument invoked by Saint-Hyacinthe, that a material soul would be composed of many material parts, none of which has the property of thought. If the parts lack that property, the whole composed of those parts will also not have that property. The reviewer argues (as Collins had done against Clarke in Britain) that some arrangements of matter do in fact have properties not found in the parts, e.g. artificial machines (pp. 42–50). The makers of clocks and automata can explain how the parts combine to produce the observed effects. The reviewer sees no reason why the brain, 'le principe de nos actions' in man and animals, cannot be the internal mechanism that works the body (pp. 49–50). At the very least, the reviewer argues, Saint-Hyacinthe has not shown the impossibility of a complex bit of matter such as the brain having thought as one of its properties. The writer in the *Bibliothèque britannique* heard the voice of Locke behind these remarks (24 (Jan.–Mar. 1747), 303 n.).

Two other reviews in the *Bibliothèque raisonnée* disturbed the writer of this letter. One of those was an account of Trembley's freshwater polyp, a discovery that posed difficulties for the believers in an immaterial principle distinct from physiology which activates man and perhaps animals. There is obvious excitement behind the review (33 (Oct.–Dec. 1744), 243–83), excitement supported by confidence in the conclusions drawn from the discovery: when cut into parts, each of the parts of the polyp grew into a whole individual. We could easily predict the disdain shown by the *Bibliothèque britannique* correspondent when the reviewer declares that the regeneration of the polyp out of parts was 'le vrai Principe actif, l'Etre indéfinissable, auquel vous donnez le nom d'*Ame*, étendu, divisible, & par conséquent composé de parties quelconques' (p. 244). Even more confidently, the reviewer went on to say:

Refusez-vous de reconnoitre l'existence d'un tel Principe, vous êtes comme forcé à donner à la Matière même la prérogative de pouvoir être animée, de pouvoir penser, d'agir & de se gouverner, dans tous les cas où elle sera arangée & disposée de la même manière que dans les différentes portions du Polype. C'en est donc fait de toute la théorie de l'Ame, enseignée jusqu'à présent par la plupart des Philosophes anciens & modernes. Cette Ame, du moins dans l'Insecte [the polyp] dont il est ici question, n'est plus *une*, elle n'est plus simple, elle est, pour ainsi dire, *multiple*, peut-être même divisible à l'*indéfini* comme la Matière, si elle n'est matière elle-même. (pp. 244–5)

The other review that disturbed this correspondent to the *Biblio-thèque britannique* was of the French translation by Barbeyrac of Cumberland's work on natural law.[19] The reviewer began the second article about this translation with some reflections on the need for a search for truth, calling attention to the difficulties that often arise. Many searchers after truth fall into error, mainly because of weakness of mind (p. 310). Some truths, such as Descartes's *cogito*, are obvious when reflected upon. There are still many questions waiting answers, e.g. 'is there a void in nature?', 'does the sun or the earth turn?', 'L'Etre pensant est-il matériel, ou est-ce quelque autre Etre entierement distinct de la Matière?' (p. 311). Since these questions are hardly relevant to Cumberland's topic, the writer of the letter may be correct in suggesting that they are somewhat gratuitous and irrelevant, another example of the tendency of the *Bibliothèque raisonnée* reviewers to inject the thinking-matter topic wherever possible.

The *Bibliothèque raisonnée* review of Reinbeck (discussed above in ch. 2) provides this writer with yet another opportunity to lament the eagerness of the journalists to launch into discussions of the possibility of matter thinking. This writer thinks it dangerous even to suggest that possibility; a strong stand should be taken against this notion when reviewing the books of Reinbeck, Saint-Hyacinthe, Gravesande, or Ansaldus. If matter does not give us the least notion of something other than figure and motion, why does the reviewer of these books seize on the 'peut-être' and suggest the possibility of thought being a property of a machine? The writer again at this point cites Locke. Among others who also accept this 'perhaps' are Toland, Collins, Morgan, Woolston, Mandeville (reminding us of that list used by Voltaire and Tabaraud). The Bible, this writer asserts, teaches us clearly that the soul is immortal and immaterial.

[19] The *Bibliothèque raisonnée* devoted two articles to this translation. The first is in 32 (Jan.–Mar. 1744), 141–62; the second (the one that is cited here) is in the same vol., Apr.–June 1744 issue, pp. 310–72. This translation was another source of knowledge of Locke for French readers. In his notes to his translation, Barbeyrac has numerous references to Locke, including one on thinking matter and Maxwell's (the English translator of Cumberland) appended survey of the Clarke–Collins debate. See Richard Cumberland, *Traité philosophique des lois naturelles* (1744), 104 n. 3.

To all such writings used by the free thinkers, this writer asks simply: 'quelle Suite d'Actes de Toute-Puissance Dieu ne devroit-il pas faire, afin d'exécuter par une Machine ce que nous concevons si aisément dans un Etre tout spirituel?' (p. 313)

There are other targets in the *Bibliothèque raisonnée* that the *Bibliothèque britannique* writer attacks in this long, spirited, dogmatic letter. This letter gives us a good measure of the reaction by traditionalists to the new views associated with the 'philosophes' in France. It also strengthens the connection, in the minds of such defenders of tradition, of Locke's role in the many discussions of thinking matter. Locke's suggestion, and the particular features of the British debate over that suggestion, surface repeatedly in books and reviews, both those for and against that version of materialism.

THE PHYSIOLOGICAL FACTOR

When Antoine-Martin Roche listed Le Camus as one of the disciples of Locke, he had in mind the way in which physiology could lend support to the notion of physical influence. No one could ignore the physiology of perceiving and acting, not even the stoutest occasionalist. What the occasionalist and pre-established harmony defenders could do was to deny a causal role for the physiology. It is possible to make that denial even when very specific correspondences are discovered or suggested between mental and brain events. Nevertheless, the more specific and detailed the correspondences were, the more difficult it became to deny physical influence. At least, some tradition-bound writers worried that, were such correspondences ever established, we would be a step closer to the clock-work man. These writers were probably correct in believing that when that sort of physiological account is combined with an ontology permitting thought to be a property of the brain, the danger of mechanizing man, of turning man into one of those machines in the great park suggested by the *Bibliothèque britannique* writer on Pyrrhonism, became more real.

In Britain, the Croonian Lectures on voluntary muscular motion addressed the question, 'how can I move my arm?' The lecturers in this series did not credit all human actions to the bodily mechanism alone, but they were concerned to give an explanation of voluntary or intentional body motion in as much physiological detail as possible.[20] I have not discovered any reviews of these British books on muscular motion in the French-language journals, but several of them *are* listed among new and forthcoming books.[21] Other English medical men were known in France (e.g. Cheyne, Mead, Hartley), but the most important work on the physiology of the body was conducted on the Continent by such men as Boerhaave, Haller, and perhaps La Mettrie. The experimental work of La Peyronie was, as we saw, reported in the journals as well. Many of the books and reviews that raised the question of thinking matter assumed some physiological events underlying awareness.

A *Bibliothèque raisonnée* review in 1746 of a book by the nephew of Herman Boerhaave is a good example of how physiological theory was linked with speculation about the nature of the soul (36: 126–54). The book was written by Abraham Kaau-Boerhaave. Its Latin title is *Impetum faciens dictum Hippocrati per corpus consentiens, philologice & physiologice illustratum, observationibus & experimentis passim firmatum*. The concept of a force or motion given to each plant or animal which becomes the life force is developed in that work. The reviewer's presentation of Kaau-Boerhaave's account of the soul should have irritated the *Bibliothèque britannique* writer on Pyrrhonism, since the reviewer remarks that the people who most vigorously insist that the soul is a spiritual substance totally different from matter are those who fear they may not survive the death of the body (p. 128). In earlier times, when the fear of being labelled a Spinozist was not possible, no one was disturbed at the notion of the soul being a body, albeit a rather special body. The reviewer cites Tertullian as an example. In more recent time, Spinozists and materialists hold the same view, regarding thought as a mode of body. The review then indicates the reactions of modern theologians to this view:

Ce sentiment, banni des Ecoles Chrétiennes déja depuis longtems, a allarmé les Théologiens. Ils sont venus avec des argumens en forme pour en faire voir les dangereuses conséquences. Si notre Ame est corporelle, nous voila,

---

[20] See my *Thinking Matter* (Minneapolis, Minn.: University of Minnesota Press; Oxford: Basil Blackwell, 1984), 172–5.
[21] Alexander Stuart's *Dissertatio de structura et motu musculari* is announced in the *Bibliothèque britannique* in 1738 (12, pt. I, pp. 210–11); Browne Langrish's *A New Essay on Muscular Motion* is listed in the *Bibliothèque raisonnée*, 10 (Apr.–June 1733), 479); Langrish's later 1747 Croonian Lectures are listed in the same journal for July–Sept. 1748 (41: 230); and James Parsons's Croonian Lecture is listed, with a brief description, in that same journal for 1746 (37 (July–Sept.), 237).

disent-ils, réduits au rang des Bêtes, nous n'avons plus rien à espérer après cette vie, puisque tout ce qui est Corps, doit être détruit & anéanti. Terreur panique. (p. 129).

The reviewer freely admits that 'the soul certainly has properties which are particular to it, but we know neither its nature nor how it acts on the body' (p. 130). Nor do we know how objects produce ideas in our awareness (p. 131).

The next section of the book describes the composition of *organized* bodies: they are made of solids and fluids which act on one another. In addition, some writers find the need for an *impulsive motion* (pp. 131–2). The reviewer comments that of course it takes motion to keep organized bodies alive, but Kaau-Boerhaave considers the impulsive motion to be 'un Etre particulier qui est *hors de Dieu* & hors du Corps qu'il n'a pas encore animé' (p. 132). It is a principle of incorporeal motion. The reviewer considers this 'being' to be an example of multiplying entities beyond necessity. The motion of bodies is not some separate, additional entity, but a simple mode of body (p. 133).

In presenting Kaau-Boerhaave's suggestion for the 'seat of the soul' (that it is the *sensorium commune*), the reviewer calls attention to La Peyronie's locating it in the *corpus callosum* (p. 142). Kaau-Boerhaave also retained the older notion of a *sensitive soul* which was corporeal, distinguishing it from 'esprit' which reasons, forms ideas, and makes judgements, and is immortal. The reviewer does not think two souls add much clarity to the account, nor does he think Kaau-Boerhaave has drawn the distinction between the two very clearly. Apparently, Kaau-Boerhaave allows some feelings, appetites, and attention, even memory, as functions of the sensitive soul. Thus, the reviewer believes that these properties of the sensitive soul make it easy for a 'philosophe' to form the conclusion that matter can think: 'Si la Matière peut penser, qu'est-il besoin de recourir à un Principe étranger qui n'a guère d'autre avantage sur l'Ame sensitive, que celui de porter son vol un peu plus haut qu'elle ne fait' (pp. 145–6). The motivation behind two souls is, the reviewer suggests, to enable Kaau-Boerhaave to hold a middle ground between his Christian beliefs and his scientific views (p. 146).

CONCLUSION

It was the scientific advances in our knowledge of the workings of the mechanism of the body which influenced many of the French 'philosophes', Diderot and d'Alembert in particular. With their announced programme, embodied in the 'Discours préliminaire' and in many entries in the *Encyclopédie* (1751–65), of basing all knowledge and theory on experience and observation, the detailed physiology of the body and the specific correlations between mental and physical states enabled some writers to resolve the relation between mind and body, making it a causal relation. Others suggested an even stronger relation, identity. The journal reviews of a variety of books which dealt with the thinking-matter issue, some of which involved Locke; the occasional comments by reviewers which the *Bibliothèque britannique* writer on Pyrrhonism interpreted as biased towards one-substance man and lending support for l'*homme machine*; that same writer's impassioned attack on the editors of the *Bibliothèque raisonnée*: all of these features give a clear indication of the conflict between orthodox traditionalists and the new radical developments in science and philosophy up to mid-century. Locke was placed by friend and foe with the radicals. The parts of his doctrine that located him there were primarily his suggestion of thought as a property of the brain and his stress on the sensory origin of ideas and knowledge. Three other aspects of his examination of human understanding helped associate Locke's doctrine with the radical literature: his limitation on knowledge, especially our inability to penetrate to the real nature of substance (material or immaterial), the prominence he gave to reason, and his general distrust of systems.

What we now need to do, in order to complete our story of the adventures of Locke's thinking matter in France, is to examine some of the better-known 'philosophes' in order to determine how their views on these issues (especially those associated with materialism) relate to those of Locke and the British controversy.

8
Locke among the 'Philosophes'

THE previous chapters of this study have presented discussions of the relation between mind and body in articles and books in eighteenth-century French literature, with an eye to filling in the background to the appearances of Locke's suggestion about the possibility of God adding thought as a property to organized matter. Those chapters have tracked this Lockian suggestion in a number of lesser-known writers, including some of the clandestine pamphlets. Voltaire has been the only major figure in the story so far, aside from the discussions of Malebranche and Leibniz on the three systems. Voltaire's role in popularizing Locke's suggestion has been central to our story. The French-language journals I have discussed were also prominent in the dissemination of Locke's thought. Those who attacked Voltaire and Locke on this topic were mainly obscure followers of Malebranche.

I have left it for this final chapter to explore some of the writings of the better-known French writers, many of whom were associated with Diderot and d'Alembert in the great *Encyclopédie*; others, such as La Mettrie and d'Holbach, contributed to what is usually thought of as 'French Materialism'. Locke's name is found in some of these writings, especially in Diderot's defence of the Abbé de Prades and in his *Encyclopédie* entry 'Locke'. Sometimes it is Voltaire's Letter XIII that is cited about Locke's thinking matter.

This final chapter is not only concerned with Locke's name and doctrines among the French 'philosophes'. It seeks to fill in from these sources the continued debate over the three systems of mind and body; the active concept of matter, especially biological matter; and the concept of materialism. I want to determine whether this French materialism, the materialism of the 'philosophes', differs in significant ways from the materialism and automatism feared by British writers who attacked Locke.

DIDEROT ON LOCKE

Diderot's entry 'Locke', in the *Encyclopédie, ou Dictionnaire raisonné des sciences, des arts et des métiers* (1751–65), is a praiseworthy presentation of some of the main features of Locke's life, with an outline of his writings. The sketch ends by ascribing to Locke that eighteenth-century accolade 'honnête homme'. The items selected for comment are indicative of what was considered valuable in his doctrines and his character. The fact of Locke's dissatisfaction with the standard course of study and methodology at Oxford is noted, as is his discovery of Descartes as a first step outside the confines of formal instruction. Locke's next move into medicine (anatomy, natural history, and chemistry) is given particular praise, not only because science in general and medicine in particular was by the *encyclopédistes* looked to as the basis for all knowledge, but also because it combined with Locke's other interests to give him a variety of perspectives from which to view man. While writing metaphysics, Diderot observes, he practised medicine: 'c'est lui seul qui a vû les phénomènes, la machine tranquille ou furieuse, foible ou vigoureuses, saine ou brisée, délirante ou réglée, successivement imbécille, éclairée, stupide, bruyante, muette, léthargique, agissante, vivante & morte.' Locke is also said to have studied the effects of the passions and interests on character-formation, perhaps referring to his close study of children.

Locke's relationship with Shaftesbury is said to be one where Locke provided the model of an intellectual life for Shaftesbury. Noting that Shaftesbury provided an income for Locke as his assistant, Diderot remarks: 'one can *acquire* a man of merit such as Locke, but one cannot *buy* him'. Locke's travels in Europe are cited, as is his retreat to Holland when Shaftesbury was suspected of treason. The role of the king in Locke's formal dismissal from Christ Church is described, as are the king's (and some of Locke's friends') efforts to get Locke to return and accept a pardon. Locke, the writer informs us with some emotion, rejected 'avec fierté' the idea of a pardon, since that would accuse him of a crime he had not committed. Locke's subsequent return to England in the fleet of William and Mary and the many offers of governmental posts are also chronicled. Locke's preference for rest and quiet led him to decline all offers at that time.

All of Locke's writings are cited, the work on education is given several paragraphs. The *Reasonableness of Christianity* (1695) is especially praised for its banishment of all mysteries in religion. The *Essay* (1690) is of course mentioned, as are *Two Treatises of Government* (1690) and the writings on money.

The comments on Locke's death reveal a certain ideal in Diderot's mind: Locke died 'dans son fauteuil, maître de ses pensées, comme un homme qui s'éveille & qui s'assoupit par intervalles jusqu'au moment où il cesse de se réveiller; c'est-à-dire que son dernier jour fut l'image de toute notre vie'. The summation of Locke's life and character is continued:

Il étoit fin sans être faux, plaisant sans amertume, ami de l'ordre, ennemi de la dispute, consultant volontiers les autres, les conseillant à son tour, s'accommodant aux esprits & aux caracteres, trouvant par-tout l'occasion de s'éclairer ou d'instruire, curieux de tout ce qui appartient aux arts, prompt à s'irriter & à s'appaiser, honnête homme, & moins calviniste que socinien.

Locke's suggestion about thinking matter appears in the final two brief paragraphs of this entry. The writer notes that 'des hommes pusillanimes' have objected to that idea but, Diderot asks: 'qu'importe que la matiere pense ou non? Qu'est-ce que cela fait à la justice ou à l'injustice, à l'immortalité, & à toutes les verités du systême, soit politique, soit religieux?' The final comment on this topic, a topic which had given rise to so much dispute in Britain and France by 1750, reflects the views about nature and matter found in Diderot's 'Entretien entre d'Alembert et Diderot' and 'La Rêve de d'Alembert':

Quand la sensibilité seroit le germe premier de la pensée, quand elle seroit une propriété générale de la matiere; quand inégalement distribuée entre toutes les productions de la nature, elle s'exerceroit avec plus ou moins d'énergie selon la variété de l'organisation, quelle conséquence fâcheuse en pourroit-on tirer? *aucune*. L'Homme seroit toujours ce qu'il est, jugé par le bon & le mauvais usage de ses facultés.

Locke could hardly have been given a stronger appraisal. Neither Leibniz nor Malebranche received that kind of praise, praise of the person more than of his doctrines. The entry, 'Léibnitzianisme, ou Philosophie de Léibniz', is a very long and detailed presentation of Leibniz's thought in all areas; the entry on Malebranche is much shorter. Both these philosophers appear in other entries, but the assessment of them as persons is missing. It was clearly Locke the man, his intellectual and moral qualities, that attracted Diderot; not that he did not use or agree with his doctrines. Diderot had not of course met Locke; his picture must have been derived from the information found in various 'éloges' that were available, but also, I suspect, from Diderot's reading of some of his writings.[1] To what extent Diderot's fulsome portrait reflects the general reputation of Locke in France by 1750, we cannot say. None of the critics of what was viewed as Locke's materialist principles characterized him as evil. Tournemine came closest to such a charge, a charge vigorously denied by Voltaire. What was said by his critics was that those principles and doctrines lent support to libertines and materialists, or that Locke's stress on the sensory origin of ideas detracted from the dignity of the Christian soul.

It was this latter doctrine which was attacked by Antoine-Martin Roche and the Abbé Mey; that doctrine also played a dramatic role in 'l'affaire de Prades'. Diderot, who was suspected of aiding and abetting de Prades, if not actually writing part of his thesis, *was* intimately involved in the aftermath of the censure of de Prades. In what he called 'Suite de l'Apologie de l'Abbé de Prades' (1752), written as if by de Prades, Diderot took on Caylus, the bishop of Auxerre.[2] It is a long, critical defence of all aspects of de Prades's thesis. The proposition of the thesis in which Locke's name became entwined, the sensory origin of ideas and knowledge, was linked by the bishop to de Prades's talk of God giving life to the already formed body. The bishop shows the usual worries about any departure from traditional doctrine, in this case that of two substances united to form a man. The bishop charges that de Prades only pays lip-service to the two-substance doctrine: de Prades leaves, he said,

---

[1] Diderot probably owes a good portion of his characterization of Locke to Pierre Coste's 'Eloge de M. Locke' which first appeared in 1705 in the *Nouvelles de la république des lettres*, later repr. in French edns. of Locke's *Essay* from 1729 on. Many of the traits cited by Diderot occur in Coste's 'Eloge', but Diderot has greatly embellished the portrait of Locke. The glowing description of Locke contains much of the flavour of the ideal 'philosophe'. See the *Encyclopédie* entry under that term.

[2] Arthur M. Wilson explains that 'Diderot wrote this adroit exercise in polemics in the name of the Abbé de Prades, who was at that time in Berlin preparing his own apology, which was to appear in two parts. Accordingly Diderot entitled his little changeling, which was on sale in Paris even before the Abbé de Prades had published his, the *Suite de l'Apologie de M. l'Abbé de Prades . . . Troisième partie*' (*Diderot* (New York: Oxford University Press, 1972), 169). It also appeared with de Prades's *Apologie* (see above, ch. 4).

man as 'une bête brute, un automate, une machine mise en mouvement' by sensory stimuli.[3] Diderot, in the voice of de Prades, confirms the bishop's fears: 'je pense trés sincèrement, et sans m'en croire moins chrétien, que l'homme n'apporte en naissant ni connaissances, ni réflexions, ni idées'. Moreover, man will stay 'comme une bête brute, un automate', if sensory stimuli fail to activate the faculties of the soul. This account, Diderot says, is the belief held by Locke, experience supports it, and it is true. Many theologians and modern philosophers also accept this account. The bishop can, of course, form notions that are more sublime and less true, but he should be careful not to give to those chimeras more existence and value than they merit.

Later in his reply, Diderot takes up the claim, carefully made by de Prades, that while sense experience convinces us of the existence of external objects, we cannot *reason* to the existence of such objects because there is no suitable relation between sensations and objects. This was a point de Prades made in his own defence. In his *Pensées philosophiques* (1746), Diderot puts the point in more precise language: 'Entre les actes extérieurs et la pensée, il n'y a point de liaison essentielle' (*Œuvres philosophiques*, p. 20), a distinction between a general 'rapport' and a 'liaison réelle' or 'essentielle' that Tournemine also drew earlier in the century. Diderot reminds Bishop Caylus of de Prades's recognition of the lack of a suitable relation. The bishop, Diderot remarks, reads that passage as saying there is no 'affinity' between sensations and objects. Since this is just what de Prades claimed, there are no grounds for the charge of materialism against de Prades. The bishop finds materialism in de Prades's acceptance of a general causal connection between the physical world and sensation; causal connections are in fact instances of physical influence. What the bishop wants is for de Prades to substitute occasionalism for physical influence. The tension between those two systems rises to the surface in the bishop's objections.

MIND AND BODY IN THE *ENCYCLOPÉDIE*

The attitude towards the three systems of mind–body relation by the writers of entries in the *Encyclopédie* vary. Pierre Tarin, a doctor on

---

[3] Caylus, as quoted by Diderot, *Œuvres complètes*, ii. 628. The language used by Caylus in this charge is almost identical to that employed by Roche. See above, pp. 73–5.

the Faculty of Medicine at Paris (Proust describes him as 'theoricien plus que praticien')[4] considered any attempt to explain the interaction as useless for medicine, but he goes on to describe correlations, praising the work of Boerhaave and Haller.[5] He stresses mechanical and physical principles for explaining the operations of the body. The same author, in the entry for 'Cerveau', summarizes what Chambers said about Dr Astruc (Tarin seems to have borrowed directly from Chambers):[6]

M. Astruc va plus loin: il prétend rendre raison de phénomenes du raisonnement & du jugement, par l'analogie qu'il suppose entre les fibres du *cerveau* & celles des instrumens de musique. Selon lui, c'est un axiome que chaque idée simple est produite par l'ébranlement d'un fibre déterminé, & que chaque idée composée est produite par vibrations isochrones de plusieurs fibres . . .

The entry 'Influence (métaphysique)' explains that this term designates the connection between soul and body which is used by the first of the three hypotheses, physical influence. The writer of this entry seems to reject this hypothesis on the grounds that we cannot comprehend how two such different substances could act on one another. Besides, Leibniz has shown that it would violate the laws of motion. The system is said to be that favoured by the ancients and it is 'le plus goûté du vulgaire'. There is a brief discussion of occasional causes, but the presentation stresses its oddity: the soldier does not move his arm and fire the cannon, God does!

Examples have a way of being repeated. Louis de Jaucourt, a close collaborator with Diderot and a doctor of medicine at the University of Leiden,[7] in the entry for 'Harmonie préetablie' illustrates a familiar criticism of Leibniz's system: 'The soul of Virgil produced the Aeneid, his hand wrote it without obeying in any way the intentions of the author'. God has decreed that the correlations will occur. Leibniz is said to regard the soul and body as two automata. The

---

[4] See Jacques Proust, *Diderot et l'Encyclopédie* (Paris: Colin, 1962), Appendix I, p. 527.

[5] Entry 'Physiologie'. Tarin remarks that there is nothing in the idea of motion that can be found in the idea of soul.

[6] The way Tarin refers to Astruc is identical to Chambers's opening reference: 'M. Astruc va plus loin'; Chambers writes, 'Dr. *Astruc* goes further'. The rest of this passage is close to a literal translation of Chambers (*Cyclopaedia* (1728)). See above, p. 107.

[7] Proust adds: 'Il fut polygraphe. Il etait membre associé de plusieurs Académies (Londres, Berlin, Stockholm, Bordeaux).'

boat example used by Bayle against Leibniz is also repeated. While admiring Leibniz, Jaucourt is uneasy with this system.[8]

The 'trois hypothèses' are also discussed in 'Cause (métaphysique)'. The author of this entry was the Abbé Claude Yvon, another writer implicated in de Prades's censured thesis. The question posed by the abbé is: 'is the soul the *physical* or only the *occasional* cause of the motions of the body?' Leibniz's pre-established harmony system is said to destroy liberty and makes the existence of an external world doubtful. The old system of real influence has been destroyed by Descartes and Malebranche. The English philosophers (he does not give any names) say that God has included in the soul a certain power to act on its own body. This system is less subtle and less refined than that of occasional causes, although the English view does seem to correspond with our natural belief: a real efficacy. But such a power is obscure and seems unlikely between a substance which is inactive in essence and another which is by its nature active. Even if we say this system of real influence explains how the body obeys the will of the soul, it cannot explain how the soul obeys the motions of the body. Clearly borrowing (without attribution) from D. R. Boullier, Yvon says of physical influence: it gives reasons for action but none for sensation. The abbé goes on to talk of my will as a mediating cause between the motions of my body and God's general will. The following remark is virtually a direct quotation from Boullier:[9] 'C'est bien une volonte efficace de Dieu qui me fait marcher: mais il ne veut me faire marcher qu'en conséquence de ce qu'il a voulu une fois pour toutes, que les mouvemens de mon corps suffisent les desirs de mon ame'. My soul is the true cause of the motions of my body because it is the cause of its volitions.

In using the Boullier material, the Abbé Yvon presents Boullier's modification of occasionalism, a modification which, with the distinction between general and particular causes, enabled Boullier to lend support to his causal account of sensation. As we know, Boullier was a strong critic of Voltaire's Letter XIII and its use of Locke's suggestion about thinking matter. Boullier wanted to have causal influence without any implication of materialism, but he also

---

[8] W. H. Barber says that Jaucourt had a 'close acquaintance with the published texts' of Leibniz; and, although he was an admirer of Leibniz, he was 'not an enthusiastic partisan of Leibnizian metaphysics, which he recognizes, have not won general approval'. See his *Leibniz in France, from Arnauld to Voltaire* (Oxford: Oxford University Press, 1955), 105.

[9] See above, ch. 5, pp. 117–19.

found the sharp separation between mind and body unsatisfactory. The Abbé Yvon's rejection of physical influence and pre-established harmony is, in the entry 'cause', more traditional, certainly more occasionalist, than the writer from whom he borrowed.

The entry 'Âme' which Yvon also wrote is more openly occasionalist and more vigorous in its attack on thinking matter. The entry starts out with the familiar quick survey of ancient thinkers. Some of the ancients believed the soul to be a quality, others a substance. They had no notion of spirituality or immateriality of the soul. Some more recent writers, e.g. Spinoza, hold that there is only one substance. Other moderns who believe with the ancients that the soul is material are Averroës, Bembo, Politian, Pomponazzi, Cardano, Hobbes. Spinoza's system is characterized as 'absurd'. Yvon then moves into the topic of thinking matter by first discussing our perception of objects. Physical causation by itself will not result in perceptual awareness. We must pay attention to what is affecting our sense organs, otherwise we will remain unaware of objects. There must be something in us that attends and considers the impressions on organs and brain. What is transmitted from objects to sense organs is unlike the contents we become aware of in perception. Particles from objects cannot be the cause of awareness. In fact, there must be some superior cause which, given the faculty we have of thought, causes us to have certain ideas in the presence of certain objects. The abbé spends another paragraph arguing that the cause of thought cannot be atoms in motion; we must recognize in man, as part of his essence, a principle which thinks and judges.

If that which thinks in us was a subtle matter, as some writers suggest, that matter could not communicate thoughts to others. All it could do would be to cause the thinking matter in others to move. There would have to be a correspondence between my thoughts and the movements of matter in you. No one, Abbé Yvon says, believes that the matter which thinks in us can directly affect the matter in others. The only way of communicating thoughts is by speech, signs, or writing. None of these can put the thinking matter in others in motion. The conclusion must be that matter does not think. Nor will it help to invoke God, as Locke does, in order to make some matter think. Two long passages from Voltaire's Letter XIII are then produced in which Voltaire refers to Locke and Stillingfleet on this topic.[10]

[*See p. 190 for n. 10*]

The entry 'Âme' does not end here, although the Abbé Yvon's contribution does. Diderot added a much more interesting supplement, mainly on the topic of the location of the soul. He starts off with a brief reference to those who believe the soul to be spiritual but extended (a view held by many of the immaterialists in Britain). These writers do not locate the soul at any particular place, Diderot says: it is in all parts of the body, existing complete in each part (a principle we have run into earlier). This view resolves some problems, Diderot thinks, but gives rise to others. Another group of philosophers think that the soul is not extended, but believe there is a particular place where it resides and exercises its function. Diderot may have Descartes in mind as representative of this group. He does not find this view very intelligible, mainly because he does not think we have any reasons for selecting one place over another in the brain.

What it turns out he means by this last remark is that if we are going to identify a part of the brain which plays a crucial role in awareness, we need to base our claim on experimental work. He names Vieussens, father and son (the former a doctor and anatomist), and Le Peyronie as researchers who have good reasons for identifying a place in the brain as the 'siege' of the soul.[11] Diderot discusses La Peyronie in some detail. What the observations and experiments made by La Peyronie have shown is that 'in whatever way we conceive that which thinks in us, it is the case that its functions are dependent upon the organization and the actual state of the body while we are alive'. He cites a number of La Peyronie's case-studies of brain-damaged patients, all supporting the conclusion that the *corpus callosum* cannot be altered or destroyed without an alteration or loss of reason and judgement. Diderot points out that Le Peyronie has shown how a fibre deranged, an inflammation, a fall, a contusion affect our cognitive performances: then it is 'adieu le

---

[10] The passages, with a few different phrases and sentence punctuation, are taken from the *Lettres écrites de Londres* (1734), 100–1.

[11] Raymond Vieussens (medical doctor at Montpellier), *Neurographia universalis, hoc est, Omnium corporis humani nervorum simul et cerebri medullaeque spinalis descriptio anatomica* (1682). This work is a detailed descriptive physiology of brain and nerves. The 'siege' of the soul is the brain. He uses animal spirit physiology, including identifying some nerves that relate to voluntary motion. The external senses are said to be the soul considered as capable of several perceptions. He uses occasionalist language: God produces sensations in the soul when physical motions touch the senses. For a long review of this work, see *Nouvelles de la république des lettres* (Nov. 1685), art. III.

jugement, la raison'. There can be no doubt that these experiments and case-studies show the close connection of the functions of the soul with the state and organization of the body.

In another entry, 'Immortalité', Diderot advances his notion that we have immortality in the memories of men; but the first paragraph of this entry argues, as had Locke earlier, that immateriality is not necessary for immortality. The soul of man is immortal (if it is) 'not because it is spiritual, but because God is just and wishes to reward and punish the good and evil men in another world'. God has created the soul out of nothing, it will return to nothing unless God wishes to conserve it. 'Le sentiment de la spiritualité et de l'*immortalité*, sont indépendans l'un de l'autre; l'ame pourrait être spirituelle et mortelle, matérielle et *immortelle*.'

DIDEROT'S PHYSIOLOGICAL MATERIALISM

Diderot had a wide knowledge of medicine and medical researchers. Jean Mayer, the editor of Diderot's *Eléments de physiologie*, indicates the authors Diderot read in this area: e.g. Charles Bonnet, Paul Joseph de Barthez, Robert Whytt, La Mettrie. Mayer does not list La Peyronie, but, from what we have just seen, it is clear that Diderot was familiar with his work. In Diderot's 'Rêve de d'Alembert', the interlocutor Bordeu describes one of La Peyronie's operations on the brain of a wounded soldier. What was useful for Diderot in La Peyronie's experimental studies was the evidence they provided of specific correlations between brain states and cognitive events. Diderot's entry 'Affection' extended that correlation to such states as love and hate, pleasure and pain. There are muscular motions in the body that accompany those affective states. The intensity of emotions corresponds with the dilation of the heart, the pulse rate, etc. Behavioural manifestations of anger are correlated with, if not a function of, bodily processes. It is, he asserts in this entry, 'in the mechanism of the body where we must look for the cause of the difference in the sensibility of different men when reacting to the same event'. Diderot goes on to use the example he and others frequently use, comparing the human body to a string instrument, such as a harpsichord: 'Nous ressemblons en cela à des instruments de musique dont les cordes sont diversement tendues; les objets extérieurs font la fonction d'archets sur ces cordes, et nous rendons tous des sons plus ou moins aigus.'

He employed the same analogy in his 'Entretien entre d'Alembert et Diderot', comparing man to a 'clavecin', with sensibility and memory added.[12] Just as the strings of the harpsichord vibrate and make sounds, so the nerves in the body are strings which vibrate and activate muscles and hence limbs move.[13] In his *Eléments de physiologie*, the point is made again: emotions such as gaiety, sadness, anger, tenderness, voluptuousness can never occur or be explained without reference to the body, to corporeal motions within the body.[14] Earlier in the same chapter of the *Eléments* Diderot attacks the traditional notion of two substances, one material, the other immaterial. Given the standard definitions of each of these kinds of substances, Diderot concludes that they are essentially incompatible. 'Is there anything more absurd than the idea of a contact between two beings, one of which has no parts and occupies no space? Is there anything more absurd than the idea of the action of one being on another without contact?' (p. 55).

From the rejection of two substances, from his assertions that all interaction requires physical motion and contact, that cognition and affection are closely linked with nerve and brain motion, it is easy for Diderot to conclude that the action of the soul on the body, or of body on soul, 'is the action of one part of the body on another part' (p. 59). He asserts unequivocally that 'memory is a corporeal quality', and that the 'only difference between a sensitive and a rational soul is a matter of physiological organization' (p. 59). Is he really saying memory and all mental processes are physical (albeit complex) events in the body, or is he only remarking (as La Peyronie, Astruc, and Collet did) the close and specific dependence of mental states and processes on particular brain states and the condition of particular nerve fibres? In the chapter of the *Eléments* on 'Animal' (ch. II, pt. I), he characterizes the difference between animals (what he there calls 'la machine de chair') and an iron or wooden machine, between man or dogs and a pendulum, as that the pendulum and the iron or wooden machine lack awareness and volition (p. 35). He was arguing there that the action of both sorts of objects are necessary, caused by some impulse either external or internal to the machine. Presumably, from what he later says about all interaction being by contact, the impulsive motion can only act by physical contact, in

[12] See *Œuvres philosophiques*, ed. P. Vernière (Paris: Garnier, 1964), 273–4.
[13] Ibid. 271–2.
[14] See the edn. of the *Eléments* by Jean Mayer (Paris: Didier, 1964), 58–9.

cases of conscious actions by acting on certain areas of the brain. In a brief discussion of 'Volonté' (ch. VI, pt. III), Diderot asserts explicitly that willing and understanding are mechanical functions of the brain and are corporeal (p. 262). Willing is the effect of a cause which activates and determines the will. Without the cause, the will is only a chimera, only a word. In that passage, Diderot applies the claim to a large range of what we would normally call 'mental' or 'affective' qualities.

La douleur, le plaisir, la sensibilité, les passions, le bien ou le malaise, les besoins, les appetits, les sensations interieures, et exterieures, l'habitude, l'imagination, l'instinct, l'action propre des organes commandent à la machine et lui commandent involontairement. Qu'est-ce en effet que la volonté, abstraction faite de toutes ces causes? Rien. (p. 262)

The difference between voluntary and involuntary action is simply that in the former *the brain* is active, in the latter it is passive (p. 263).

Late in this work, in part III: 'Phénomenes du cerveau', in chapter IX: 'Maladies', Diderot reaffirms that all sensations, all affections are corporeal. Consequently, 'there is a physical medicine which is equally applicable to body and mind', a statement recalling for us Le Camus's programme (p. 301). Diderot seems, then, to hold not only that sensation, memory, emotions are *caused by* matter in motion, but that they are themselves material. But what was his concept of matter? It differs markedly from the passive, inert, and inactive matter of the immaterialists in Britain and even from the matter of Malebranchians in France. Newton's matter had the properties of attraction and repulsion, but there was a question as to whether these were natural or added properties. Biological matter, e.g. muscle tissue, the matter out of which animals and man (and plants) are made, has for Diderot the properties of sensibility and irritability: it is *essentially* active. When Diderot says that all sensations and affections are corporeal, he is not saying they are properties of corpuscular matter. Those who in Britain attacked Locke's suggestion of thinking matter did not have any very specific notion of living matter or of the brain. They were fixated on the matter they knew, corpuscular, inactive matter, matter with the properties of extension, impenetrability, and motion. They did not look beyond that particular metaphysic of matter. When Diderot says that thought is a function of the organization of the brain, he is asserting a rather different claim from that Locke was understood to have made by his attackers in Britain or in France. British thinking matter is not the same as French 'matière pensante'.

Still it is not clear precisely what Diderot meant by saying sensations, memory, and affections are corporeal. Did he mean that they were particular kinds of brain events, different from the motions of nerves or the contracting of muscles? Even to say that the emotions are nothing without their causes, that emotion words are only words, fails to tell us precisely what he understands to be the effects of those causes. If he means by 'anger' or 'sadness' the *feelings* we experience when we are sad or angry, those feelings are not identical with their mechanical or biological causes. The ambiguity of the assertion that sensations are corporeal is of course found not only in Diderot. It is a problem facing most writers who fancy materialism. As we shall see, that ambiguity is prominent in La Mettrie's writings.

LA METTRIE'S DUALISM OF PROPERTIES

La Mettrie's *Traité de l'âme* first appeared in 1745 with the title *Histoire naturelle de l'âme*. It was reprinted with that same title in 1747. In his *Œuvres philosophiques* (1751), the work carries the title of *Traité de l'âme*.[15] In that work, as Verbeek has convincingly shown, La Mettrie has borrowed from a variety of authors, ancient and modern. Among ancient writers we find Aristotle, Tertullian, and Gassendi; among the moderns Descartes, Malebranche, Haller, Boerhaave. It is difficult to find a consistent or unified view which can be ascribed to La Mettrie. Nevertheless, the *Traité* is useful for bringing together a body of writings dealing with the topics related to this study, topics of mind and body, mental and physical properties. This style of writing by surveying a vast body of literature on set topics or themes concerning the soul had become almost a distinct *genre*. In some cases, for example with d'Argens or Mirabaud, the compiler's own views can be discerned. The lack of unity, even the incompatible passages, in La Mettrie's *Traité* illustrate the difficulty writers had in sorting out the difference between 'caused by' or 'explained by' and 'are identical with' or 'the same as'.

[15] In the discussion that follows, I have used the reprint ed. with notes and commentary by Theo Verbeek: *Le Traité de l'âme de La Mettrie* (2 vols., Utrecht: OMI-Grafisch Bedrijf, 1988). Page references are to the works edn. of 1751 used in facsimile by Verbeek. The editor's extensive notes and commentary give an exhaustive account of the various sources from which La Mettrie borrowed in this work.

The *Traité* tells us that matter has two basic properties: extension and the power or ability to receive different 'forms' (p. 87). La Mettrie defines 'form' as 'the different states or modifications' matter is able to acquire. The most important forms are motion (including, I think, self-motion) and the faculty of feeling ('sentiment'). The term 'sentiment' stands for a generic psychological property; its variants are sensing, imaging, having ideas, recollecting. Even though these are properties or forms of *matter* (of *organized* matter such as the brain), they are not neurophysiological. Of course, mechanical, physiological events are close accompaniments of these psychological events. Only sensitive beings have these mental properties.

As many tracts did, so La Mettrie discusses the location, the 'siege', of the soul. He is reviewing and presenting the views of previous writers in these pages; hence the persistence of the term 'soul'. In so far as we can extract La Mettrie's own beliefs from his survey and use of the writings of others, we might say that the term 'soul' is for him a code word for 'soul properties' (i.e. mental properties). He does not think we can discover the essence or nature of soul or body (p. 86), but we can discover by experience and observation those properties some philosophers ascribe to an immaterial substance they call 'soul'. Some of these writers did use literal language about the 'residence' of the soul. Other writers, including Descartes, also used functional language: the place where the soul exercises its function. How the soul functions in or on the brain is never explained, other than to say it moves nerves or animal spirits. In the passages in La Mettrie's *Traité* (pp. 110–23), he speaks of the soul being extended. Many British writers also talked of the soul being extended, but, like Locke, they usually made it clear that its extension was of a different kind from the extension of corpuscular bodies. La Mettrie seems to suggest two kinds of extension when he criticizes those who think all extension requires *solidity* (p. 90). Nevertheless, since he wants to talk of properties, not of substances (and especially not of an immaterial substance), the concept of extension for these psychological forms is not important. A dualism of properties will have to give some account of the status (the ontic status) of both kinds of property, but that is not an easy task, nor did anyone that I know really give such an account. The result of this failure is that it becomes easy to think of both kinds of properties as being the same, as both being brain processes or states. In some writers, there is a confusion between the motion of animal spirits and the feelings they (or the vibrating nerve strings) arouse or the ideas they are said to cause. Brain traces tend to be taken for ideas.

In the *Traité* there is a fair amount of detail on the physiology of sense perception. There are also a number of passages in which he indicates specific fibres as the source of particular ideas and feelings. In general, there is a recognition, common at that time, of the effects of physiological defects on mood and mental states. As we have seen, most writers on physiology were familiar with these dependencies. Where physical influence entered these accounts was in the discussions of the relation between physical objects and perceptual awareness. The material presented by La Mettrie in this work uses causal language for this relation. Objects are said to *strike* sense organs, thereby disturbing the nerves in the relevant organ. The motion of animal spirits is said to modify and transmit the disturbance to the brain, to the sensorium. It is in the sensorium that the sensitive soul receives the sensations. Do the animal spirits modify the motions into sensations, or does this change occur only at the point where the sensitive soul is affected? Sometimes La Mettrie (or those from whom he borrows) speaks of sensations being transmitted to the soul, not to the brain. There is no sensation without a change in the sense organs, or in the surface of the nerves of that organ. No bodies enter the nerves. Details on the correlations between brain states and mental events are found on pp. 107, 112, 121–3. On p. 111, he also speaks of the diversity of motions of the animal spirits excited in the nerves as giving birth to different sensations. There is also an important passage distinguishing between those faculties that are purely mechanical and those that properly belong to sensitive beings. It may be that this distinction reveals a modification to the standard view of the Cartesian beast-machine: it has only the mechanical faculties. I may be reading too much into this distinction of kinds of faculties, but there is a suggestion, I think, that the later term, 'l'homme machine', is to be taken as going beyond the purely mechanical notion of man. La Mettrie's man has the sensitive faculties as well (see e.g. p. 98).

Is there any support for this suggestion about the nature of *l'homme machine* in La Mettrie's work of this title?[16] The first two-

---

[16] References to this work are to Aram Vartanian's edn., *La Mettrie's L'Homme machine: A Study in the Origins of an Idea* (Princeton, NJ: Princeton University Press, 1960). There are several references to Locke in this work, one to the thinking-matter suggestion, one to Locke's talking parrot.

thirds of that work are concerned to stress, through many examples, the tight dependence on or correlation between bodily events and mental and affective states. In the last third of that work he begins to draw his conclusions and to state his own views. He asks, since all the faculties of the soul depend on the organization of the brain and body, why cannot we say that matter (brain and body) has the mental and affective properties? The properties he most often mentions are awareness and feelings. He makes statements such as that the matter of the bodily organs can feel remorse, once that matter 'has acquired with time the faculty of feeling' (p. 180). We are not told what is involved in the acquisition by the sense organs or brain of the faculty of feeling, but it is important for us to note this qualification. La Mettrie lists some examples of matter being active: the chicken runs after its head is cut off, a frog's legs move when stimulated even after death. He also cites the polyp which had caused so much excitement when it was discovered (p. 181). The heart also, even in newly dead men, is active. All these *facts* prove, he says, that each fibre or part of organized bodies moves itself (pp. 181–2). He says that the location of the innate *force* that activates these fibres and organs is in the fibres and organs themselves, although there is some suggestion that some parts of the body play a more central role than others. The brain, for example, is the source which animates the whole, the source of our feelings, pleasures, passions, thoughts: 'the brain has muscles for thinking, as the legs do for walking' (p. 183). Even defects of the imagination (an important faculty for him) can be explained in terms of the power or force of the brain. There is a relation of sympathy between the muscles of the brain and the imagination. Appeals to a soul in order to explain mental and affective experiences are appeals to the Holy Spirit (p. 184)! What La Mettrie stresses is the *material unity* of man. Appeals to a soul as well as the body to explain mental and affective phenomena use two entities where one will do.

He speaks of activating the animal spirits which in turn mechanically move the limbs. He asserts repeatedly that *the body is a machine*; sometimes it is said to be a clock (pp. 186, 190). Getting close to his general conclusion, he comments: 'I believe that thought is so little incompatible with organized matter, that it seems to be a property of it, just as are electricity, impenetrability, extension, etc.' (p. 192). Even more decisively, he says that

to be a machine, to feel, think, know how to distinguish good from evil, as blue from yellow, to be born with intelligence and instinct for morality, and to be only an animal, are things which are no more contradictory than to be an ape or parrot and know how to find pleasure. (p. 192)

He then states his main conclusion: 'man is a machine and there is in the universe only one substance diversely modified' (p. 197). Man is the kind of machine just described. The phrase 'diversely modified' indicates that *l'homme machine* has feelings and thoughts, makes moral and aesthetic judgements, as well as being extended, having parts that interrelate mechanically. In other words, the *body machine* is not the same as *l'homme machine*: the latter is the body machine after it has acquired the 'human' properties of thought and feeling. The one-substance language he sometimes uses does not result in a reduction of all properties to one sort. Nor does it over-look differences in the combinations and forms matter can take. That there is a very tight dependence of events, such as sensing, reflecting, recalling, having ideas, on the mechanical and physio-logical features of the human body does not lead to a metaphysical monism of qualities. Causal dependence is not identity. Even if we say that there is just one kind of active principle, one sort of basic force at work in the body, that makes the heart beat and the brain think and feel, the heart beating is one kind of event, being aware of my heart beating is another kind of event. The ontology towards which La Mettrie seems to be inclined includes matter *and* its various properties. There is still a dualism in his view, not a dualism of substances, but a dualism of properties: mechanical ones *and* cognitive and affective ones.

BARON D'HOLBACH'S SYSTEM

We have come across the name 'Mirabaud' in Chapter 3, the author of another of those surveys of ancient authors supporting thought as a property of matter. Astruc named Mirabaud as a follower of Locke. By this time, at the end of our story, Mirabaud is dead (he died in 1760), but his name was used by d'Holbach as the pseud-onymous author of his own *Système de la nature* (1770), a work whose doctrines d'Holbach must have felt Mirabaud would have approved.[17] D'Holbach is much more precise, and gives many more details of a system whose metaphysics rests on matter and motion

[17] *Système de la nature, ou des lois du monde physique et du monde moral*, new edn., with notes and corrections by Diderot (2 vols., 1821; repr. Hildesheim: G. Olms, 1966).

than do other writers. He also employs the principle (which came to be called 'Locke's principle') about the sensory origin of ideas, praising him for rejecting innate ideas (i. 198–200). Where the specificity is important for us is in its clear recognition of the active matter which is necessary for such a system.

The difference between British thinking matter and French 'matière pensante' is decisively illustrated by d'Holbach's contrast early in his *Système*. He distinguishes two senses of 'nature'. One sense of this term refers to a mass of dead, purely passive matter, lacking all properties, a concept not far from the one used by Locke in sketching his scenario for Bishop Stillingfleet. With matter of this sort, d'Holbach admits we would be forced to seek outside nature for a principle of motion and action (i. 29). On the other hand, if by 'nature' we mean (what in fact d'Holbach believes is true) a whole of parts with properties, parts which are in constant interaction and which

gravitent vers un centre commun, tandis que d'autres s'éloignent, et vont à la circonférence, qui s'attirent et se repoussent, qui s'unissent et se séparent, et qui par leurs collisions et leurs rapprochemens continuels produisent et décomposent tous les corps que nous voyons,

then there is no need to look for supranatural forces to account for the formation of bodies and the phenomena we observe (i. 29–30). Man is matter of this second sort, which in time acquires the qualities of feeling, thinking, and reasoning.

Sometimes he writes as if he is not saying thought *is* motion, only that it *results from* motion (e.g. i. 93). Later, d'Holbach says that 'the generation of sensations, perceptions and ideas, as well as their association and connections in the brain' are only the results of successive impulses which the external sense organs transmit to the brain. The faculty of thinking reacts to and becomes aware of those external disturbances (i. 136–7). But d'Holbach is no better than other writers at explaining the precise connection between that faculty and the brain.

Where he is most effective is in showing the difficulty, if not absurdity, in the two-substance view of man. Against all evidence of experience, the defenders of spiritual or immaterial substance make man double: 'il se regarda comme un tout composé par l'assemblage inconcevable de deux natures différentes, et qui n'avaient point d'analogie entre elles' (i. 94). This gratuitous supposition of *l'homme physique* and *l'homme moral* has been, he says, adopted by most philosophers today (i. 95). Chapter VII continues to attack the notion of two substances, mainly by showing that no one has explained how two such different substances could interact. The dogma of a spiritual soul 'offers in effect only a vague idea, or rather no idea at all' (i. 118).

D'Holbach's account of sensation, perception, and ideas attempts to give an analysis in terms of matter and motion, modifications of the brain; but he occasionally speaks of thoughts, reflection, imagination, and judgement as modifications of the soul (i. 138). Sometimes, sensory modifications are said to be in the brain, but also 'en moi' (i. 136). Other passages describe the brain feeling and being aware of ideas caused by the motion in nerves (i. 137). To think or reflect is, he says, 'sentir ou apercevoir en nous-mêmes les impressions, les sensations, les idées que donnent les objets qui agissent sur nos sens, et les divers changemens que notre cerveau ou organe intérieur produit sur lui-même (i. 137–8). Clearly, d'Holbach would like to say that all 'mental' operations, all the intellectual faculties, which we like to attribute to the soul, are really only modifications or ways of being of the brain, but he cannot avoid speaking of the brain also being the place of feeling (i. 141). He does not, I think, succeed in reducing fear, for example, or sadness, to the 'tremblement dans les membres', to 'la pâleur sur le visage', or to the tears that flow from our eyes (i. 141).

Whether or not we think he has been successful in his efforts at reduction, it is easy to see how his readers, already fearful of what the 'philosophes' and materialists had done to the concept of man, saw the *Système* as an instantiation of *l'homme machine*, taken as a mechanical but flesh and blood automaton. How else could they react to a passage such as the following:

Une idée, qui n'est qu'une modification imperceptible de notre cerveau, met en jeu l'organe de la parole, ou se montre par les mouvemens qu'elle excite dans la langue; celle-ci fait à son tour naître des idées, des pensées, des passions dans des êtres pourvus d'organes susceptibles de recevoir des mouvemens analogues, en conséquence desquels les volontés d'un grand nombre d'hommes font que leurs efforts combinés produisent une révolution dans un état, ou même influent sur notre globe entier. (i. 197)

Whether or not he has been successful in reducing ideas, thoughts, passions, and will to motions of the machine of the body, readers would have had a difficult time not to assume he had. Even if we think the reductive programme has been (or can be) successful, it is important to remember d'Holbach's distinction between the 'old' dead, inactive matter and the 'new', active, and interactive matter with which he worked.

VOLTAIRE'S ADMIRATION OF LOCKE

Voltaire has been one of the main characters in our story. His admiration for Locke and his doctrines continued to be reflected in his writings after 1733–4, in subsequent reprints of Letter XIII and 'Lettre sur l'âme' and in some of his other writings. In various works, Locke is described as 'Le modeste et sage Locke',[18] as 'le seul métaphysicien raisonnable',[19] as a modest man 'qui ne feint jamais de savoir ce qu'il ne sait pas'.[20] Locke appears in Voltaire's popular *Elémens de la philosophie de Neuton* (1738; repr. 1741, 1744), first as the man who persuaded Newton that all our ideas come from the senses (1744 edn., p. 32), then as being too gullible in believing those travellers' tales about the custom in some countries of eating children (pp. 33–4). Locke's talking Brazilian parrot is similarly treated in *Le Philosophe ignorant* (ch. XXXV). There, and in the *Elémens*, Voltaire admonishes Locke for denying any common notion in all men of good and evil. He wanted to agree with Locke on no innate ideas while at the same time accepting that eighteenth-century notion of a moral sense, a built-in reaction to what is good and evil as part of human nature.[21] In this same work, he says that Locke persuaded Newton of another point: 'que Dieu a donné aux animaux (qui semblent n'être que matiere) une mesure d'idées, & les mêmes sentiments qu'à nous' (p. 37).

---

[18] 'Poème sur la loi naturelle' (1756), in *Œuvres complètes* (Paris: Garnier, 1878), ix. 452–53 n. 2. This and some of the following passages from Voltaire are nicely collected by R. Naves, in his edn. of the *Lettres philosophiques* (Paris: Garnier, 1988), notes to Letter XIII.

[19] Voltaire's 'Mémoires pour servir à la vie de M. Voltaire', *Œuvres complètes* (Garnier edn.), i (1883), 21: 'je le regardais comme le seul métaphysicien raisonnable, je louais surtout cette retenue si nouvelle, si sage en même temps et si hardie, avec laquelle il dit que nous n'en saurons jamais assez par les lumières de notre raison pour affirmer que Dieu ne peut accorder le don du sentiment et de la pensée à être appelé *matière*'.

[20] Voltaire's *Le Philosophe ignorant* (1766), in *Œuvres complètes* (Garnier edn.), xxvi. 74–8.

[21] A more extended discussion of this point is contained in ch. XXXIV of Voltaire's *Le Philosophe ignorant*.

Chapter VI of part I of the *Elémens* addresses the question of the union of soul and body. While admitting that Newton has not discussed this question, or that of the formation of ideas, Voltaire gives a summary account of the four opinions of that topic. Three of these opinions on mind–body are the familiar ones, the 'trois hypothèses' which have appeared so often in our story. (1) The ancients believed that there is nothing above or besides matter. They also regarded ideas in our understanding as similar to wax impressions. Voltaire then makes a comment which appears to go against some of his earlier remarks about Locke and thinking matter.

Les Philosophes qui ont voulu ensuite prouver que la matiere pense par elle-même, ont erré bien davantage; car le vulgaire se trompoit sans raisonner, & ceux-ci erroient par principes; aucun d'eux n'a pû jamais rien trouver dans la matiere, qui pût prouver qu'elle a l'intelligence par elle-même. (p. 40)

(2) The second and most generally received opinion about ideas is that they are the result of the interaction of two substances. This view is based on the experience we believe we have of interaction between our body and our will. The objection to this view of interaction is that the motion conveyed from objects to sense organs could not affect the soul unless the soul was corporeal (p. 43). (3) The third system is that of occasionalism, which Voltaire finds implausible and which reduces man to an instrument of God (pp. 43–4). (4) The fourth system is that of pre-established harmony. The two-clocks analogy is cited, the example found in Jaucourt's *Encyclopédie* entry 'Harmonie' is repeated here also (Virgil's hand wrote the *Aeneid* without the influence of his will). Voltaire finds this part of Leibniz's philosophy unacceptable, but he goes on to praise many other of Leibniz's doctrines.

The rationale for including this chapter on mind and body in his commentary on Newton is not clear. Nor can we pick out one of the four systems as the one favoured by Voltaire. What *is* apparent from this discussion, and from other of his writings, is that he failed to find the metaphysics of two substances at all useful or informative. In his *Traité de métaphysique* (1796), Voltaire says we can never know substances of either sort since all we discover are properties: 'Since we are unable to have any notions except by experience, it is impossible for us ever to know what matter is' (ch. VIII). In that same *Traité*, thinking matter is discussed at some length (ch. V). There, Voltaire agrees with those who attack this notion that, if thought was a composition of material parts, thought would have to be extended and divisible. But if thought is a property of God, a property which God gives to matter, there would be no reason for that property to be extended or divisible. It would then be like other properties given to matter by God, e.g. motion, gravitation. The way in which gravitation acts on bodies is as hidden from us as the way thought acts on our bodies. Locke's name does not appear in this discussion, but there are clear echoes of Letter XIII and even of some sentences in Voltaire's correspondence with Tournemine. There are also in this work a few paragraphs on personal identity which follow Locke's account, again without his name (ch. VI).

In a long note added to the third part of his 'Poème sur la loi naturelle' (1756), he reminds the reader that Locke was convinced of the limitation of human knowledge and held a belief in the infinite power of God. Thus, Locke said that we know the nature of our soul only by faith. In terms of knowledge, 'l'homme n'a point par lui-même assez de lumières pour assurer que Dieu ne peut pas communiquer la pensée à tout être auquel il daignera faire ce présent, à la matière elle-même'.[22] Cartesians spend too much time over the question whether the human understanding is a substance or a faculty. Voltaire affirms that the faculty that animals have of self-motion is not a substance (a being apart) but a gift from the creator: 'Locke says that the same Creator is able to make a gift of thought to any being he chooses'. On this hypothesis, Voltaire asserts, 'thought granted to be an element of matter is not less pure, not less immortal than it is on any other hypothesis'.[23] This is what Locke says, without affirming that this hypothesis is true. Locke merely talks of what 'Dieu eût pu faire et non ce que Dieu a fait'. Locke, Voltaire assures us, was aware of man's insignificance in relation to God. It is this awareness and the recognition of God's power which some have characterized as impiety in Locke. Partisans of Locke, who are convinced of the immortality of the soul, are even called 'materialists'. The conclusion of this long, effusive note touches on other aspects of Locke's thought which Voltaire also admired. For example, Locke was the first 'qui ait fait voir ce que c'est que l'identité, et ce que c'est que d'être la même personne, le même *soi*; il est le premier qui ait prouvé la fausseté du système des idées innées'.[24]

---

22 In Naves's edn., p. 223.
23 Ibid. 224.
24 Ibid. 225.

In *Le Philosophe ignorant* (1766), in a chapter on Locke (ch. XXIX), Voltaire lists a number of truths which Locke has convinced him of, e.g. that nothing enters our understanding except via the senses; that there are no innate ideas; that he does not always think; that to say the will is free is absurd (it is the man that is free). Locke's account of personal identity is also presented again, although with too much emphasis on memory. Thinking matter is prominent in this chapter on Locke.

In chapter IV of his *Lettres à S. A. Mgr. Le Prince* *** [i.e. C. G. F. de Brunswick-Lunebourg] *sur Rabelais et sur d'autres auteurs accusés d'avoir mal parlé de la religion chrétienne* (1767), Voltaire admits that Locke's *Reasonableness* is a bit unorthodox in what it requires us to believe, but hardly unchristian. People have said Locke does not believe the soul is immortal because he was persuaded that 'God, the absolute master of all, is able to give (if he wishes) feeling and thought to matter'.[25] Chapter IV is devoted to English authors, the very same as appear in that list in Letter XIII: Locke, Toland, Tindal, Woolston. There is also a chapter on Vanini and another on Spinoza.

Voltaire keeps returning to Locke's suggestion about thinking matter. In an addition in 1770 to his *Dictionnaire philosophique*,[26] a short section in the entry 'Âme' is devoted to 'Des doutes de Locke sur l'âme'. In that section, the 4. 3. 6 *Essay* passage is quoted in Coste's translation. This passage contains, Voltaire comments, the 'words of a profound, religious, and modest man'. As he usually insisted in his correspondence, Voltaire says again in this section that Locke does not say matter does think, only that our knowledge is such that we cannot say it is impossible for God to give some matter such a property. The whole of antiquity was also of this opinion; writers then regarded the soul as a very delicate matter, hence matter is able to think and feel. A few other references follow to Gassendi, Descartes, Church Fathers, and Malebranche.

Another section added to the 1770 *Dictionnaire* entry on the soul is on the souls of animals. Locke is also supported in his anti-Cartesian claim that the soul does not always think. Voltaire reminds the reader that he was persecuted for agreeing with Locke on this simple point: 'Ce qui n'avait produit en Angleterre que quelques

---

[25] *Œuvres complètes* (Garnier edn.), xxvi. 483–4.
[26] *Dictionnaire philosophique*, in *Œuvres complètes* (Garnier edn.), xvii (1878).

disputes philosophiques produisit en France les plus lâches atro-
cités: un Français fut la victime de Locke'.

CONCLUSION

There are other references to Locke in Voltaire's writings. The
sample we have taken confirms a rather central role for Locke in
Voltaire's philosophical writings and in some of his autobiographical
comments. Even in his *Métaphysique*, Voltaire did not develop a
systematic account of those issues related to Locke's suggestion or to
the questions about mind and body, or perception, which we have
discovered were linked together in the reactions to and use of
Locke's doctrines by French-language writers. But Voltaire's
repeated remarks about Locke from 1733 to at least 1770 kept
Locke's name before the reading public. As well, Diderot's praise
of Locke; the references to him in entries in the *Encyclopédie*; the
discussions in these sources of the three systems; the mention of
medical writers such as La Peyronie for the tight and specific
correlation of mental and bodily states; the emergence of more
systematic attempts to formulate a materialism by La Mettrie and
most extensively by d'Holbach: all of these help us to appreciate the
context towards which the occasionalist critics of Locke pointed.
What I think those critics failed to anticipate was the change in the
concept of matter taking place among medical researchers, a change
which enabled other writers such as La Mettrie, Diderot, and
d'Holbach to formulate a more dynamic notion of man, man as a
unified biological organism with many diverse properties. Thought
and feeling (in all their modes) take their place alongside properties
such as irritability, muscular contractions, blood flow, and numerous physical processes taking place in organs, nerves, and brain.

Locke's suggestion, which his contemporaries in Britain attacked,
which Voltaire popularized in France, which writers such as Roche,
Astruc, Gerdil, and Mey thought they saw spreading in France, came
out of a quite different ontology with a different concept of matter.
Locke began the process of removing substance from our explanation and understanding of the world (just as Bishop Stillingfleet
charged), not by an overt rejection of substance-talk but (1) by arguing that we have only a very vague idea of substance, especially of
immaterial substance, (2) by substituting the scientific language of
the corpuscular theory wherever possible, and (3) by simply not

using the concept of substance in his new account of the moral person. He was not entirely free from the concept, however. Even in his reply to Stillingfleet's attack on the 4. 3. 6 passage, Locke employed substance-talk in order to illustrate for the bishop what he understood by the *possibility* of God adding thought to a suitably organized bit of matter.

Among the 'philosophes', then, Locke took his place with the many other writers invoked to illustrate and help convince their readers of the new view of man that was emerging. With his reputation as an honest man and a serious thinker, Locke was a 'modern' whom they could praise and use, even though he had not developed a detailed account, a metaphysic, of thinking matter. Locke's strong stress on experience and observation and his rejection of traditional concepts fitted nicely into the programme of the 'philosophes', especially of Diderot and d'Alembert.

General Conclusion

W H A T have we learned from following the adventures of Locke's thinking matter across the Channel in France? It is always salutary to discover in philosophy's history topics and debates which occur in our contemporary world. The central topic of our story, how are we to understand the relation between mental and physical events, especially between mind and our own body, is one of the major interests today among philosophers and cognitive psychologists. The vocabulary of the eighteenth-century discussions differs from that used today, the level of detail in present-day discussions is far greater than anything found in eighteenth-century writers. What may be more prominent in those older discussions are the ontological questions: one substance, two substances, or no substances? Those in the eighteenth century who reacted to the suggestion of two different kinds of properties belonging to one substance saw these efforts as a threat to their concept of man and human nature. These critics of what they saw as materialism (one substance, two kinds of properties) were not satisfied until they had a model which kept the two substances distinct and apart, interaction occurring only through God's causal intervention.

Were those in Britain who saw Locke's suggestion as a move towards a clockwork man, or those in France who considered the growing knowledge of the physiology of nerves and brain as supporting *l'homme machine*, justified in their fears? If mental and affective states are caused by external and internal physical events (i.e. if the system of physical influence were true), is the result a materialism of matter and motion? Those in the eighteenth century who thought the answer to his question was 'yes' were aided in that belief by the disappearance in accounts of man of the two-substance ontology. An ontology of one substance infamously advocated by Spinoza and tacitly accepted by many others disturbed traditional views and made difficult the task of understanding the possibility of such an ontology preserving the dualism of mind and matter within a two-property ontology. It is just such a dualism, a duality of kinds of properties (mental and physical), that is, I think, found in La Mettrie and even in passages in d'Holbach. A dualism of properties is made even more feasible when we realize that the matter of our body is itself dynamic and active, as Diderot believed. One question remains: if, as seems to be the case, mental properties *causally* depend upon bodily events and processes, does not such dependence give the mental a subordinate role? Even more to the point, does a causal *explanation* of mental events (assuming that such is possible) lead to a *reduction* of the mental to the physical? Causal dependence does not turn effects into their causes. The very attempt to explain the one kind of property in terms of the other already recognizes two kinds of property. Whether or not we think materialistic explanations, explanations in terms of matter and motion or electrical-chemical events in the brain, do in fact explain all that needs to be explained in affective and cognitive states, those explanations start from and presuppose an ontology of two kinds of properties, two sorts of events.

Following the reception of Locke's suggestion has had other benefits, historical and methodological lessons. As with the reconstruction in Britain of the reactions to that suggestion, so tracing its appearances in French-language books and journals has enabled us to examine at, as it were, the micro-level some of the attempts to deal with new ideas by many less well-known writers in less glamorous contexts, along with some of the standard authors. The challenge to traditional metaphysics by the substitution of two-property for two-substance dualisms, by the stress on experience and observation rather than established authority, by the growing use of medical and biological science for the solutions to mind–body relations has been illustrated in Britain and now in France by following the theme of thinking matter. That is proved to have been a powerful and focusing theme in both countries. The reactions to that theme in France were perhaps more diverse and, in some instances, more radical than in Britain.

The adventures of Locke's suggestion in France can be described as 'picaresque' because of the way this suggestion appears, re-appears, is attacked and defended in so many places and in such different contexts. Picked up by some of the clandestine tracts; cited as the centre of a supposed group of 'disciples' by occasionalist protectors of tradition; given prominence by the great Voltaire, whose defence was in turn attacked by the German Reinbeck and the

French writer on animal souls D. R. Boullier; implicated in that amusing 'affaire de Prades' at the Sorbonne; attacked by several abbots; defended at great length by the Swiss Cuenz; making frequent appearances in the leading journals of the day; mentioned in entries in the *Encyclopédie*; Locke himself dubbed an 'honnête homme' and described as a 'philosophe' by no less a person than Diderot: these are rather unusual adventures for what I take to be a conceptual aside by Locke in his *Essay*. The spread of that suggestion (and, we must not forget, of some of the British controversy it engendered) in France was aided by Condillac's seizing 'Locke's principle' about the sensory origin of ideas (and the rejection of innate ideas), a principle which reinforced the general scientific attitudes of the French 'philosophes' towards experience and observation as the bases for knowledge.

The fact that Locke's suggestion elicited such widespread reactions in France is an indication of the stature Locke had as one of the leading English philosophers. The rapid translation into French of his books increased the access to his doctrines. One result our story has not produced is an understanding of the reception of all of Locke's books and doctrines in France. From notices and discussions in the journals, it is evident that these were widely known. In his valuable (but now generally overlooked) study, Thomas Webb[1] remarks that, after Voltaire's Letter XIII, Locke became 'the Philosopher *à la mode*', even, Webb adds, in the salons of Paris and the gardens of Versailles where 'fine gentlemen descanted with fine ladies on the origin of ideas' (p. 6). Webb goes on to make an even more intriguing claim: 'Even the heroines of the stage amused their audience with disquisitions on the original, certainty, and extent of knowledge' (p. 6), precisely the programme of the *Essay* as announced by Locke. The only reference Webb gives to support this latter claim is to Dugald Stewart's *Dissertation*, first published in 1821.[2] Stewart's editor, Hamilton, cites only one play, albeit written by a very popular playwright, where the heroine does indeed spend a

---

[1] Thomas E. Webb, *The Intellectualism of Locke: An Essay* (Dublin: William McGee & Co., 1857).

[2] Dugald Stewart, *Dissertation Exhibiting the Progress of Metaphysical, Ethical, and Political Philosophy, Since the Revival of Letters in Europe*, ed. Sir William Hamilton (Edinburgh: Constable, 1854). Locke's *Essay* 'was not only read by the learned, but had made its way into the circles of fashion at Paris'. A note at this point speaks of 'allusions to Locke's doctrine in the dramatic pieces then in possession of the French stage' (pt. I, p. 222).

number of long speeches outlining, without naming the source, Locke's programme. That play was *La Fausse Agnès* (1757) by Néricault Destouches.[3] It would be interesting to know of other plays with such obvious Lockian references and language; even better would be to have support for Webb's other claim that Locke was discussed in salons and gardens!

Locke's influence in France is usually seen through Condillac's claim that his account of sensation and knowledge followed Locke's. By the time the early nineteenth-century French historians are lecturing and writing, Locke is linked with what Victor Cousin labelled 'the School of Sensualism'.[4] Cousin sealed Locke's fate in being tied to that label, at least until Webb challenged it. Webb was driven to strong words about Cousin: 'M. Cousin's criticism is not only an insult to the memory of Locke—it is an insult to Philosophy and to common sense' (p. 13). Webb does his best to correct Cousin's one-sided reading of Locke. It is a worthwhile question to ask, 'how does such an obvious misreading of Locke ever get started?' A more important project would be to trace the reception of Locke's doctrines and books in France, and not only in France. No one has really undertaken such a project.

One way into such a comprehensive project would be to follow the thinking-matter suggestion as it was reacted to in other countries, e.g. in Portugal, Italy, and Germany. Nicholas Jolley has given us an account of Leibniz's strong rejection of Locke's suggestion, but I suspect there was a wider reaction in Germany.[5] A chance finding of an Italian book attacking d'Holbach, with discussions of Locke's suggestion, Voltaire's Letter XIII, La Mettrie, and others, suggests that there is a research project on Locke and eighteenth-century

---

[3] See Hamilton's note U, pp. 552–6, for his citation and outline of the play. The play can be found in *Œuvres dramatiques de N. Destouches* (new edn., 4 vols., 1820), iv. 1–142. The play was apparently first performed on 12 Mar. 1759. In Act II, Scene xii, Angélique urges an examination of 'our knowledge in general, the degrees of knowledge, its extent and reality'. The next part of her programme would be to deal with universal or general propositions, maxims, principles, etc. In subsequent speeches, Angélique refers to innate ideas: some people are said to accept them, she rejects them. Real and chimerical ideas, true and false ideas, the connection and relation of ideas: all these are cited (iv. 133–7).

[4] See Victor Cousin, *Cours de l'histoire de la philosophie*, vol. ii: *Histoire de la philosophie du XVIIIe siècle* (new edn., Paris: Didier, 1841) or his *Philosophie de Locke* (Paris: Didier, 1861).

[5] Nicholas Jolley, *Leibniz and Locke: A Study of the 'New Essays on Human Understanding'* (Oxford: Oxford University Press, 1984).

Italy waiting to be done.[6] It is even more obvious that there is a rich research project on Locke in eighteenth-century Portugal.[7] The logic books that Carvalho mentions in his long introduction to his edition of the Portuguese translation of an abridgement of the *Essay* indicate not just reactions in that country to Locke's infamous suggestion, but some adoptions of other aspects of his thought. My guess is that if archival material still exists in Portugal, e.g. in church or government files, we might discover some fascinating reactions to the 'materialism of John Locke'.

Tracing the appearance of Locke's suggestion in other countries in the eighteenth century may well reveal other specific uses and evaluations of his more central doctrines. Such detailed examination of tracts and pamphlets, speeches, reviews, and journal articles in each country may even show the misleading nature of Cousin's stereotyping of Locke as a sensualist. At the very least, such projects would help us construct a detailed understanding of the reception, use, and criticism of Locke's philosophy in eighteenth-century Europe. We do not have as yet such a comprehensive understanding.

---

[6] D. Antonmaria Gardini, *L'anima umana e sue proprieta dedotte da'soli principi di ragione . . . contra i materialisti* (1781).

[7] I have already referred to the Portuguese translation of an abridgement of the *Essay*. See above, Introduction, n. 4. See also J. S. Yolton and J. W. Yolton, 'Locke's Suggestion of Thinking Matter and Some Eighteenth-Century Portuguese Reactions', *Journal of the History of Ideas*, 45 (1984), 302–7. Holland is of course another country that needs to be examined for Locke's role there. Richard Ashcraft has recently added to our biographical knowledge of Locke's role in the English dissident groups prior to 1688: *Revolutionary Politics and Locke's Two Treatises of Government* (Princeton, NJ: Princeton University Press, 1986). Rosalie Colie's much earlier study, *Light and Enlightenment* (Cambridge: Cambridge University Press, 1957), began the work that needs to be done on Locke's doctrines in the Netherlands. I believe scholars there are active again on this very important context for Locke's doctrines.

Bibliography
Compiled by Jean. S. Yolton

1. Eighteenth-Century Sources
(a) Books and Articles

L'Âme matérielle (œuvre anonyme), ed. with intro. and notes by Alain Niderst, Publications de l'Université de Rouen (Paris: Nizet, 1969). 245 p.

ARGENS, JEAN-BAPTISTE DE BOYER, Marquis d', *La Philosophie du bon-sens, ou Réflexions philosophiques sur l'incertitude des connoissances humaines*, enlarged and corrected edn., *Avec un examen des remarques de M. l'abbé d'Olivet et de l'Académie françoise* (The Hague: Pierre Paupie, 1768). 3 vols. in-12⁰. 1st publ. 1737 with imprint: Londres: Aux dépens de la Compagnie (xii, 444 p. in-12⁰).

ARNAULD, ANTOINE, *Des vrayes et des fausses idées, contre ce qu'enseigne l'auteur de la Recherche de la verité* [Malebranche] (Cologne: Nicolas Schouten, 1683). [6], 339 p. in-12⁰.

[ASTRUC, JEAN], *Dissertation sur l'immatérialité et l'immortalité de l'âme* (Paris: La Veuve Cavelier & fils, 1755). [2], xv, 444 p. in 12⁰. Consecutively paged with this but with a separate title-page is his *Dissertation sur la liberté*.

BACHAUMONT, LOUIS PETIT DE, *Mémoires secrets* . . . See § 2 below under this title.

BASSELIN, ROBERT, *Dissertation sur l'origine des idées, où l'on fait voir, contre Mr. Descartes, le Révérend Père Malebranche, et Messieurs de Port-Royal, qu'elles nous viennent toutes des sens, et comment* (Paris: François de Laulne & Jean Musier, 1709). [8], 75 p. in-12⁰.

BAXTER, ANDREW, *An Enquiry into the Nature of the Human Soul; Wherein the Immortality of the Soul Is Evinced from the Principles of Reason and Philosophy* (3rd edn, London: A. Millar, 1745). 2 vols. in-8⁰. 1st pub. 1733 (?); 2nd edn. 1737.

BAYLE, PIERRE, *Dictionnaire historique et critique*, 3rd edn., rev., corrected, and enlarged by the author (Rotterdam: Michel Bohm, 1720). 4 vols. infolio. 1st pub. 1697. For its continuation, see Chaufepié, J. G. de.

—— 'An Account of the Life of John Locke, Esq; Extracted from Mr. Bayle's Historical and Critical Dictionary', *American Magazine*, 2 (Sept. 1744), 540–4.

[BERKELEY, GEORGE], *Siris: A Chain of Philosophical Reflexions and Inquiries concerning the Virtues of Tar Water, and Divers Other Subjects connected together and Arising one from another*, by G.L.B.O.C. (Dublin: Printed by M. Rhames for R. Gunne, 1744). 261 p. in-8º.

[BERKELEY, GEORGE], *Recherches sur les vertus de l'eau de goudron, où l'on a joint des Réflexions philosophiques sur divers autres sujets importans, traduit de l'Anglois . . . avec deux lettres de l'auteur* (Amsterdam: Pierre Mortier, 1745). xxiv, 343 p. in-8º. Transl. of *Siris*.

[BOUGEANT, GUILLAUME-HYACINTHE], *Amusement philosophique sur le langage des bestes* (Geneva: Pierre Gosse, 1757). [2], 79 p. in-12º. 1st publ. 1739.

[BOULLIER, DAVID R.], *Apologie de la métaphysique, à l'occasion du 'Discours préliminaire de l'Encyclopédie'* [by d'Alembert], *avec les sentimens de M*** sur la critique des 'Pensées' de Pascal par Voltaire, suivis de trois lettres relatives à la philosophie de ce poète* (Amsterdam: J. Catuffe, 1753). 183 p. in-12º. 'Trois lettres' repr. in *Guerre littéraire*, q.v.

[——] *Court Examen de la thèse de Mr. l'abbé de Prades, et observations sur son Apologie* (Amsterdam: M. M. Rey, 1753). xxiv, 165 p. in-12º.

—— *Discours philosophiques: Le Premier sur les causes finales, le second sur l'inertie de la matière, et le troisieme sur la liberté des actions humaines* (Amsterdam, Paris: Guillyn, 1759). xxxviii, 271 p. in-12º.

[——] *Essai philosophique sur l'âme des bêtes, où l'on traite de son existence et de sa nature, et où l'on mêle par occasion diverses réflexions sur la nature de la liberté, et où l'on réfute diverses objections de Mr. Bayle* (Amsterdam: F. Changuion, 1728). xvi, 300 p. in-8º. The 2nd edn. has the subtitle: *Où l'on trouve diverses réflexions sur la nature de la liberté, sur celle de nos sensations, sur l'union de l'âme et du corps, sur l'immortalité de l'âme. Seconde edition, à laquelle on a joint un Traité des vrais principes qui servent de fondement à la certitude morale* (Amsterdam: F. Changuion, 1737, 2 vols. in-12º), with a dedication to Fontenelle signed '*Boullier*'.

[——] *Lettres critiques sur les Lettres philosophiques de Mr. de Voltaire, par rapport à notre âme, à sa spiritualité et à son immortalité, avec la défense des Pensées de Pascal contre la critique du même Voltaire, par M**** ([Paris,] Saint-Omer: Imprimerie de Fertel, 1753). 215 p. in-12º.

[——] *Lettres sur les vrais principes de la religion, où l'on examine le livre de 'La Religion essentielle à l'homme', avec la défense des 'Pensées' de Pascal contre la critique de Voltaire, et trois lettres relatives à la philosophie de ce poète* (Amsterdam: J. Catuffe, 1741). 2 vols. in-12º.

[——] *Pièces philosophiques et littéraires* (s.l.: s.n., 1759). viii, 294, 24 p. in-12º. Includes 'Lettre sur l'esprit philosophique de notre siècle'.

[——] 'Réflexions sur quelques principes de la philosophie de Mr. *Locke*, à l'occasion des "Lettres philosophiques" de Mr. de Voltaire', *Bibliothèque françoise*, 20 (1735), 189–214.

[BOURSIER, LAURENT-FRANÇOIS], *De l'action de Dieu sur les créatures: Traité dans lequel on prouve la prémotion physique par le raisonnement et où l'on examine plusieurs questions qui ont rapport à la nature des esprits et à la grace* (Lille: J.-B. Brovellio, 1713). 6 vols. in-12°. Also pub. Paris: F. Babuty, 1713 (2 vols. in-4°).

BUFFIER, CLAUDE, *Les Principes du raisonnement, exposés en deux logiques nouvelés, avec les remarques sur les logiques qui ont eu le plus de réputation de notre temps* (Paris: P. Witte, 1714). xxxii, 526 p. in-12°.

—— 'Traité des véritez de consequence, ou Les Principes du raisonement', in his *Cours de sciences sur des principes nouveaux et simples* (Paris: Guillaume Cavelier & Pierre François Giffart, 1732), cols. 745–892. Repr. of his 'Principes du raisonnement'.

—— 'Traité des premières vérités et de la source de nos jugements', in his *Œuvres philosophiques*, notes and intro. by Francisque Bouillier (Paris: Adolphe Delahays, 1843), 1–309. 1st pub. 1724.

CAMPBELL, ARCHIBALD, *The Necessity of Revelation, or An Enquiry into the Extent of Human Powers with Respect to Matters of Religion, Especially Those Two Fundamental Articles, the Being of God, and the Immortality of the Soul* (London: Printed by W. Bowyer at the Expence of the Society for the Encouragement of Learning, 1739). [12], 417 p. in-8°.

CAYLUS, CHARLES-D.-G. DE, *Instruction pastorale de Monseigneur l'évêque d'Auxerre, sur la vérité et la sainteté de la religion, méconnue et attaquée en plusieurs chefs par la thèse soutenue* [par de Prades] *en Sorbonne le 18 novembre 1751* ([Régennes?] 1752). [8], 80 p. in-4°.

CHAMBERS, EPHRAIM, *Cyclopaedia, or An Universal Dictionary of Arts and Sciences* (London: Printed for James and John Knapton [*et al.*], 1728). 2 vols. in-folio.

[CHAUDON, LOUIS MAYEUL], *Dictionnaire anti-philosophique, pour servir de commentaire & de correctif au Dictionnaire philosophique, & aux autres livres qui ont paru de nos jours contre le Christianisme*, new enlarged edn. (Avignon: Veuve Girard, F. Seguin & A. Aubanel, 1769). 2 vols. in-8°. 1st publ. Avignon, 1767.

CHAUFEPIÉ, JACQUES-GEORGES DE, *Nouveau Dictionnaire historique et critique, pour servir du supplément ou de continuation au Dictionnaire historique et critique de Mr. Pierre Bayle* (Amsterdam: Z. Chatelain [*et al.*]; Paris: Pierre de Hondt, 1750–6). 4 vols. in-folio.

CLARKE, SAMUEL, *A Collection of Papers, Which Passed between the Late Learned Mr. Leibnitz and Dr. Clarke in the Years 1715 and 1716, Relating to the Principles of Natural Philosophy and Religion; with an Appendix, to which are added, Letters to Dr. Clarke concerning Liberty and Necessity, from a Gentleman of the University of Cambridge* [Richard Bulkeley], *with the Doctor's Answers to them; also Remarks upon a Book, entituled A Philosophical Enquiry concerning Human Liberty* [by Anthony Collins] (London: James Knapton, 1717). [2], xii, [3], 416, 46 p. in-8°. Known as the Leibniz–Clarke Collection.

CLARKE, SAMUEL, Collins–Clarke exchange. See under Collins, Anthony.

COLLET, FRANÇOIS-JOSEPH, *Quaestio medica quodlibetariis disputationibus . . . Praeside M. Petro Bercher . . . , An sua sit in cerebro cuique ideae fibra?* (held at the Faculty of Medicine, Paris, 27 Jan. 1763) (Paris: Typis Viduae Quillau, 1762). [2], 8 p. in-4°.

[COLLIBER, SAMUEL], *Free Thoughts concerning Souls, in Four Essays*: I. *On the Humane Soul Consider'd in Its Own Nature*; II. *Of the Humane Soul Compared with the Souls of Brutes*; III. *Of the Supposed Prae-existent State of Souls*; IV. *Of the Future States of Souls. To which is added, An Essay on Creation* (London: R. Robinson, 1734). xiii, 168 p. in-8°.

[——] *An Impartial Enquiry into the Existence and Nature of God . . . With an Appendix concerning the Nature of Space and Duration* (London: Printed; and Sold by the Booksellers, 1718). 230 p. in-8°.

[COLLINS, ANTHONY], 'A Letter to the Learned Mr. Henry Dodwell; Containing Some Remarks on a (Pretended) Demonstration of the Immateriality and Natural Immortality of the Soul, in Mr. Clarke's Answer to his Late Epistolary Discourse, &c.', incl. in Samuel Clarke's *A Letter to Mr. Dodwell . . . The Sixth Edition. In This Edition are Inserted the Remarks on Dr. Clarke's Letter to Mr. Dodwell, and the Several Replies to the Doctor's Defences thereof* (London: J. and J. Knapton, 1731). 475 p. in-8°. Collins's 'Letter' was 1st pub. 1707; Clarke's in 1706. This 6th edn. includes four defences and replies by Clarke, and four by Collins, all with separate title-pages, all previously published.

CONDILLAC, ÉTIENNE BONNOT DE, *Essai sur l'origine des connoissances humaines; ouvrage où l'on réduit à un seul principe tout ce qui concerne l'entendement humain* (Amsterdam: P. Mortier, 1746). 2 vols. in-12°.

—— *Œuvres philosophiques*, ed. Georges Le Roy, Corpus général des philosophes français: Auteurs modernes, 33 (Paris: Presses universitaires de France, 1947). 3 vols.

—— *Traité des sensations* (London, Paris: De Bure ainé, 1754). 2 vols. in-12°.

—— *Traité des systêmes, où l'on démêle les inconvenients et les avantages* (Amsterdam, Leipzig: Arkstée & Merkus, et se vend à Paris chez Jombert, 1771). [4], 448 p. in-12°. First pub. The Hague, 1749 (2 vols.).

COSTE, PIERRE, 'Lettre de Mr. Coste à l'auteur de ces Nouvelles, à l'occasion de la mort de M. Locke', *Nouvelles de la république des lettres* (Feb. 1705), 154–77. Repr. in the French transl. of Locke's *Essay concerning Humane Understanding*, beginning with the 2nd edn. (1729).

CROUSAZ, JEAN-PIERRE DE, *De mente humana: Substantia a corpore distincta et immortali, dissertatio philosophico-theologica* (Groningen: Typis Gesinae Elamae, 1726). viii, 269 p. in-12°.

—— *De l'esprit humain, substance différente du corps active, libre, im-*

mortelle: Verités que la raison démontre et que la révélation met au-dessus de tout doute (Basle: J. Christ, 1741). 606 p. in-12°. Transl. of *De mente humana*.

—— *Examen de l'Essay de Monsieur Pope sur l'homme* (Lausanne: M. M. Bousquet, 1737). xiv, 214 p. in-12°.

—— *A Commentary on Mr. Pope's Principles of Morality, or Essay on Man . . . And Some Cursory Annotations by the Translator* [Samuel Johnson] (London: E. Curll, 1738). xvi, 79 p. Trans. of the *Examen*.

—— *An Examination of Mr. Pope's Essay on Man, Translated from the French of Mr. Crousaz* [by Elizabeth Carter] (London: A. Dodd, 1739). [2], viii, 227 p. in-12°.

—— *Examen du pyrrhonisme ancien et moderne* (The Hague: P. de Hondt, 1733). 766 p. and index, in-folio.

—— *Réflexions sur l'ouvrage intitulé La Belle Wolfienne, auxquelles on a joint plusieurs éclaircissemens sur le Traité de l'esprit humain* (Lausanne, Geneva: M.-M. Bousquet, 1743). v, 213 p. in-12°. 1st publ. 1743 without 'Éclaircissemens'.

—— *Système de réflexions qui peuvent contribuer à la netteté et à l'étendue de nos connoissances, ou Nouvel essai de logique* (Amsterdam: F. L'Honoré, 1712). 2 vols. in-8°.

—— *A New Treatise of the Art of Thinking, or A Compleat System of Reflections concerning the Conduct and Improvement of the Mind, Illustrated with Variety of Characters and Examples Drawn from the Ordinary Occurrences of Life* (London: Tho. Woodward, 1724). 2 vols. in-8°. Trans. of *Système de réflexions*.

[CUENZ (or CUENTZ, KÜNZ), CASPAR], *Essai d'un sisteme nouveau, concernant la nature des esprits spirituels, fondé en partie sur les principes du célèbre Mr. Locke, philosophe anglois, dont l'auteur fait l'apologie* (Neufchatel [*sic*]: De l'Imprimerie des editeurs du Journal helvétique, 1742). 4 vols. in-8°. Vols. ii and iv have variant subtitles: ii: *qui renferme principalement la défense ou l'apologie de Mr. Locke*; iv: *dans lequel on repond principalement à diferentes objections*.

CUMBERLAND, RICHARD, *Traité philosophique des loix naturelles . . . Traduit du latin par Monsieur Barbeyrac, . . . avec des notes du traducteur, qui y a joint celles de la traduction anglaise* (Amsterdam: P. Mortier, et se vend à Paris chez Huart, 1744). xxviii, [2], 435, [9] p. in-4°. 1st pub. 1672 as *De legibus naturae disquisitio philosophica*; English trans. 1692 as *A Brief Disquisition on the Law of Nature*; 1727 as *A Treatise of the Law of Nature*.

DAGOUMER, GUILLAUME, *Philosophia ad usum scholae accommodata* (Paris: P. Aubouin [*et al.*], 1702–3). 3 vols in-12°.

DENESLE, —, *Examen du matérialisme, relativement à la métaphysique* (Paris: Imprimerie de Vincent, 1754). 2 vols. in-12°.

DESCARTES, RENÉ, 'Regulae ad directionem ingenii, ut & inquisitio veritatis per lumen naturale', in his *Opuscula posthuma, physica et mathematica* (Amsterdam: Apud Janssonio-Waesbergios, 1701 (6 parts in 1 vol., separately paged)), pt. IV (90 pp.).

—— *Traité de l'homme*, in *Œuvres philosophiques*, ed. Ferdinand Alquié (Paris: Garnier, 1963), i (1618–37), 379–480. 1st separately pub. as *De homine* (1662), and as *Traité de l'homme* 1664.

—— *Les Passions de l'âme*, in *Œuvres philosophiques* (Paris: Garnier, 1973), iii (1643–50), 939–1103. 1st pub. separately 1649.

Dictionnaire anti-philosophique. See Chaudon, L.-M.

DIDEROT, DENIS, *Eléments de physiologie*, ed. with intro. and notes by Jean Mayer, [Publications de la] Société des textes français modernes (Paris: Didier, 1964). lxxxi, 387 p. Written 1774–8; 1st pub. in his *Œuvres complètes*, ed. J. Assézat, ix (1878).

—— 'Entretien entre d'Alembert et Diderot', in *Œuvres philosophiques*, 247–84. Written in 1769, but not pub. until 1830.

—— *Œuvres complètes*, chronological edn.; intros. by Roger Lewinter (Paris: Le Club français, 1969–73). 15 vols.

—— *Œuvres philosophiques*, ed. with intro., bibliography, and notes by Paul Vernière (Paris: Garnier, 1964). xl, 649 p.

—— *Pensées philosophiques*, in *Œuvres philosophiques*, ed. P. Vernière (1964), 1–72. 1st pub. 1746.

—— 'Le Rêve de d'Alembert', in *Œuvres philosophiques*, pp. 285–371. Written in 1769, but not pub. until 1830.

—— 'Réponse à l'Instruction pastorale de l'Evêque d'Auxerre [Caylus]', in *Œuvres complètes*, ii (1969), 618–66.

—— 'Suite de l'Apologie de M. l'abbé de Prades', in *Œuvres complètes*, ii (1969), 603–66. Incl. 'Réponse'; 1st pub. 1752 as 3rd part of de Prades's *Apologie*, q.v.

[DILLY, A.], *Traité de l'ame et de la connoissance des bêtes, où après avoir demontré la spiritualité de l'ame de l'homme l'on explique par la seule machine, les actions les plus surprenantes des animaux, suivant les principes de Descartes* (Amsterdam: George Gallet, 1691). [22], 276 p. in-12°.

DITTON, HUMPHREY, *A Discourse concerning the Resurrection of Jesus Christ, in Three Parts: I. The Consequences of the Doctrine Are Stated Hypothetically, II. The Nature and Obligation of Moral Evidence Are Explain'd at Large, III. The Proofs of the Fact of Our Saviour's Resurrection Are Propos'd, Examin'd and Fairly Demonstrated to Be Conclusive. Together with an Appendix concerning the Impossible Production of Thought from Matter and Motion, the Nature of Human Souls, and the Hypothesis of* τὸ πάν; *as also, concerning Divine Providence, the Origin of Evil, and the Universe in General* (2nd edn., London: J. Darby, and Sold by Andr. Bell and B. Lintott, 1714). xvi, 510 p. in-8°. 1st pub. 1712.

[ELLIS, JOHN], *Some Brief Considerations upon Mr. Locke's Hypothesis, That the Knowledge of God Is Attainable by Ideas and Reflexion; Wherein Is Demonstrated, upon His Own Principles, That the Knowledge of God is Not Attainable by Ideas of Reflexion, Being an Addition to a Book Lately Publish'd, entitled The Knowledge of Divine Things from Revelation* [by John Ellis] (London: J. Watts, and sold by B. Dod, J. Fletcher at Oxford, and T. Merrill at Cambridge, 1743). [4], 51 p. in-8°.

Encyclopédie, ou Dictionnaire raisonné des sciences, des arts et des métiers, ed. D. Diderot and J. d'Alembert (Paris: Briasson, 1751–65). 17 vols. in-folio & 11 vols. of 'Recueil de planches'. Vols. 8–17 pub. Neuchâtel: S. Fauche, 1765.

An Essay towards Demonstrating the Immateriality and Free-Agency of the Soul, in Answer to Two Pamphlets: one intitled, A Philosophical Enquiry into the Physical Spring of Human Actions, &c., Supposed to Have been Wrote by Mr. Samuel Strutt; and the other intitled, A Philosophical Enquiry concerning Human Liberty, Supposed to Have Been Wrote by Anthony Collins, Esq; (London: J. Shuckburgh in Fleetstreet, 1760 [misprint for 1740]. xvi, 136 p. in-8°. The imprint date of 1760 is presumably a typographical error for 1739 or 1740, since the publication of this anonymous work is noticed in the *Bibliothèque britannique*, 14 (Jan.–Mar. 1740), 432.

Examen de la religion, dont on cherche l'éclaircissement de bonne foy, in *L'Evangile de la raison: Ouvrage posthume de M. d. M.* . . . (s.l.: s.n., 1764), 121–207. 1st pub. clandestinely 1745.

FONTENELLE, BERNARD LE BOVIER DE, *Entretiens sur la pluralité des mondes*, ed. with intro. and notes by Alexandre Calame, [Publications de la] Société des textes français modernes (Paris: Nizet, 1966). lii, 210 p. 1st pub. 1686.

—— 'Réflexions sur l'argument de M. Pascal et de Mr. Locke concernant la possibilité d'une vie à venir', in *Nouvelles libertés de penser*, q.v.

FORMEY, JEAN-HENRI SAMUEL, *La Belle Wolfienne, avec deux lettres philosophiques, l'une sur l'immortalité de l'âme, & l'autre sur l'harmonie préétablie* (The Hague: J. Neaulme, 1741–53). 6 vols. in-12°. Facsimile repr. in C. von Wolff's *Gesammelte Werke* (Hildesheim: G. Olms, 1983), pt. III, vols. xvi–xvii.

—— *Histoire abrégée de la philosophie* (Amsterdam: H. Schneider, 1760). iv, 320 p. in-8°.

GARDINI, ANTONMARIA, *L'anima umana e sue proprieta dedotte da'soli principi di ragione . . . contra i materialisti e specialmente contro l'opera intitolata, Le Bon-sens* [by Holbach] (Padua: Nella Stamperia del Seminario, Appresso Giovanni Manfré, 1781). xx, 284 p. in-8°.

GERDIL, GIACINTO SIGISMONDO, Cardinal, *Défense du sentiment du P. Malebranche sur la nature et l'origine des idées, contre l'examen de Mr. Locke* (Turin: Imprimerie royale, 1748). [14], xxxix, 246, [22] p. in-4°.

GERDIL, GIACINTO SIGISMONDO, Cardinal, *L'Immaterialité de l'âme démontrée contre M.* Locke, par les mêmes principes par lesquels ce philosophe démontre l'existence & l'immatérialité de Dieu avec des nouvelles preuves de l'immatéralité de Dieu et de l'Âme, tirées de l'Ecriture, des Peres & de la raison (Turin: Imprimerie royale, 1747). [22], 283 p. in-4°.

[GOURLIN, PIERRE-SÉBASTIEN, Abbé], *Observations importantes au sujet de la thèse de M. l'abbé de Prades soutenue en Sorbonne le 18 novembre 1751, censurée par la Faculté de théologie le 27 janvier 1752, et condamné par M. l'archévêque de Paris le 29 du même mois* (s.l.: s.n., 1752). 342 p. in-12°.

GRAVESANDE, WILLEM JACOB STORM VAN 'S, *Introduction à la philosophie, contenant la metaphysique et la logique, traduite du latin* (Leiden: J. & H. Verbeek, 1737). x, 473 p. in-8°. Trans. of his *Introductio ad philosophiam: Metaphysicam et logicam continens* (Leiden: J. & H. Verbeek, 1736).

—— *Œuvres philosophiques et mathémathiques de Mr. G. J. 'sGravesande* (Amsterdam: M. M. Rey, 1774). 2 vols.

Guerre littéraire, ou Choix de quelques pièces de M. de V***, avec les réponses, pour servir de suite et d'éclaircissement à ses ouvrages ([Lausanne]: 1759). cxl, 183 p. in-8°. A collection of thirteen items by Voltaire or attributed to him, some about him, some by J. Vernet, the first of which is 'Trois lettres sur la nature de notre âme, & sur son immortalité, à l'occasion des Lettres philosophiques de Mr. de Voltaire' by David Boullier.

GUISI, —, *Démonstration de la réligion chrétienne contre les athées & les déïstes* [c.1737].

—— *Pensées, ou Conjectures sur l'union de l'âme avec le corps* [1737?]. The author was a native of Aarau, in Switzerland. I have been unable to locate a copy of either of his works.

HARTLEY, DAVID, *Observations on Man, His Frame, His Duty and His Expectations* (London: S. Richardson [*et al.*], 1749). 2 vols. in-8°. Facsimile repr. Delmar, NY: Scholars' Facsimiles & Reprints, 1976.

HILDROP, JOHN, *Free Thoughts upon the Brute Creation, or An Examination of Father Bougeant's Philosophical Amusement, &c., in Two Letters to a Lady* (London: R. Minors, 1742). [4], 64 p. in-8°.

[HOLBACH, PAUL-HENRI DIETRICH, Baron d'], *Système de la nature, ou des lois du monde physique et du monde moral*, par M. Mirabaud (London: s.n., 1770). 2 vols. in-8°. Facsimile repr. Geneva: Slatkine, 1973.

—— *Système de la nature . . .*, new edn. with notes and corrections by Diderot (Paris: E. Ledoux, 1821). 2 vols. in-8°. Facsimile repr. Hildesheim: G. Olms, 1966.

HUME, DAVID, *An Abstract of a Book Lately Published, Entituled, A Treatise of Human Nature, Wherein the Chief Argument of That Book Is Farther Illustrated and Explained* (London: C. Borbet, 1740). 32 p. in-8°. 'Reprinted [in facsimile] with an introduction by J. M. Keynes and P. Sraffa' (Cambridge: Cambridge University Press, 1938). xxxii, 32 p.

— *Essais philosophiques sur l'entendement humain* (Amsterdam: J. H. Schneider, 1758). 2 vols. in-8°. Trans. by J. B. Mérian and pref. by J. H. S. Formey of *Philosophical Essays concerning Human Understanding* (1748), later entitled *An Enquiry concerning Human Understanding*. There were a further 3 vols. issued 1759–60, vols. iii–iv with half-title only: *Œuvres philosophiques de Mr. D. Hume*; and vol. v with half-title: *Œuvres de Mr. Hume*. Vol. iii is a trans. by Mérian of *Natural History of Religion*; iv, also trans. by Mérian, contains *Dissertations sur les passions, sur la tragédie*, and *Règle du goût*. Vol. v, trans. by J. B. R. Robinet, contains *Essais de morale*.

— *The Letters of David Hume*, ed. J. Y. T. Greig (Oxford: Oxford University Press, 1932). 2 vols.

— *A Treatise of Human Nature: Being an Attempt to Introduce the Experimental Method of Reasoning into Moral Subjects* (London: J. Noon, 1739–40). 3 vols. in-8°.

— *A Treatise of Human Nature*, ed. with analytical index, by L. A. Selby-Bigge. 2nd edn., with text revised and variant readings by P. H. Nidditch (Oxford: Oxford University Press, 1978).

JACKSON, JOHN, *A Dissertation on Matter and Spirit; with Some Remarks on a Book Entitled, An Enquiry into the Nature of the Human Soul* [by Andrew Baxter] (London: J. Noon, 1735). viii, 56 p. in-8°.

[LA BARRE DE BEAUMARCHAIS, ANTOINE DE], *Amusemens littéraires, ou Correspondance politique, historique, philosophique, critique & galante* (Frankfurt: Varrentrapp, 1738–9). 3 vols. in-8°. Repr. The Hague: J. van Duren, 1740.

LADVOCAT, LOUIS-FRANÇOIS, *Nouveau Sistème de philosophie, établi sur la nature des choses connuës par elles-mêmes* (Paris: Nicolas Le Breton, 1728). 2 vols. in-12°.

LA METTRIE, JULIAN OFFRAY DE, *Histoire naturelle de l'âme* (The Hague: J. Néaulme, 1745). xii, 398 p. in-12°. Repr. 1747 with title: *Traité de l'âme*.

— *Le Traité de l'âme de La Mettrie*, ed. with historical intro. and commentary by Theo Verbeek (Utrecht: OMI-Grafisch Bedrijf, 1988). 2 vols.

— *La Mettrie's L'Homme machine: A Study in the Origins of an Idea*, ed. with introductory monograph and notes by Aram Vartanian (Princeton, NJ: Princeton University Press, 1960). 264 p. 1st pub. 1748.

LA PEYRONIE, FRANÇOIS GIGOT DE, 'Observations par lesquelles on tâche de découvrir la partie du cerveau où l'âme exerce ses fonctions', *Mémoires de l'Académie royale des sciences* (1741), 199–218.

LE CAMUS, ANTOINE, *Médecine de l'esprit, où l'on cherche, 1. le méchanisme du corps qui influe sur les fonctions de l'ame, 2. les causes physiques qui rendent ce méchanisme ou défectueux ou plus parfait, 3. les moyens qui peuvent l'entretenir dans son état libre et le rectifier lorsqu'il est géné* (2nd edn., Paris: Ganeau, 1769). xii, 359 p. in-4°. 1st pub. 1753 with different subtitle: *Où l'on traite des dispositions et des causes physiques qui influent sur les operations de l'esprit et des moyens de maintenir ces operations dans un bon état* (2 vols. in-12°).

LE CLERC, JEAN, 'Eloge du feu M. Locke', *Bibliothèque choisie*, 6 (1705), 342–411. English trans. separately pub. as *The Life and Character of Mr. J. Locke* (1706).

LEIBNIZ, GOTTFRIED WILHELM, *Leibniz–Clarke Collection*. See Clarke, Samuel, *A Collection* . . .

—— *Philosophical Papers and Letters: A Selection*, trans. and ed. with intro. by Leroy E. Loemker (2nd edn., Synthèse Historical Library, Dordrecht: Reidel, 1970). xii, 736 p. 1st pub. 1956.

—— *Theodicy: Essays on the Goodness of God, the Freedom of Man and the Origin of Evil*, ed. with intro. by Austin Farrer (New Haven, Conn.: Yale University Press, 1952). 448 p. Repr. LaSalle, Ill.: Open Court, 1985. Originally pub. 1710.

LELAND, JOHN, *A View of the Principal Deistical Writers that Have Appeared in England in the Last and Present Century, with Observations upon Them, and Some Account of the Answers that Have Been Published against Them; in Several Letters to a Friend* (2nd edn., with additions, London: B. Dod, 1755). 2 vols. in-8°.

—— *A View of the Principal Deistical Writers . . . A Supplement to the First and Second Volumes . . . To Which Is Added the Late Lord Bolingbroke's Letters on the Study and Use of History, as far as Relates to the Holy Scriptures* (3rd edn., corrected and enlarged, with index, London: B. Dod, 1756). xvi, 368, [40] p. in-8°.

[LELARGE DE LIGNAC, JOSEPH-ADRIEN], *Elémens de métaphysique, tirés de l'expérience, ou Lettres à un matérialiste sur la nature de l'âme* (Paris: Desaint & Saillant, 1753). 453 p. in-12°.

LE MASSON DES GRANGES, DANIEL, Abbé, *Le Philosophe moderne, ou L'Incrédule condamné au tribunal de sa raison* (Paris: Despilly, 1759). xxiv, 300 p. in-12°.

LOCKE, JOHN, 'Extrait d'un livre anglois qui n'est pas encore publié, intitulé Essai philosophique concernant l'entendement, où l'on montre quelle est l'étenduë de nos connoissances certaines, & la manière dont nous y parvenons. Communiqué par Monsieur Locke', *Bibliothèque universelle et historique*, 8 (1688), 49–142. Also issued separately with title: *Abrégé d'un ouvrage* . . . (1688).

—— *An Essay concerning Humane Understanding: In Four Books* (London: Eliz. Holt for Thomas Basset, 1690). [12], 362, [22] p. in-folio. 2nd edn. pub. 1694; 3rd 1695; 4th 1700; 5th 1706; all but the 3rd containing expansions.

—— *An Essay concerning Human Understanding*, ed. with intro., critical apparatus, and glossary by Peter H. Nidditch, Clarendon Edition of the Works of John Locke (Oxford: Oxford University Press, 1975). liv, 867 p.

—— *Essai philosophique concernant l'entendement humain, où l'on montre quelle est l'étendue de nos connoissances certaines, & la maniere dont nous y parvenons*, trans. Pierre Coste (Amsterdam: Henri Schelte, 1700). [58], 936, [24] p. in-4°. Trans. of *Essay concerning Human Understanding*, 4th edn. (1700).

—— *Essai philosophique*, 2nd edn., rev., corrected, and enlarged by translator (Amsterdam: Pierre Mortier, 1729). xlvi, 595, [16] p. in-4°. Incorporates most of the changes added in the 5th edn. (1706), and includes Coste's biographical letter from the *Nouvelles de la république des lettres* (under Coste, above).

—— *An Abridgment of Mr. Locke's Essay concerning Human Understanding* [by John Wynne] (London: A. and J. Churchill, and Edw. Castle, 1696). [8] 310, [10] p. in-8°. Abridgement of bks. II–IV, with a one-page summary of bk. I. The 2nd edn. (1700) expanded to include new chapter 'Of the Association of Ideas' (2. 23) and 'Of Enthusiasm' (4. 19) from the 4th edn.

—— *Abrégé de l'Essay de M. Locke, sur l'entendement humain*, trans. J. P. Bosset (London: Jean Watts, 1720). [8], 286, [2] p. in-8°. A trans. of Wynne's 'Abridgment', with a summary of bk. 1 supplied by Le Clerc's extract in the 'Notice V' from the *Bibliothèque universelle et historique*, 17 (1690), 399–427.

—— *Saggio filosofico di Gio. Locke su l'umano intelletto*, trans. and commentary by Francesco Soave (Milan: Gaetano Motta, 1775–6). 3 vols. in-12°. Trans. of Wynne's 'Abridgment' with exceedingly extensive notes by Soave.

—— 'Ensaio philosophico sobre o entendimento humano: resumo dos livres I e II recusado pela Real Mesa Censória e agora dado ao prelo com introdução e apendices. Publicados por Joaquim de Carvalho', *Boletim da Biblioteca da Universidade de Coimbra*, 20 (1951), 1–215. Contains a long historical intro. by Carvalho (pp. 1–70), followed by a trans. of Wynne's abridgement of bk. 2, preceded by an adaptation of Le Clerc's abridgement of bk. 1, possibly following Bosset, made in mid-18th century. This work also published separately in 1951.

—— *The Reasonableness of Christianity, as Demonstrated in the Scriptures* (London: A. & J. Churchill, 1695). [4], 304 p. in-8°.

—— Locke–Stillingfleet exchange. Bishop Edward Stillingfleet attacked Locke's *Essay* in his *Discourse in Vindication of the Doctrine of the Trinity* (1696) and Locke replied in *A Letter to Edward Ld Bishop of Worcester concerning Some Passages Relating to Mr. Locke's Essay . . . in a late Discourse of His Lordship's, in Vindication of the Trinity* (1697). Stillingfleet counterattacked with *The Bishop of Worcester's Answer to Mr.*

Locke's Letter concerning Some Passages Relating to His Essay of Humane Understanding ... (1697). Again, Locke replied: *Mr. Locke's Reply to the Right Reverend the Bishop of Worcester's Answer to His Letter, concerning Some Passages Relating to Mr. Locke's Essay ... in a Late Discourse of his Lordships, in Vindication of the Trinity* (1697). Stillingfleet's reply to this pamphlet was *The Bishop of Worcester's Answer to Mr. Locke's Second Letter, Wherein His Notion of Ideas is Prov'd to be Inconsistent with It Self and with the Articles of the Christian Faith* (1698). Locke's final salvo was *Mr. Locke's Reply to the Right Reverend the Lord Bishop of Worcester's Answer to His Second Letter, Wherein, besides Other Incident Matters, What His Lordship Has Said concerning Certainty by Reason, Certainty by Ideas, and Certainty of Faith; the Resurrection of the Same Body; the Immateriality of the Soul; the Inconsistency of Mr. Locke's Notions with the Articles of the Christian Faith, and Their Tendency to Sceptism, Is Examined* (1699). Locke's statements, with some quotations from Stillingfleet, are included as footnotes in the 5th edn. of the *Essay* (1706). Only the argument about 'thinking matter' in the 4. 3. 6 passage is included as a footnote in the 2nd French (1729) and subsequent French edns.

[LUZAC, ÉLIE], *Essai sur la liberté de produire ses sentimens* (s.l.: Au pays libre, pour le bien public, 1749). 124 p. in-8°.

[——] *L'Homme plus que machine: Ouvrage qui sert à refuter les principaux argumens sur lesquelles on fonde le matérialisme* (2nd edn., Göttingen: Chez l'auteur, 1755). 176 p. in-12°. 1st edn. (140 p.) pub. without subtitle 1748.

MALEBRANCHE, NICOLAS, *Œuvres complètes*, gen. ed. A. Robinet (Paris: J. Vrin, 1958–70). 21 vols. Some vols. in 2nd edn. (1969–72). Vols. i–iii contain *De la recherche de la vérité*, ed. Geneviève Rodis-Lewis, original edn. 1674–5. Vol. xii contains *Entretiens sur la métaphysique et sur la religion*, ed. Robinet; original edn. 1688. The 'Eclaircissements' to *De la recherche de la vérité* 1st pub. 1678, as a supplementary vol. iii; ed. Rodis-Lewis, they are vol. iii of these *Œuvres*. *Réflexions sur la prémotion physique* (1st pub. 1715), here ed. Robinet, are contained in vol. xvi (1958).

[MALLET, EDMÉ], *Essai sur l'étude des belles-lettres* (Paris: L.-E. Ganeau, 1747). xvi, 271 p. in-8°.

MAUBEC, —, 'Docteur', *Principes phisiques de la raison et des passions des hommes* (Paris: D. Girin, 1709). 205 p. in-12°.

MAYNE, JOSÉ, *Dissertação sobre a alma racional, onde se mostrão os sólidos fundamentos da sua immortalidade, e se refutão os erros dos materialistas antigos e modernos* (Lisbon: Regia officina typografica, 1778). [8], xx, 118 p. in-12°.

MAYNE, ZACHARY [supposed author], *Two Dissertations concerning Sense and the Imagination; with an Essay on Consciousness* (London: J. Tonson, 1728). [8], 231 p. in-8°.

[Mey, Claude, Abbé], *Essai de métaphysique, ou Principes sur la nature et les opérations de l'esprit* (Paris: Desaint, 1756). 398 p. in-12°.

[——] *Remarques sur une thèse soutenue en Sorbonne le samedi 30 octobre 1751 par M. l'abbé de Loménie de Brienne, présidé par M. Buret* ([Paris], 1751). 29 p. in-12°.

[Mirabaud, Jean-Baptiste de], 'De l'âme et de son immortalité', in *Le Monde, son origine et son antiquité*, ed. with a pref. by J.-B. Le Mascrier (London, 1751), pt. I.

[——] 'Sentimens des philosophes sur la nature de l'ame, par J.-B. Mirabeau [*sic*]', in *Nouvelles libertés de penser*, q.v.

Nicéron, Jean-Pierre, 'John Locke', in his *Mémoires pour servir à l'histoire des hommes illustres dans la république des lettres*, i (Paris: Briasson, 1729), 35–49.

Nicole, Pierre, *Essais de morale* (Paris, 1733–71). 25 vols. First *Essais* published in 1671. Facsimile repr. of this edn., which incorporates other 'instructions', pub. Geneva: Slatkine, 1971.

Nouvelles Libertés de penser (Amsterdam [i.e. Paris: Piget], 1743). 205 p. in-12°. Contains the following: 'Réflexions sur l'argument de M. Pascal et de M. Locke concernant la possibilité d'une vie à venir, par Fontenelle'; 'Sentimens des philosophes sur la nature de l'âme, par J.-B. de Mirabau [i.e. Mirabaud]'; 'Traité de la liberté, par Fontenelle'; 'Réflexions sur l'existence de l'âme et sur l'existence de Dieu [anon.]'; 'Le philosophe, par Du Marsais'.

Perronet, Vincent, *Some Enquiries, Chiefly Relating to Spiritual Beings: in Which the Opinions of Mr. Hobbes, with Regard to Sensation, Immaterial Substance and the Attributes of the Deity Are Taken Notice of; and Wherein Likewise Is Examined How Far the Supposition of an Invisible Tempter Is Defensible on the Principles of Natural Reason* (London: F. Giles [*et al.*], 1740). vi, 105 p. in-8°.

Philosophical Society of Edinburgh, *Essays and Observations, Physical and Literary, Read before a Society in Edinburgh and Published by Them* (Edinburgh: G. Hamilton and J. Balfour, 1754–71). 3 vols. in-8°. Incl. essays by Henry Home (Lord Kames) and John Stewart.

Pluche, Antoine, Abbé, *Le Spectacle de la nature, ou Entretiens sur les particularités de l'histoire naturelle, qui ont paru plus propres à rendre les jeunes gens curieux et à leur former l'esprit* (Paris: Veuve Estienne, 1732–50). 9 vols. in-12°. There were numerous later edns. and trans.

Pope, Alexander, *Essay on Man*, ed. Maynard Mack (London: Methuen, 1950). xc, 186 p. 1st pub. 1733.

—— *Essai sur l'homme, par M. Pope*, trans. Étienne de Silhouette (s.l.: s.n., 1736). xxx, 109 p. in-8°.

POPE, ALEXANDER, *Essai sur l'homme, par M. Pope*, trans. Abbé du Resnel (Utrecht: E. Néaulme, 1737). xxiv, 90 p. in-12º.

PRADES, JEAN-MARTIN DE, Abbé, *Apologie de M. l'abbé de Prades* (Amsterdam [i.e. Berlin], 1752). 3 parts in 1 vol. in-8º. Contains: 'Thèse soutenue en Sorbonne le 18 novembre 1751, par J. M. de Prades' [in Latin and French]; 'Apologie de M. l'abbé de Prades' [by Prades and Abbé Yvon]; 'Suite de l'Apologie de M. l'abbé de Prades, ou Réponse à l'Instruction pastorale de M. l'évêque [Caylus] d'Auxerre' [by Denis Diderot].

RASSIELS DU VIGIER, — DE, *Traité de l'esprit de l'homme, où l'on verra la preuve de son existence, l'origine de ses idées pendant son union avec le corps* (Paris: J. Jombert, 1714). 287 p. in-8º.

REINBECK, JOHANN GUSTAV, *Réflexions philosophiques sur l'immatérialité de l'âme raisonnable, avec quelques remarques sur une lettre dans laquelle on soutient que la matière pense*, trans. J. H. S. Formey (Amsterdam, Leipzig: Arkstée & Merkus, 1744). [32], 323, [7] p. in-12º. Trans. of *Philosophische Gedancken über die vernünfftige Seele und derselben Unsterblichkeit, nebst einigen Anmerckungen über ein französisches Schreiben, darin behauptet werden will, dass die Materie dencken* (Berlin, 1740).

[ROCHE, ANTOINE-MARTIN], *Traité de la nature de l'âme, et de l'origine de ses connoissances, contre le système de Mr. Locke et de ses partisans* (Paris: Veuve Lottin & J. H. Butard, Desaint et Saillant, 1759). 2 vols. in-12º.

SAINT-HYACINTHE, THÉMISEUL DE (pseud. of HYACINTHE CORDONNIER), *Recherches philosophiques sur la necessité de s'assurer par soi-même de la vérité, sur la certitude de nos connoissances, et sur la nature des êtres* (London: J. Nourse, 1743). 514 p. in-8º.

SINSART, BENOÎT, *Recueil de pensées diverses sur l'immatérialité de l'âme, son immortalité, sa liberté, sa distinction d'avec le corps, ou Réfutation du matérialisme; avec une réponse aux objections de Mr. Cuentz et de Lucrèce le philosophe* (Colmar: Imprimerie royale, 1756). 376 p. in-8º.

TABARAUD, MATHIEU-MATHURIN, *Histoire critique du philosophisme anglais, depuis son origine jusqu'à son introduction en France inclusivement* (Paris: L. Duprat-Duverger, 1806). 2 vols. in-8º.

TIPHAIGNE DE LA ROCHE, CHARLES-FRANÇOIS, 'Essai sur la nature de l'âme, ou Examen de cette célébre proposition de M. Locke: Dieu peut donner, s'il veut, à certains amas de matière, disposés comme il le juge à propos, la faculté d'appercevoir et de penser', in his *Bigarrures philosophiques* (Amsterdam, Leipzig: Arkstée & Merkus, 1759), i. 115–244; ii. 207–94.

TOLAND, JOHN, *Letters to Serena, containing: I. The Origin and Force of Prejudices, II. The History of the Soul's Immortality among the Heathens, III. The Origin of Idolatry and Reasons of Heathenism; as also, IV. A Letter to a Gentleman in Holland, Showing Spinosa's System of Philosophy to Be without Any Principle or Foundation; V. Motion Essential to*

Matter, in Answer to Some Remarks by a Noble Friend on the Confutation of Spinosa. To All Which Is Prefix'd, VI. *A Preface, Being a Letter to a Gentleman in London Sent Together with the Foregoing Dissertations, and Declaring the Several Occasions of Writing Them* (London: Bernard Lintot, 1704). [49], 239 p. in-8°.

VIEUSSENS, RAYMOND, *Neurographia universalis, hoc est, Omnium corporis humani nervorum simul et cerebri medullaeque spinalis descriptio anatomica* . . . (new edn., Lyons: J. Certe, 1684). 252 p. in-folio. 1st pub. 1682.

VOLTAIRE, F.-M. AROUET DE, *Elémens de la philosophie de Neuton, contenant la métaphysique, la théorie de la lumière, et celle du monde* (new edn., London [i.e. Paris]: s.n., 1741). viii, 5–12, 471 p. in-8°. Repr. 1744; 1st pub. Amsterdam 1738, with title *Elémens de la philosophie de Neuton, mis à la portée de tout le monde*).

—— *Lettres à S.A. Mgr. le Prince* *** [C. G. F. de Brunswick-Lunebourg] *sur Rabelais et sur d'autres auteurs accusés d'avoir mal parlé de la religion chrétienne*, in *Œuvres complètes* (ed. Garnier), xxvi. 469–526. 1st pub. 1767.

—— *Letters concerning the English Nation* (London: C. Davis and A. Lyon, 1733). [16], 253, [18] p. in-8°. English-language edn. preceded the French.

—— *Lettres écrites de Londres sur les Anglois, et autres sujets, par M. D. V*** (Basle: s.n., 1734). [8], 228, [19] p. in-8°. Later known as 'Lettres sur les Anglois' or 'Lettres philosophiques'.

—— *Lettres philosophiques*, ed. with intro. and commentary by Gustave Lanson (3rd edn., Paris: Hachette, 1924). 2 vols.

—— *Lettres philosophiques, ou Lettres anglaises, avec le text complet des remarques sur les Pensées de Pascal*, ed. with intro. by Raymond Naves; illus. edn.; Classiques Garnier (Paris: Garnier, 1988). xx, 304 p.

—— *Lettre de M. de V*** avec plusieurs pièces de différens auteurs* (The Hague: Pierre Poppy, 1738). 178 p. in-12°.

—— 'Mémoires pour servir à la vie de M. de Voltaire, écrit par lui-meme (1759)', in his *Œuvres complètes* (Garnier), i. 1–65.

—— *Le Philosophe ignorant* (Geneva: Cramer, 1766). viii, 171 [i.e. 169] p. in-8°.

—— 'Poème sur la loi naturelle', in his *Œuvres complètes* (Garnier), ix. 433–64. 1st pub. 1756 under the title *La Religion naturelle: Poème en quatre parties*.

—— *Traité de métaphysique*, ed. H. Temple Patterson (Manchester: University Press, 1937). xiv, 76 p. 1st pub. in *Collection complète des œuvres de Voltaire*, xxxii (Édition Cramer in-4°) in 1796; 1st separately pub. 1834.

—— *Œuvres complètes de Voltaire* (Kehl: Imprimerie de la Société littéraire typographique, 1785–9). 70 vols. in-8°. Known as the Kehl edition.

—— *Œuvres complètes de Voltaire*, 'nouvelle édition, avec notices, préfaces, variantes, table analytique, les notes de tous les commentateurs et des notes nouvelles, conforme pour le texte à l'édition de Beuchot . . . (Paris: Garnier, 1877–85). 51 vols. Vols. xvii–xx contain his *Dictionnaire philosophique*, 1st pub. 1764.

VOLTAIRE, F.-M. AROUET DE, *Œuvres complètes de Voltaire* = *Complete Works*, gen. ed. W. H. Barber (Geneva: Institut et Musée Voltaire; Oxford: Voltaire Foundation, 1968–present). In progress; vols. i–lxxxiv contain literary works; vols. lxxxv–cxxxv, correspondence, chiefly ed. Th. Bestermann.

WOLFF, CHRISTIAN (or CHRISTIAN VON), *Gesammelte Werke*, ed. and rev. J. Ecole [*et al.*] (Hildesheim: G. Olms, 1962–present). Pub. in 3 sections; includes some facsimiles.

[WOLLASTON, WILLIAM], *The Religion of Nature Delineated* (London: S. Palmer, 1725). 219 p. in-4°. 1st pub. privately 1722.

(*b*) *Periodicals*

Académie royale de chirurgie, Mémoires de l'Académie . . . , 1–2 (1761–9) (new edn., Paris: Impr. royale). Vol. 2, pp. xxxiij–li contains biography and 'Eloge' of La Peyronie.

Bibliothèque angloise, ou Histoire littéraire de la Grande-Bretagne, 1–15 (1717–28), Amsterdam: Veuve de Paul Marret. Ed. Armand Boisbeleau de la Chapelle, and others.

Bibliothèque britannique, ou Histoire des ouvrages des savans de la Grande-Bretagne (Apr./June 1733–Jan./Mar. 1747), The Hague: Pierre de Hondt. 25 vols. in-12°. Ed. Pierre Desmaizeaux and Jean-Frédéric Bernard, and others. Facsimile repr. Geneva: Slatkine, 1969.

Bibliothèque françoise, ou Histoire littéraire de la France, 1–42 (1723–46), Amsterdam: Jean-Frédéric Bernard. Ed. J.-F. Bernard, Denis-François Camusat, Claude-Pierre Goujet, H. du Sauzet, Bel, and François Garnet.

Bibliothèque germanique, ou Histoire littéraire de l'Allemagne et des pays du nord, 1–50 (July/Sept. 1720–41), Amsterdam: Pierre Humbert. Vols. for 1733–41 ed. Formey. Continued by *Journal littéraire d'Allemagne, de Suisse et du nord*, q.v. Facsimile repr. Geneva: Slatkine, 1969.

Bibliothèque raisonnée des ouvrages des savans de l'Europe (July/Dec. 1728–Jan./June 1753), Amsterdam: Wetstein & Smith. 52 vols. in-16°. Ed. chiefly by J. Barbeyrac, A. Boisbeleau de la Chapelle; intended as a successor to *Bibliothèque ancienne et moderne* (ed. Jean Le Clerc).

Bibliothèque universelle et historique, 1–25 (Jan. 1686–Oct. 1693), Amsterdam. Ed. Jean Le Clerc. Vol. 26, containing an index to all vols., pub. 1718.

Histoire des ouvrages des savans, par Monsr. B*** [Jacques Basnage de Beauval], 1–25 (Sept. 1687–June 1709), Rotterdam [etc.]: Reinier Leers.

Journal de Trévoux (commonly so called): *Mémoires pour l'histoire des sciences et des beaux arts* (Jan. 1701–Dec. 1767), Trévoux [Switzerland]: Imprimerie de SAS. 878 parts in 265 vols. in-8°. Pub. later in Lyons, then in Paris. Facsimile repr. Geneva: Slatkine, 1967.

Journal des sçavans, 1–13 (5 Jan.–30 Mar. 1665; 4 Jan. 1666–Nov./Dec. 1792), Paris. Superseded by the *Journal des savants*, pub. 1797 and, after a hiatus, from 1816 to the present.

Journal helvétique (1738–Aug. 1769) [Neuchâtel]. Issued as the literary part of the *Mercure suisse*, q.v.; ed. L. Bourget.

Journal littéraire d'Allemagne, de Suisse et du nord, 1–2 (1741–1742/3), Amsterdam. Successor to the *Bibliothèque germanique*. Superseded by the *Nouvelle bibliothèque germanique*.

Mémoires secrets pour servir à l'histoire de la république des lettres en France, depuis 1762 à nos jours, ou Journal d'un observateur, 1–36 (1777–89), London: John Adamson. Originally circulated in manuscript, the journal covers events from 1762 to 1787. Ed. M. de Bachaumont, it is also known as the '*Mémoires de Bachaumont*'.

Mercure suisse, ou Recueil de nouvelles historiques, politiques, littéraires et curieux (1732–69), Neuchâtel. Issues for 1738–69 include the *Journal helvétique*, (q.v.).

Nouvelle Bibliothèque, ou Histoire littéraire des principaux écrits qui se publient, 1–19 (Oct./Dec. 1738–Apr./June 1744), The Hague: P. Paupie. A continuation of the *Bibliothèque françoise*. Ed. the Marquis d'Argens, Barbeyrac, C. P. Chais, and others.

Nouvelles de la république des lettres, 1–40 (Mar. 1684–Apr. 1689; 1699–1710; Feb. 1716–May/June 1718), Amsterdam: H. Desbordes. Ed. Pierre Bayle until Feb. 1687; by D. de Larroque, Jacques Bernard, and others. Those issues ed. Bayle are repr. in his *Œuvres diverses* (1727).

Nouvelles ecclésiastiques, ou Mémoires pour servir à la constitution Unigenitus (1713/Feb. 1728–1803), s.l. (later Utrecht, then Paris). 75 vols. in-4°. 1st vol. covering 1713–28 originally circulated in manuscript.

Observateur: Ouvrage poligraphique et périodique, 1–2 (8–18 June 1736), Amsterdam: J. Rijkhoff le fils. Usually called *Observateur poligraphique*; ed. J.-B. le Vilain de la Varenne.

Le Pour et contre: Ouvrage d'un goût nouveau, dans lequel on s'explique librement sur tout ce qui peut intéresser la curiosité du public, 1–20 (1733–40), Paris: Didot. Another edn. pub. The Hague, 1733–8. Ed. Abbé Prévost. Facsimile repr. Geneva: Slatkine, 1967.

2. Secondary Sources

ASHCRAFT, RICHARD, *Revolutionary Politics & Locke's Two Treatises of Government* (Princeton, NJ: Princeton University Press, 1986). xxii, 613 p.

BARBER, W. H., *Leibniz in France, from Arnauld to Voltaire: A Study in*

French Reactions to Leibnizianism, 1670–1760 (Oxford: Oxford University Press, 1955). xi, 276 p.

BLOCH, OLIVIER (ed.), *Le Matérialisme du XVIIIe siècle et la littérature clandestine; Actes de la Table ronde des 6 et 7 juin 1980, organisé à la Sorbonne à Paris, avec le concours du C.N.R.S.*, Bibliothèque d'histoire de la philosophie (Paris: J. Vrin, 1982). 288 p.

BROCKLISS, LAWRENCE W. B., *French Higher Education in the Seventeenth and Eighteenth Centuries: A Cultural History* (Oxford: Oxford University Press, 1986), xiii, 544 p.

CARAYOL, ELISABETH, *Thémiseul de Saint-Hyacinthe, 1684–1746*, Studies on Voltaire and the Eighteenth Century, vol. 221 (Oxford: Voltaire Foundation, 1984). 278 p.

CIORANESCU, A., *Bibliographie de la littérature française du dix-huitième siècle* (3 vols., Paris: Éditions du CNRS, 1969).

CLAIR, PIERRE, 'Libertinage et incrédules (1665–1715)', *Recherches sur le XVIIe siècle*, 6 (1983), 1–294.

COLIE, ROSALIE L., *Light and Enlightenment: A Study of the Cambridge Platonists and the Dutch Arminians* (Cambridge: Cambridge University Press, 1957).

COUPERUS, MARIANNE (ed.), *L'Étude des périodiques anciens: Colloque de Utrecht, 9–10 janvier 1970* (Paris: Nizet, 1972). 221 p.

—— *Un Périodique français en Hollande: Le Glaneur historique (1731–1733)*, Publications de l'Institut d'études françaises et occitanes de l'Université de Utrecht, 6 (The Hague: Mouton, 1971). 340 p.

COUSIN, VICTOR, *Cours de l'histoire de la philosophie* (rev. edn., 3 vols., Paris: Didier, 1841; vol. ii has special title: *Histoire de la philosophie du XVIIIe siècle*. Based on course material taught 1828–30).

—— *Philosophie de Locke* (4th edn. rev. and enlarged, Paris: Didier, 1861; extracted and expanded from his *Cours de l'histoire de la philosophie*).

DESTOUCHES, PHILIPPE NÉRICAULT, *La Fausse Agnès, ou Le Poète campagnard*, in his *Œuvres dramatiques de N. Destouches*, iv (new edn., Paris, 1820), 1–142.

DOE, JANET, 'Jean Astruc (1684–1766): A Biographical and Bibliographical Study', *Journal of the History of Medicine and Allied Sciences*, 15 (Apr. 1960), 184–97.

EMILSSON, EYJOLFUR K., *Plotinus on Sense-Perception: A Philosophical Study* (Cambridge: Cambridge University Press, 1988). ix, 179 p.

JOLLEY, NICHOLAS, *Leibniz and Locke: A Study of the 'New Essays on Human Understanding'* (Oxford: Oxford University Press, 1984). xiii, 215 p.

Le Journalisme d'ancien régime, questions et propositions: Table ronde, CNRS, 12–13 juin 1981, Textes et documents, Société française d'étude du XVIIIème siècle (Lyons: Presses universitaires de Lyon, 1982). 413 p.

KEYNES, GEOFFREY, *Bibliography of George Berkeley, Bishop of Cloyne: His Works and His Critics in the Eighteenth Century*, Soho bibliographies (Oxford: Oxford University Press, 1976). xxvii, 285 p.

KNAPP, RICHARD G., *The Fortunes of Pope's Essay on Man in 18th-Century France*, Studies on Voltaire and the Eighteenth Century, vol. 82 (Oxford: Voltaire Foundation, 1971), 156 p.

LEU, HANS JACOB (ed.), *Helvetisches allgemeines eydgenössisches oder schweitzerisches Lexicon* (20 vols., Zurich: Hans Ulrich Denzler, 1747–65).

MACK, MAYNARD, *Collected in Himself: Essays Critical, Biographical and Bibliographical on Pope and Some of His Contemporaries* (Newark: University of Delaware Press, 1982). 569 p.

MOSSNER, ERNST CAMPBELL, *The Life of David Hume* (Oxford: Oxford University Press, 1954). xviii, 683 p.

NAVILLE, PIERRE, *D'Holbach et la philosophie scientifique au XVIIIe siècle*, rev. and enlarged edn., Bibliothèque des idées (Paris: Gallimard, 1967; 1st pub. 1943 with title *Paul Thiry d'Holbach et la philosophie scientifique au XVIIIe siècle*). 495 p.

PROUST, JACQUES, *Diderot et l'Encyclopédie* (2nd edn., Paris: A. Colin, 1967; 1st edn. 1962). 624 p.

SCHØSLER, JØRN, *Bibliographie des éditions et des traductions d'ouvrages philosophiques français et particulièrement des écrivains obscurs, 1680–1800*, Études romanes de l'Université d'Odense, vol. 22 (Odense: Odense University Press, 1986). 283 p.

—— *La Bibliothèque raisonnée (1728–1753): Les Réactions d'un périodique français à la philosophie de Locke au XVIIIe siècle*, Études romanes de l'Université d'Odense, vol. 21 (Odense: Odense University Press, 1985). 78 p.

SPINK, JOHN S. 'Un abbé philosophe: L'Affaire de J.-M. de Prades', *Dix-huitième siècle*, 3 (1971), 145–80.

STEWART, DUGALD, *Dissertation First: Exhibiting the Progress of Metaphysical, Ethical, and Political Philosophy, Since the Revival of Letters in Europe*, ed. Sir William Hamilton (Edinburgh: Constable, 1854; 630 p. 1st pub. 1821 as a prefix to the *Supplement to the 4th, 5th and 6th editions of the Encyclopaedia Britannica*, i. 1–166).

THOMSON, ANN, *Materialism and Society in the Mid-Eighteenth Century: La Mettrie's 'Discours préliminaire'*, Histoire des idées et critique littéraire, no. 198 (Geneva: Droz, 1981; xii, 278 p. Includes text of the 'Discours').

VARTANIAN, ARAM, *Diderot and Descartes: A Study of Scientific Naturalism in the Enlightenment* (Princeton, NJ: Princeton University Press, 1953). vi, 336 p.

WADE, IRA O., 'Notes on the Making of a *Philosophe*: Cuenz and Bouhier', in Charles G. S. Williams (ed.), *Literature and History in the Age of Ideas:*

Essays on the French Enlightenment Presented to George R. Havens (Columbus, Ohio: Ohio State University Press, 1975), 97–123.

WEBB, THOMAS, *The Intellectualism of Locke: An Essay* (Dublin: William McGee & Co., 1857). ix, 192 p.

WELLMAN, KATHLEEN, 'Medicine as a Key to Defining Enlightenment Issues: The Case of Julien Offray de la Mettrie', *Studies in Eighteenth-Century Culture*, 17 (1987), 75–89.

WILSON, ARTHUR M., *Diderot* (New York: Oxford University Press, 1972). xviii, 917 p.

YOLTON, JEAN S. and YOLTON, JOHN W., 'Locke's Suggestion of Thinking Matter and Some Eighteenth-Century Portuguese Reactions', *Journal of the History of Ideas*, 45 (1984), 302–7.

YOLTON, JOHN W., 'Hume's *Abstract* in the *Bibliothèque raisonnée*', *Journal of the History of Ideas*, 40 (1979), 157–8.

—— *John Locke and the Way of Ideas*, Oxford Classical and Philosophical Monographs (Oxford: Oxford University Press, 1956). x, 235 p.

—— 'Méthode et métaphysique dans la philosophie de John Locke', *Revue philosophique de la France et de l'étranger*, 163 (Apr.–June 1973), 171–85.

—— *Perceptual Acquaintance from Descartes to Reid* (Minneapolis, Minn.: University of Minnesota Press; Oxford: Basil Blackwell, 1984). x, 248 p.

—— *Thinking Matter: Materialism in Eighteenth-Century Britain* (Minneapolis, Minn.: University of Minnesota Press; Oxford: Basil Blackwell, 1984). xiv, 238 p.

Index

Académie royale de chirurgie 103 n., 228

Académie royale des sciences, *Mémoires* 103, 104 n., 221

Addison, Joseph 146

Alembert, Jean Le Rond d' 2, 51 n., 75, 92 n., 111, 157–8, 181, 182, 206, 214, 218, 219; see also *Encyclopédie, ou Dictionnaire* ...

Algarotti, Francesco, Count 45 n.

Alquié, Ferdinand 218

L'Âme matérielle 39 n., 55–7, 213

analogy 95, 96, 116, 192, 202

Anaxagoras 39

animal(s) 77, 115, 125, 131, 132–3, 166–7, 203; souls of 80, 94, 110, 122, 162, 173, 209

animal machines 29, 47, 112–13, 115, 128, 166, 170, 173–4, 196

animal spirits 26–8, 66, 67, 71, 73, 86 n., 105, 107, 113, 114, 152–3, 190 n., 195–7

Ansaldus, Casto Innocente 169–70, 177

Argens, J. B. de Boyer, marquis d' 58, 69–72, 76 n., 80, 194, 213, 229

Arianism 43

Aristotle, and Aristotelianism 39, 86, 93, 143, 194

Arnauld, Antoine 21, 144, 145, 213

Ashcraft, Richard 211 n., 229

Assézat, J. 218

Astruc, Jean 8, 60, 63–6, 106–7, 108, 172, 187, 192, 198, 205, 213

atheists and atheism 11, 58, 59, 71, 80, 140, 175

atoms 33–4, 149, 170

Augustine, Saint 27

automaton, automata 1 n., 13, 24, 53, 108, 111, 112–16, 124–5, 131–4, 176, 182, 186–7, 200; corporeal 36; immaterial or spiritual 33–4, 36, 83, 128

Averroës 71, 189

Bachaumont, L. P. de 103 n., 213, 229

Bacon, Francis 39

Barber, W. H. 148 n., 188 n., 228, 229

Barbeyrac, J. 54 n., 76 n., 128 n., 177, 217, 228, 229

Barthez, Paul-Joseph de 191

Basnage de Beauval, Jacques 30, 32

Basselin, Robert 92 n., 123, 213

Baxter, Andrew 161, 163–5, 167–8, 213, 221

Bayle, Pierre 2 n., 11, 17, 18–19, 31, 33, 38, 40 n., 41, 43, 51 n., 56, 57, 58, 79, 80 n., 132, 188, 213, 214, 215, 229

Béguelin, N. 10 n., 12 n., 14–15

Bel, — 42 n., 228

Bembo, Pietro 189

Benitez, Miguel 56 n.

Berkeley, George 81 n., 100 n., 124, 134, 151–5, 213

Bernard, Jacques 57 n., 229

Bernard, Jean-Frédéric 41, 42 n., 228

Bernier, F. 56

Bestermann, Theodore 41 n., 44 n., 45, 228

Bibliothèque ancienne et moderne 159

Bibliothèque angloise 159, 228

Bibliothèque britannique 6, 9, 41, 79, 80, 141, 159–67, 178, 179, 181, 219, 228

Bibliothèque choisie 2, 159

Bibliothèque françoise 42, 214, 228, 229

Bibliothèque germanique 14, 228, 229

Bibliothèque raisonnée 6–7, 9, 54 n., 80, 103, 129 n., 134–5, 140–1, 151–5, 158 n., 159–61, 167–72, 174–8, 179, 181, 228

Bibliothèque universelle et historique 1, 159, 222, 223, 228

Bionens, — de (=Théodore Crinsoz) 7, 168

Bloch, Olivier 51 n., 55, 56 n., 57 n., 58 n., 64 n., 65 n., 230

Blount, Charles 59

Boerhaave, Herman 24, 179, 187, 194

Boisbeleau de la Chapelle, Armand 54 n., 228